Knowledge Management in the Public Sector

Knowledge Management in the Public Sector

A Blueprint for Innovation in Government

David E. McNabb

Routledge
Taylor & Francis Group

LONDON AND NEW YORK

First published 2007 by M.E. Sharpe

Published 2015 by Routledge
2 Park Square, Milton Park, Abingdon, Oxon OX14 4RN
711 Third Avenue, New York, NY 10017, USA

Routledge is an imprint of the Taylor & Francis Group, an informa business

Library of Congress Cataloging-in-Publication Data

McNabb, David E.
  Knowledge management in the public sector : a blueprint for innovation in government /
by David E. McNabb.
    p. cm.
  Includes bibliographical references and index.
  ISBN-13: 978-0-7656-1727-9 (cloth : alk. paper)
  ISBN-10: 0-7656-1727-7
  1. Knowledge management. 2. Organizational learning. 3. Public administration—
Information technology—Case studies. 4. Electronic government information—Case
studies. I. Title.

HD30.2.M398 2006
352.3'8—dc22   2006005776

ISBN 13: 9780765617286 (pbk)
ISBN 13: 9780765617279 (hbk)

For Meghan, Michael, and Sara.

Contents

List of Tables, Figures, and Boxes

Tables

Figures

Boxes

Introduction

Knowledge . . . is inexhaustible. Once produced . . . knowledge can be
used repeatedly—it will not disappear. In fact, it only increases!
Digital knowledge can be copied and never missed. It can be given
away but still kept. Digital knowledge can be distributed instantly. It is
non-linear; it defies the theory of economy of scale. Knowledge is the
key element of wealth in the information age.
(Fast, William R., 2002, Knowledge Strategies)

[Government] organizations are increasingly implementing knowledge
management (KM) strategies to maximize the benefits of what they
know to help improve the efficiency and effectiveness of their business
operation. KM is a collaborative and integrative approach to creating,
capturing, organizing, accessing, using, and reusing intellectual
assets—to get the right information to the right people at the right time
to support management and decision-making.
(Office of the Inspector General, U.S. Dept. of State, 2003, Knowledge
Management at the Department of State, Monthly Activities Report [July])

The term *public sector* refers to the functioning agencies and units at the
federal, state, county, municipal, and local levels of government. The sector
includes all agencies, government corporations, the military, and departments,
agencies, and miscellaneous units that perform some form of public service.
They range in size from the largest federal department down to the smallest
special district, such as a mosquito abatement district or a community library
district. For this text, the public sector does not include those organizations
considered to be *nonprofit organizations* (NPOs), although many similar management principles apply to both NPOs and government. All business enter-
prises, regardless of their form, their structure, or the focus of their activities,
constitute the profit-centered portion of the economy, and are part of the
private sector. As such, they are not a major concern in this text.

Private- and public-sector managers use the same business tools; usually,
however, organizational improvement programs and management techniques
are first developed, tested, and proved effective in private-sector organizations.

Typically, only later are these innovations adopted in government. This text is about how government managers and administrators are adopting the public-sector-developed concepts and practices known as *knowledge management.*

Knowledge management incorporates ideas and processes from many different sources and technologies; a wide variety of disciplines, techniques, and processes contribute to the art and science of managing knowledge in organizations. One government observer found references to more than twenty different disciplines and information and communication technologies in this evolving management tool:

- Artificial intelligence (AI),
- Business process improvement (including process modeling, ABC costing, process simulation, functional economic analysis, etc.),
- Change management,
- Cognitive science,
- Complexity theory,
- Computer-supported collaborative work (GroupWare),
- Computer science and engineering,
- Computer user interface design,
- Data administration/standardization,
- Data mining,
- Decision support systems,
- Document management,
- Electronic publishing,
- Expert systems,
- Library and information science,
- Organizational science,
- Performance support systems and appraisal,
- Relational and object databases,
- Semantic networks,
- Text search and retrieval,
- And more.

Butler, Feller, Pope, Barry, and Murphy (2003, 83) also described KM as a multidisciplinary domain of interest, with origins in philosophy, economics, organization theory, information systems, marketing, management strategy, innovation research, and organizational learning. Elements of these disciplines have been brought together to result in a management philosophy and set of tools and processes founded on four basic tenets: (1) knowledge is created in the minds of people; (2) knowledge can be captured, put on paper, entered into a computer system, put to work, or simply remembered; (3) following a fundamental characteristic of the human mind, knowledge is classified, combined, modified, and reorganized. Technology makes it easier to recapture knowledge by making it possible to search using key words or phrases; and (4) knowledge is shared; as it is shared, it is recycled, modified, and enlarged.

Common Challenges, Responsibilities, and Trends

Public-sector managers and administrations face many challenges and new responsibilities in the twenty-first century. Just a few of the more salient of these challenges are defending the homeland against terrorist actions, preventing the spread of infectious diseases, maintaining a reliable stream of social security income, continuing to support the transition from welfare to work, ensuring that our education systems meet the needs of students both young and old, and repairing an aging and in many cases decaying physical infrastructure (U.S. GAO 2004). Further exacerbating the effects of these and other challenges are a number of social and economic trends that hinder the ability of governments to carry out their appointed tasks. Among the key trends impacting the way government must act today and in the future are:

- A global reaction and response to the threat of terrorism and other physical threats to our personal and national security.
- The globalization of society that will continue to increase the interdependence of businesses and industries, national and regional economies, markets for products and services, civil societies, and national governments.
- The shift to market-oriented, knowledge-based public services, and the continued pressures for privatization of government services.
- A demographic mega-shift taking place in many industrialized societies, including more legal and illegal migration, an aging and more diverse population in the United States and elsewhere, and zero or negative population growth.
- Continued rapid advances in science and technology—and the blending of the two, as in biotechnology—and the opportunities and challenges these advances represent—including the potential for adverse public reaction to such advances.
- The many challenges and opportunities facing governments for maintaining and improving the quality of life for their citizens, families, communities, and nations in general, including getting control of rising healthcare costs.
- The challenges government managers and administrators face with the changing and increasingly diverse nature of government structures (such

as collaborations across jurisdictions) and tools, including e-government.
- A continuing demand that governments do more with less, and for greater accountability for the actions of government. This global trend is driving a movement for improving the performance of governments. This movement goes by many names, such as "reinventing government" and "management transformation." A primary feature of the movement is public- and private-sector partnerships.

Globally, governments have been forced to become more adept at grappling with these and other challenges. At the federal level, this trend is manifested by the impact such administrative mandates as the Government Performance and Results Act (GPRA), the Legislative Branch Appropriations Act (LBAA), and others are having on government agency and department operations and structures. GPRA, for example, has mandated a management shift that emphasizes results-oriented performance (strategic) planning, measurement, and reporting. A five-part framework directs agency progress under the LBAA: leadership, strategic human capital management, performance measurement, organizational alignment, and communications. The goal of these performance initiatives is to eventually link all future resources to results.

Throughout the federal government—and increasingly at the state and local levels as well—a far-reaching dialogue is under way in which new answers are being framed for such questions as what should constitute government in the information economy, what governments should do, and what should be left to the private sector or managed through collaborative public-/private-sector partnerships. Driving this dialogue is the need for government agencies to continue to transform their organizational cultures from the traditional hierarchical, bureaucratic models to open, flat, and worker-empowered organizations where change is welcomed. For this transformation to occur, a number of shifts in the way government operates must take place. These include shifts from:

- Processes to results,
- Stovepipes to matrices (matrixes),
- Hierarchical to flatter and more horizontal structures,
- An inward focus to a customer and stakeholder focus,
- Micromanagement to employee empowerment,
- Reactive behavior to proactive approaches,
- Avoiding new technologies to embracing and leveraging them,
- Hoarding knowledge to sharing knowledge,
- Avoiding risk to managing risk, and
- Protecting turf to forming partnerships and collaborative teamwork.

The overriding goal of these shifts in focus is to achieve a fundamental transformation in government departments, agencies, and units. In order to make that transformation happen, the GAO recommends that the first priority of a government agency is to strengthen its capacity to perform its mission by carrying out the following six tasks:

1. Demonstrate top leadership commitment to the organizational transformation,
2. Involve key constituents and other stakeholders in developing their required strategic plans and organizational transformations,
3. Use the strategic plan as the foundation for aligning activities, core process, and resources to support mission-related outcomes,
4. Establish a communications strategy to foster transformation, create shared expectations, and build involvement,
5. Develop annual goals and a system for measuring performance, and
6. Strategically manage its human capital to support the accomplishment of the agency's objectives.

Why Another Book on Knowledge Management?

If there is one thing about knowledge management that everyone can agree on, it is the fact that its proponents have been more than prolific in talking and writing about it. Early in the new century, a university colleague found that more than 300 books had already been published on the subject. Other than some minor details, most of those authors agreed on the basic principles and fundamental structures of this emerging discipline. They also agreed that managing the knowledge they had was as, or more, important for a business as managing all their other assets. Considered in this light, another book on knowledge management may be like preaching to the converted.

However, this is not intended to be "just another book on knowledge management." Most of the books on KM are concerned with the way it is or should be used in business. KM in government (or, more formally, in the public sector) has been all but ignored. For that reason, this book is *only* concerned with KM in the public sector. It looks at KM in federal, state, and local government.

Structure of the Book

This book is organized into four major sections. The first—Foundations of Knowledge Management—establishes the bonds and interconnectedness of learning, knowledge, and innovation as fundamental organizational transformation concepts. After a brief historical overview of the evolution of a stream of management initiatives, knowledge management is introduced as a logical result of this progression. The next chapter introduces readers to some of the fundamental constructs found in the growing body of literature for this new discipline in the context of a self-regulating and -organizing social system. These concepts are incorporated into a model that illustrates the entire knowledge management system from raw data to organizational payoffs.

Part 2—Transforming Government with KM—expands on each of the major constructs introduced in the components of KM model introduced in chapter 1. In the five chapters included in this section readers will be shown how information technology and personal work processes transform data to information, and information into knowledge; how KM transforms silo mentalities into knowledge-valuing cultures; how selected KM processes are able to transform organizational isolates into valued participants; how KM contributes to fostering innovation in government; and how learning and innovation contribute to transforming a traditional government bureaucracy into a learning organization.

Part 3—KM Systems in the Public Sector—begins with a brief review of the argument that public-sector management (and, hence, knowledge management) is different than private-sector management. These arguments tend to focus on the lack of the profit motive as the major contributor to these differences (if any). The section also compares the role of the chief information officer (CIO) with a newer position, that of the public-sector chief knowledge officer (CKO).

Part 4—Stories of Public-Sector KM in Action—provides readers with a number of example case studies that illustrate how KM has been implemented in a variety of different government organizations. The last section in the book provides a review of a chain of intellectual activity that is shaping the drive to make knowledge management a full-fledged academic discipline. The consensus is that although early KM initiatives focused on IT applications, more recent manifestations of KM emphasize the social and behavioral aspects of the KM concept. In some circles, this is referred to as "second generation" or "new knowledge management" (McElroy 2003).

Acknowledgments

Few if any books on management in either the public or private sectors are ever written without drawing upon the contributions of the many researchers, practitioners, administrators, and academics that have passed along the same road previously. Certainly, this book owes a large debt of gratitude to the many pioneers in this new management discipline, and to the many public servants—military and civilian, federal, state, and local—who have shared their knowledge, time, expertise, and passion for the use and promise of knowledge management. I thank you all and wish you continued success as you labor to make the governments of tomorrow better than those that came before. Although I willingly recognize the help and guidance received, I take full responsibility for any errors of commission or omission that may appear in the final manuscript.

I owe a large debt of gratitude to a number of my colleagues at Pacific Lutheran University. The PLU School of Business provided both moral and financial assistance during my research for the book, including providing matching funds to attend several distant and local government KM conferences. I am profoundly grateful for his support in this and earlier endeavors. Dr. Thad Barnowe, PLU professor of management, gave much welcome guidance in his recommendations and suggestions for improvements to the manuscript. Other faculty members who have contributed significantly to the evolution of the ideas that emerged in the form of this book include professors Jim Albers, Eli Berniker, Bruce Finnie, and Chung-Sing Lee.

I wish also to thank my editor at M.E. Sharpe, Mr. Harry Briggs, who supported the concept for the book from our very first conversation. I also wish to thank the anonymous reviewers of the book proposal for their encouragement and excellent advice.

This book is dedicated first to the members of my family for their support —past, present, and future—and to my colleagues and friends at universities in the United States and Riga, Latvia. I wish them well as they continue on the search for truth and understanding in this new century, eagerly facing ever-new challenges, and secure in the knowledge that educating the young men and women of the world is surely one of the noblest of professions.

Part 1

Foundations of Knowledge
Management

1

Historical Foundations of KM

*When the [US] Department of Defense invented the Internet in the
1960s as a communications network for defense research purposes,
no one could have foreseen how it would transform society three
decades later. Today, the Internet has become a part of the daily life
of [citizens around the globe].*
(Ho 2002, 434)

*Information technology (IT) has become one of the core elements of
managerial reform, and electronic government (e-government) may
figure prominently in future governance. IT has opened many
possibilities for improving internal managerial efficiency and the
quality of public service delivery to citizens.*
(Moon 2002, 424)

This book is about the use of knowledge management (KM) systems and
processes by government organizations to improve the ways they operate
and the ways that they deliver public services to citizens. Improving organizational performance includes making it possible for agencies to become
more innovative in carrying out their missions, while at the same time becoming more accountable to the publics they serve. The organizational drive
is to harness the existing knowledge in government agencies to foster creative problem solving by government workers at all levels. Knowledge management is a key component in this new way of functioning.

Chapter Objectives

This chapter has been framed on a set of objectives that are designed to
help readers:

- Gain an introduction to the field of knowledge management and its evolution into an accepted principle for public-sector administration and management.
- Understand how KM is an essential component in the transforming government and e-government movements.
- Understand that, although significant differences exist between the private and public sectors, many management concepts and processes—such as knowledge management—are equally applicable in both sectors.
- Recognize that KM is only the latest in a long tradition of management methods and programs that have been designed to enable the leveraging of organizational knowledge and experience.
- Understand how KM helps government organizations make the highly desirable shift from reactive agencies to learning organizations.
- Understand that KM enables greater innovation and creativity in government organizations.

Business managers and managers of public agencies are often told that management in the two sectors is inherently different. It is not the purpose of this book to seek to say whether that statement is true or not. However, it does deal with the question: *Is the way KM is acquired and implemented in government really any different than it is in business and industry?* Depending upon with whom you're conversing, you would still hear *yes, no,* or *maybe.* This book proceeds on the premise that those who support the difference argument are probably right.

Writing on the use of executive information systems in government, one group of observers had this to say about differences between the private and public sectors:

> Differences between private and government organizations are at the core of public administration theory and have been the topic of an ongoing stream of research. . . . Differences have been found, for example, in personnel management, decision making and information systems. (Watson and Carte 2000, 373)

Watson and Carte also identified these bases for the differences: environmental factors, the ways in which sector organizations interact with their environments and with their stakeholders, and fundamental differences in organizational structures and processes. Also, because public organizations have less interaction with the market, they are not as influenced by rewards and punishments associated with market controls. Finally, public sector organizations:

- Are more constrained in their choices of procedures,
- Perform activities that are mandated by political forces,
- Face more external formal controls and specifications on their actions,
- Deal with greater external influence on what they do and how they do it,
- Gain approval from a wide variety of stakeholders,
- Have multiple, often contradictory, objectives,
- Have less autonomy and control over decision making and human resources,
- Are less able to devise incentives for staff performance,
- And are often forced to have their failures—large and small—aired in the public press.

The editorial director of the industry journal *KMWorld* prefaced a special supplement on best practices in government in the June 2005 issue of the magazine, in which he stated flatly, "The point being: government is different." However, then speaking for KM consultants and IT vendors, he added, "But as 'different' as government can be, it can also be very familiar" (Moore 2005, S2).

Three of what may be the greatest differences are (1) the government's move toward enterprise architectures—the mandate for all agencies to identify commonalities of use in IT so that cost savings can be gained through bulk purchases; (2) government's long history of learning how to work with regulatory issues in the use of KM and IT; and (3) the driving force of public policy that forces government agencies to respond to legislative and executive mandates.

An IT industry spokesperson was quoted in the same special supplement preface of *KMWorld,* speaking on the regulatory experience of government: "Government is in on the forefront of regulatory compliance because they have had compliance mandates for decades." In industry, corporate standards on the use of IT are still fairly new; many businesses are just beginning to understand the sensitivity and discoverability of electronic records—as the officers, managers, and directors of Enron and Anderson Consulting learned to their dismay.

Government purchases of KM systems and support are also driven by public policy—a point that the private sector does not have to deal with. Moore quoted another industry spokesperson, Gary Ward, vice president of sales for X1 Technologies: "You can have the most amazing technology in the world, but if there is not a policy imperative driving the adoption, it [selling to the government] is going to be difficult sledding in the public sector." Summarizing his views on the differences, Moore concluded, "In government the driving impetus is from public policy and budget pressure. In the private sector, the driving impetus is business performance and . . . budget pressure."

Evolution of KM in the Public Sector

Many observers feel that KM is really nothing new. Rather, it should be considered the latest component in the government's fifty-plus-year effort to integrate information technology (IT) into operations to improve performance and make government agencies and departments more accountable. By 2005, the latest development in this progression had become a global movement to reform the way governments serve their citizens; around the world that movement is referred to as *e-government.* One leading enterprise software and knowledge systems industry spokesperson described the foundation for this movement in these terms:

> Governmental organizations worldwide are facing several challenges as administrative, executive and judicial bodies continue to evolve into an electronic work environment. Pushed by paperwork-reduction mandates, requirements to handle increase workloads with fewer personnel and the rapid adoption of electronic communication channels by taxpayers and citizens, governments are often on the forefront of adopting new approaches to electronic information management. (McKinnon 2005)

Tacit knowledge is knowledge held in the minds of the men and women who hold, use, and share what they know about things and how to do what they do. Explicit knowledge is knowledge that has been or can be written down and contained in documents and other media.

Three converging trends are behind the drive by public-sector organizations to gain better control of their information infrastructure and management of the tacit and explicit knowledge held by their personnel and in knowledge repositories in the organization. The first trend is the expected high turnover in knowledge workers as large numbers of the baby-boom generation retire; a number of studies have cited the coming loss of senior project and technical managers as the greatest risk facing the public sector at the start of the new century.

The second trend is a global acceleration of the push to implement e-government; agencies at all levels have been increasing the amount and variety of online services available to citizens. Many government agencies are also providing mobile communications capability for their knowledge workers, thus enabling them to communicate as information is gathered. Such electronic tools as personal handheld devices, smart phones, tablets, and laptop computers have freed knowledge workers from the tyranny of being chained to a desk.

The third trend is continued emphasis on *Enterprise Architecture Initiatives* (i.e., shared services) to achieve greater operational efficiencies and implement Web-based service delivery. Agencies must comply with enterprise architecture analyses mandated by the Office of Management and Budget (OMB) before they can replace or acquire new information technology. McKinnon described this mandate as "the constant battle to develop operational efficiencies in the face of budget and program cutbacks." It means that all government agencies must include IT acquisitions in their strategic plans. They must also establish common network platforms for e-mail, and all information and knowledge management systems.

What KM Does

KM is about managing information to make the most of the knowledge in an organization in order to benefit from finding and applying innovative answers to old and new questions. Information and communications technology constitutes one of the three chief building blocks of knowledge management. The other two are the people who use knowledge and the processes that have been developed to enable and enhance knowledge capture and sharing (Joch 2004).

Technology has made it possible for KM to evolve into what it has become today—a key management tool that is necessary for agencies and institutions to function and flourish in today's knowledge economy. Few would argue with Peter Drucker's 1995 conclusion that the world has entered upon a postindustrial economy characterized by globalization, increasingly sophisticated information and communications technology, and a knowledge society. Nonaka (1991) added that in this new economy the only certainty is that knowledge is the only sustainable source of competitive advantage (Butler et al. 2003).

This chapter presents a brief review of how early knowledge management concepts evolved over the first decade or so of KM's existence, to the point where by the middle of the first decade of the twenty-first century, KM had become a normal way of operating in many federal, state, and local governments. Administrators and managers agree that KM's blend of technology, people, and processes holds a key to organizational improvement, if not even for survival, in the face of an environment characterized by heightened political polarity, severely limited resources, and demands for government agencies at all levels to do more with less.

What KM Does Not Do

Amrit Tiwana included a list of things that KM does not do for organizations in the second edition of his *Knowledge Management Toolkit*. These points were offered as a way for KM system designers and government purchasing agents to "cleanse" themselves of intense vendor pitches:

- KM is not knowledge engineering. Rather, KM falls into the domains of management and information systems, not computer science.
- KM is not only about digital networks; it is about management processes. Technology is an enabler, not a driver.
- KM is not about building a smarter internal communications network (intranet). Nor are they the same. KM is about knowledge and experience.
- KM is not about a one-time investment in technology. It is a future-oriented investment that requires consistent attention and evaluation.
- KM is not about "enterprise-wide *infobahns*" (information highways in organizations). KM should not be confused with enterprise information systems. The primary focus is on helping the right people have access to the right knowledge at the right time. (Tiwana 2002, 8)

The Evolution of KM and KM Systems

When examined objectively, KM and knowledge management systems (KMS) may be considered to be the latest manifestation in a logical progression of governments' concerns with data, information, and knowledge. A representation of this evolutionary process is displayed in Figure 1.1.

The federal government's current concern with improving the performance of government agencies can be traced as far back as 1943, when the first book that included a call for local governments to measure their performance and offered guidelines for government to follow was published. However, government reformers had to wait a long time for the federal government to act on that recommendation; it was not until July of 1993 that Congress finally passed the Government Performance and Results Act (GPRA). GPRA required all agencies to develop strategic plans, set goals and objectives, and begin to measure their progress toward those goals (Aristigueta 2002).

Although computers had been in use in agencies for many years, government's generally heightened interest in information and communications technology began in earnest in the late 1980s. It took a more substantial form during the Clinton/Gore administrations of the 1990s and emerged in full bloom in the administration of President George W. Bush. In the 1990s under President Clinton the performance improvement program was called *reinventing government;* after 2002, the movement became the less dramatic but equally innovative concept of *e-government.*

The first wave in this evolutionary process began in the late 1950s and 1960s with the installation of mainframe computers to process large amounts of data. Among the heaviest users of computers for this purpose were the Census Bureau, the Department of Commerce, and the military. During the decade of the 1970s, as computer hardware and software gained more power and new appli-

Figure 1.1   **From Data Processing to Full Knowledge Management Systems**

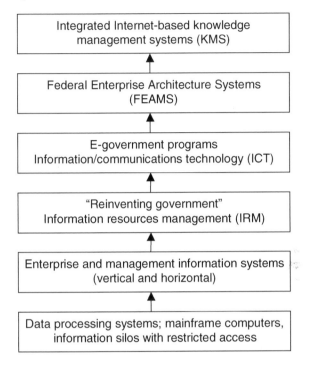

cations developed, more agencies looked to the new promise of computers to store, process, codify, process, and synthesize the reams of data governments must collect and retain. A key development at this time was the appearance of a variety of vertical management information systems.

A problem with these systems was that they tended to be largely agency or application specific, and unable to communicate with other systems. Thus, access to the information they contained remained restricted to members of the unit. It was impossible to share others' information and, more importantly, learn from earlier mistakes. Overly customized systems that are unable to meet performance requirements remain a major problem in government.

An Executive Information Systems Solution?

A solution for some of these difficulties was the internal development in the late 1970s of a few broadly based executive information systems (EISs). It was not until the mid-1980s that commercial systems became available (Watson and Carte 2000). Although the early EISs were developed for only a few highest-level executives, they soon evolved to be able to support all top management teams, and, in some large firms, can today serve a hundred or more users.

The importance of these executive systems to the development of comprehensive knowledge management systems in the late 1990s cannot be overemphasized. For example, EISs are designed to provide many of the following services:

- Extract, filter, compress, track, and indefinitely store critical data,
- Provide online status reports, trend analyses, and exception reports,
- Provide "drilldown" capability to access supporting detail or underlying data,
- Conduct data analysis, using such tools as spreadsheets and data mining,
- Support decision support systems,
- Access and integrate a broad range of internal and external information,
- Provide support for such electronic communications as e-mail and computer conferencing,
- Prepare and present graphics, tables, and textual information,
- Provide organizing support, such as electronic calendars,
- Are user-friendly and require little or no formal training to use.

The Drive for Coordination and Control

By the 1990s, it was clear that some higher-level coordination and control was needed over the acquisitions and applications of IT systems by agencies. A single organization was needed to oversee IT resources (Lee and Perry 2002). The federal government's answer was to place information resources management (IRM) under the auspices of the Office of Management and Budget. Tasks and responsibilities included oversight of planning and budgeting for all federal agency activities associated with acquiring, storing, processing, and distributing data and information.

While OMB began its coordination and control over IT, others in government were envisioning an even greater role for IT in all levels of government. They dreamed of using the lessons learned in the private sector's use of IT to introduce the same private-sector productivity gains in government. Government was to be more businesslike. That meant higher performance standards, stronger performance measurement, and stricter accountability for results. Their vision became codified in the reinventing government initiatives issued from the Clinton White House.

According to Qiao and Thai (2002), the National Performance Review

Table 1.1

Twentieth-Century Efforts to Reform Government

Year	Reform effort or program
1905	Commission on Department Methods (Keep Commission)
1910	President's Commission on Economy and Efficiency (Taft Commission)
1921	Joint Committee on Reorganization
1936	President's Committee on Administrative Management (Brownlow Committee)
1947	First Hoover Commission
1960	Task Force on Government Reorganization
1969	Advisory Council on Executive Organization (Ash Council)
1977	Carter Reorganization Effort
1982	President's Private Sector Survey on Cost Control (Grace Commission)
1987	National Commission on the Public Service (Volker Commission)
1993	National Performance Review (Gore Commission)

Source: Yuhua 2002, 91.

(NPR) Act, which gave life to the reinventing government movement, may have been the most important reform of the twentieth century. It came at a time when there was higher-than-ever demand for changing the way governments function. However, like everything else that happens in Washington, most of the concepts and proposals included in NPR were not new. There were at least eleven earlier attempts at reinventing the bureaucracy, as the list in Table 1.1 illustrates.

President Clinton included a number of e-government initiatives in his June 2000 first Webcast address. A key proposal revealed in the address was a plan to put all online resources offered by the federal government on a single Web site, www.Firstgov.gov. Not long afterward, many state and local governments expanded their adoption of IT for similar purposes.

The adoption of e-government at the federal level became more of a reality in February of 2002, when newly elected President George W. Bush described what came to be known as the *President's Management Agenda* (PMA) in his annual budget submission to Congress. PMA was offered as a way of getting government to be more focused on citizens and results. A large component in the mechanism for making this happen was expanding the role of electronic government. Under the Bush plan, e-government focused on Internet-based technology in its efforts to make it easier for citizens and businesses to interact with government agencies and departments (OMB 2005a). In addition, adoption of the e-government initiative was promised as a way to save taxpayer dollars and streamline citizen-to-government communications.

Box 1.1

The Federal Enterprise Architecture Program

Federal Enterprise Architecture (FEA): FEA is a business model–based* initiative designed to provide a common framework for improving such areas of federal government operations as budget allocations and budget and performance integration, horizontal and vertical information sharing, performance measurement, cross-agency collaboration, e-government, and component-based architectures, among others. Led by the Office of Management and Budget, the fundamental purpose of FEA is to identify opportunities to simplify processes and unify work across agencies and within the lines of business of the federal government. A key goal of FEA is to help agencies become a more citizen-centered, customer-focused government that maximizes investments to better achieve mission outcomes.

Federal Enterprise Architecture Management System (FEAMS): FEAMS is a Web-based management information repository and analysis system designed to provide agencies with access to initiatives aligned to the federal enterprise architecture (FEA) and associated references models. FEAMS was issued by the OMB in December of 2003 to provide users with an intuitive approach to discover and potentially leverage information technology components, business services, and capabilities across the federal government.

Source: www.whitehouse.gov/omb/egov/a-1-fea.html. 2003.
*According to the OMB, the business reference model is based on the government's "lines of business" and its services to the citizen, independent of the agencies and offices involved. Thus, one line of business may include two or more traditional agencies.

OMB employed a business-practices model called *federal enterprise architecture* (FEA) to guide agencies in the analysis of their current and future information and communications technology (ICT) needs and implementation of identification of common practices and systems. The application template is called the *Federal Enterprise Architecture Management System* (FEAMS). Both models are described in Box 1.1.

As noted earlier, the drive to implement e-government has become a global phenomenon. In 2005, however, not all attempts to bring the public to

Figure 1.2   **Key Components of Early E-Government Systems**

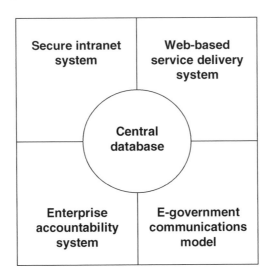

taking advantage of the many opportunities e-government affords them were successful. The United Kingdom had surprising difficulties in getting the public to use the e-government Web sites established for citizen transactions (Perera 2005). Although nearly all of the 400 local governments in the UK were expected to have established e-government services by the end of 2005, a "digital divide" exists between the UK citizens who have access to computers and those who do not. The UK government reports that e-government use is low even among those who do have access. One of the mistakes contributing to this low usage rate is the failure of the UK e-government designers to take full advantage of the potential in their first contact Web site, Directgov; this site is the UK equivalent of the U.S. first access site, FirstGov. Rather than containing links to local government Web sites, the content of Directgov is mainly limited to policy statements.

KM and E-Government—Evolutionary Stage

The E-Government Act of 2002 (H.R. 2458/S. 803), which became effective on April 17, 2003, established an Office e-government and authorized appointment of an e-administrator within the OMB.

Developing a coordinated federal, state, and local policy on the use of information technology is a key goal of the program. Working with state, local, and tribal governments, the general public, and the private and nonprofit sectors, the e-government office is charged with finding innovative ways to: (1) improve the performance of governments in collaborating on the use of information technology to improve the delivery of government information and services; (2) set standards for federal agency Web sites; and (3) create a public directory of government Web sites. Figure 1.2 illustrates how the components of early e-government systems interact.

Originally, e-government included four fundamental components: First, a secure government intranet and central database was established to enhance communication and collaboration between agencies. Second, a system for the Web-based delivery of government services was developed. Third, taking a page from the private sector, an e-commerce model customized to fit governments' needs was developed to provide greater efficiency in transactions such as government contracts and procurement. Finally, provisions for gaining greater and more open accountability were included (Moon 2002). These components were supported by such technologies as electronic data interchange, electronic filing systems, interactive voice response, voice mail, e-mail, Web service delivery, virtual reality, and many others.

Under the form established in PMA, the purpose of the new e-government initiative is to improve the management and performance of the federal government by focusing on operational areas where deficiencies are most apparent and where the government could begin to deliver concrete, measurable results. PMA includes five federal government-wide initiatives and ten program-specific initiatives that apply to a subset of federal agencies. For each initiative, PMA established clear, government-wide goals (termed *Standards for Success*), and developed action plans to achieve the goals. The five government-wide initiatives are:

- *Budget and Performance Integration (BPI):* BPI includes efforts to ensure that agency and/or program performance is routinely considered in funding and management decisions, and the programs are monitored to make sure they achieve expected results and work toward continual improvement.
- *Competitive Sourcing (CS):* This initiative calls for agencies to regularly examine activities performed by the government to determine whether it is more efficient to obtain such services from federal employees or from the private sector (often referred to as *outsourcing*).
- *Expanded Electronic Government (EEG):* This refers to actions designed to ensure that the federal government's $60-billion annual investment in information technology (IT) significantly improves the government's ability to serve citizens, and that IT systems are secure and delivered on time and on budget.
- *Improved Financial Performance (IFP):* IFP is concerned with accu-

rately accounting for the taxpayers' money and giving managers timely and accurate program cost information to improve management decisions and control costs.

- *Strategic Management of Human Capital (SMHC):* SMHC consists of processes to ensure the right person is in the right job, at the right time, and is not only performing, but performing well. It is closely associated with Human Resources Planning (HRP).

To monitor and maintain agency progress, the OMB publishes a government-wide quarterly scorecard, in which it reports individual department and agency progress on the five initiatives. An example of how the scorecard is used to push for compliance with the five-point agenda is a published e-mail warning from OMB that it would downgrade the Agriculture Department from a yellow to a red—the lowest rating—on the competitive-sourcing section of the quarterly management scorecard unless the U.S. Forest Service allowed outside suppliers to bid on at least 100 information and communications technology jobs by the end of the 2005 fiscal year.

Despite what many consultants and knowledge management government personnel would like us to believe, and the federal government's wholesale adoption of information technology, knowledge management in the public sector remains very much a work in progress. This is particularly so at the state and municipal government levels. Acceptance of knowledge management principles and programs by the states mirrors the difficulties states are experiencing in the IT-component level of KM.

From IT to FEA to KM

In the last decade of the twentieth century a small group of academics, management consultants, information technology people, and business leaders came to the realization that the key to an organization's success—or survival—in the new information economy lay in their ability to employ the technology increasingly available to collect, distribute, store, and use the knowledge that made them distinctive (DCMA 2004). Out of this consensus came a realization that what has come to be known as knowledge management has a direct and important contribution to make in implementing and sustaining e-government.

Voss, Roeder, and Marker (2003) have identified three aspects of knowledge management support for the idea that ICT can contribute to success in e-government. First, *intellectual capital* is the basis for cooperative actions that involve multi-party processes, and which often include public participation. This intellectual capital resides in stakeholder organizations with different roles and knowledge backgrounds. Intellectual capital is contained in an organization's recorded information and its human talent. The term reflects the understanding that information is a growing part of every organization's assets. Such information is often either inefficiently archived or simply lost, especially in large, physically dispersed organizations such as federal agencies.

Second, the combined knowledge management concepts of *learning organizations* and *process optimization* are core elements in both the reinvention of government and the e-government models. The role of learning in organizations gained international awareness with the appearance of Peter Senge's *The Fifth Discipline* in 1990. Nonaka and Takeuchi's *The Knowledge-Creating Company* in 1995 also focused on organizational strategies for creating new knowledge as a tool for gaining a competitive advantage.

A learning organization is one that has learned how to modify the way it operates as a result of new information, knowledge, and insights. The key product of the process is development of a *knowledge chain*. The chain identifies processes for collecting knowledge and producing, customizing, and delivering knowledge when and where it is needed. For applying the concept to government, this means

> finding the materials [and processes] suitable to feed the knowledge chain:
> a) to identify the fragments of knowledge that could be efficiently reused
> but, above all, accepted; b) to represent and formalize such fragments to
> the tractable (stored, analyzed, understood, customized, and eventually
> transferred). (Bresciani, Donzelli, and Forte 2003, 49)

The goal of process optimization is to increase the efficiency of organization processes with regard to time, costs, and quality through effectively managing the organization's knowledge. To achieve these goals, topic-oriented intranet networks are developed to acquire and distribute knowledge across organizations and organizational processes.

Third, the concept of a *knowledge base* is important to cooperative planning processes in e-government. The term *knowledge base* has traditionally referred to the data produced by the knowledge-acquisition and compilation phases of creating an expert system application. But that definition is now often broadened to include every imaginable corporate intellectual (and technological) asset. In this way, the knowledge base refers to the complete collection of all expertise, experience, and knowledge of those within a public organization.

Unlike their counterparts in business and industry, federal, state, and local government agencies have been forced by laws and organizational (often presidential) initiatives into absorbing electronic information and communication systems into every possible aspect of their operations as a way of becoming more efficient and effective. Interestingly, this mandate to improve the way government operates is a global pattern, not exclusively a North American phenomenon (Auditore 2003).

Even while governments are being told to become more efficient and technologically savvy, there is also a global movement under way to shrink government, to make it more responsive to citizens' needs, and to improve its accountability. In brief, the mandate is to reform government along the lines of business. This reform includes the privatization of programs and activities wherever possible. Globally, these initiatives are collectively referred to as *electronic government*, or simply *e-government*.

What Is E-Government?

E-government has been defined as consisting of actions to produce and deliver government services to citizens, not in the traditional face-to-face manner, but instead through the use of communications technology. A more inclusive definition would include the application of any information and/or communications technology used to "simplify and improve transactions between governments and other actors, such as constituents, businesses, and other governmental agencies" (Moon 2002, 424). Thus, e-government involves the use of information and communications technologies (ICTs) to ensure that citizens and businesses receive better quality services, mainly through such electronic delivery channels as the Internet, digital TV, mobile phones, and related technology.

A Global Reform Movement

Many governments worldwide are developing and implementing e-government strategies and programs (Borras 2003). International examples of e-government reforms include such programs as Public Service 2002 in Canada, Next Steps and Modernizing Government in the UK, Renewal of Public Service in France, Financial Improvement Program in Australia, Administrative Management Project in Austria, Modernization Program for the Public Sector in Denmark, and the Major Options Plan in Portugal (Haque 2001). The European Union is providing encouragement and incentives for such programs to all EU member states through its "eEurope" initiative (Aichholzer 2003).

The results of an international study of e-government jointly sponsored by the United Nations and the American Society for Public Administration contained the following description of e-government:

> E-government includes the use of all information and communication tech-
> nologies, from fax machines to wireless palm pilots, to facilitate the daily
> administration of government . . . [and] improves citizen access to govern-
> ment information, services and expertise to ensure citizen participation in,
> and satisfaction with the government process . . . it is a permanent commit-
> ment by government to improving the relationship between the private citi-
> zen and the public sector through enhanced, cost-effective and efficient
> delivery of services, information and knowledge. It is the practical realiza-
> tion of the best that government has to offer. (Moon 2002, 425)

Although there are differences among strategies adopted by different governments, Bresciani, Donzelli, and Forte (2003) have identified a "common
roadmap" government agencies are following on their path toward e-government implementation. Four common checkpoints on that roadmap include:
(1) establishment of a government-wide communication infrastructure to
enable cooperation among the different public-sector components, both at
the central and local levels; (2) creation of the appropriate ICT infrastructure; and (3) establishment of relevant channels for service delivery. Fundamental for the first three steps and recognized as the key for efficiently
managing e-government evolution is (4) transformation of the public agency
into a *learning organization*, in which high knowledge sharing, information
reuse, and strategic application of the acquired knowledge and lessons learned
regularly occur.

The e-government movement in the United States is a logical extension of
the reinventing government movement that began in the late 1980s, and which
was codified with the publication in 1992 of David Osborne and Ted Gaebler's
Reinventing Government. E-government moved from concept to reality during the administration of President Bill Clinton, who professed the belief
that e-government offered a means of overcoming the time and space barriers that in the past had limited delivery of government services. The very
nature of the public sector has resulted in mixed signals regarding the benefits of KM, as one Italian study has indicated:

> Public [sector organizations] . . . are characterized by the presence of very
> diverse kinds of actors (e.g., citizens and businesses, employees and ad-
> ministrators, politicians and decision makers—both at the central and local
> level), each of them with its own objectives and goals. Thus, in general, e-
> government applications have to operate in a social environment charac-
> terized by a rich tissue of actors with strong interdependent intents. Due to
> this complex network of interrelated objectives, synergies and conflicts
> may be present. (Bresciani, Donzelli, and Forte 2003, 51)

Forging a Definition for KM

Now that the connection between data processing, MIS, reinventing government, e-government, federal enterprise architecture, and knowledge management has been established, we can take a closer look at KM and KM systems. Knowledge management has been defined in a number of different ways—a fact that many authors point to as being one of the reasons why KM has not achieved greater acceptance among organizational managements.

One of the more commonly seen definitions is that provided by Nonaka and Takeuchi (1995), who defined KM as the substantiated understandings and beliefs in an organization about the organization and its environment. They also differentiated between two types of knowledge: explicit and tacit. Explicit knowledge is codified, easily translated and shared facts and information; it exists in reports and other documents. Tacit knowledge is personal knowledge that is hard to confirm and share with others; it is the private understanding and *knowing* that people have about issues, problems, services, and products. A major task of KM is to turn tacit knowledge into explicit knowledge.

Amrit Tiwana (2002) defined knowledge management as a changing mix of workers' experience, values, expert insight, and intuition that provides an environmental framework for evaluating and incorporating new experiences and information. It resides in the minds of workers, but is often expressed in the culture of the organization, including its routines, processes, systems, and norms (this definition is similar to many of the definitions for human capital).

Is It Just Another Fad?

To some, KM is considered just another management fad, like Management by Objectives (MBO) and Total Quality Management (TQM). Moreover, knowledge and knowledge management are seen by some as simply other names for information and information technology (Fuller 2002; T.D. Wilson 2002). To others, KM represents a major paradigm shift in management thinking. This change was brought about by the shift from an industrial to an information economy, in which knowledge is now an organization's most valuable resource, and one which should be managed and utilized wisely. It is important to remember that KM has both a technological and a social side. And, it is a management discipline that is still in its formative stage. Thus, the arguments of both its critics and its champions have some credibility.

The Two Worlds of KM

Traditionally, the practice of knowledge management has united the orbits of two worlds: the world of information and communications technology, and the world of people at work. This second aspect is often referred to as the "people side" or "soft side" of the knowledge management discipline. It is also the least understood and most problematic; it is also now considered the most important side of KM. The ability of an organization to grow its knowledge base depends upon the extent to which members exchange and combine existing information, knowledge, and ideas.

The technology side of KM has been where the money is. As a result, suppliers (*vendors* in government parlance) of computer hardware and software dominated the literature, conferences, and spending on KM for the first decade of its development. Beginning in the first years of the new century, however, this trend began a shift to a greater emphasis on applications. This has meant that applications integrators and KM systems consultants, including a growing number of academics, are contributing more to the growth of the KM discipline.

Conventional wisdom suggests a caveat for anyone hoping to pin reductions in spending and improvements in government performance and accountability to any rationality imposed on the government's purchase and use of technology, as John Nicolay pointed out in a *Public Administration Quarterly*:

> Two issues are clear: there exists no theoretical underpinning for the use of information technologies as an agent of change in the public service and, two, at the federal level, technology itself is regarded as a positive investment while human capital is not. (Nicolay 2002, 65)

KM at the Local Level

Like the rest of the industrialized world, today America and Americans live, work, and play in a cultural and economic environment that is permanently shaped by global access to information. More and more, this means access to information via the Internet. Over the last decade and a half, the economies of many industrialized nations underwent a wave of technological change that has significantly reshaped nearly every aspect of both the private and the public sectors. Information-age technologies are changing people's values and the nation's interests (Acs 2002; Ho 2003). Access to information—and to the knowledge that results from the application of information and communications technology to problem solving and decision making—has influenced the way businesses operate, the ways consumers purchase goods and services, and the ways that government at all levels provides public services.

Before the growth of the Internet, the federal government was already applying information and communications technology to improve operating efficiency, but primarily for internal communications and managerial purposes. This growth in Internet usage and e-commerce that occurred during the 1990s in the private sector soon pressured the public sector to serve citizens electronically in what is recognized globally as the "e-government" initiative (Ho 2002, 434).

Although the e-government movement has been widely accepted at the federal level, its acceptance appears to be moving less rapidly at the local level. In 1997, for example, only 8.7 percent of local governments in the United States had their own Web sites (Eddowes 2003). An international survey conducted in 2000 on the extent of e-government at the local level was sent to nearly 3,000 local governments with populations greater than 10,000; only a little more than half (51 percent) responded. The results showed that 85.3 percent of the municipalities responding had a Web site and 57.4 percent had an intranet. Only 46 cities reported having had a Web site for longer than five years. Despite these encouraging results, the survey was less sanguine about local governments moving farther toward adoption of full e-government programs; only 114 cities (8.2 percent of respondents) reported having a comprehensive e-government strategy or master plan to guide their future e-government initiatives (Moon 2002).

The slow growth of e-government and knowledge management among local governments has been echoed by a number of studies that report a local perception that investments in the technology do not result in commensurate positive gains in productivity and performance. The redistribution argument states that IT may not improve the productivity of the entire public sector; rather, it only redistributes benefits within government, such as giving one organization a competitive advantage. Poor measurement, the most commonly reported reason, refers to the use of labor productivity measures that measure only the number of outputs, not their quality. The lag in time required for an organization to receive full benefit from its investments in IT may be because such investments often require extensive restructuring of workflow and infrastructure before full benefits are seen. Additionally, not all workers may participate in the use of the IT at the same time; some administrators and workers will remain emphatically computer illiterate.

This leads to the last argument, that investing in IT will not by itself improve productivity. Training and a cultural change are often needed. Moreover, the investment may be larger than actually needed, thus contributing to poor results. After studying data from all fifty states, Lee and Perry concluded that, although IT does have a positive impact on economic performance (as measured by gross state product), alone, it was not found to significantly increase agency productivity. Far greater economic benefits appear to accrue to those organizations who marry information and communications technology with knowledge management theory to build knowledge management systems that synergistically magnify the benefits of each item (Butler et al. 2003).

Conclusion

KM is a set of processes, practices, and management philosophies that exist to collect, process, store, and make available the organizational knowledge that enables government agencies to be more proficient and competitive in the delivery of public services.

KM and knowledge management systems (KMS) may be the latest manifestation of governments' concerns with data, information, and knowledge. This interest began in the late 1950s and 1960s with the growth of large-scale adoption of data processing with mainframe computers and batch processing. By the 1970s, a few organizations were employing internally developed Executive Information Systems (EISs). These, in turn, evolved into a variety of management information systems and commercially available EIS products. By the late 1980s, the reinvent government effort allowed government leaders to take advantage of the widely available computer capabilities in government agencies to introduce private-sector management practices into government, including total quality management, performance appraisals, and cost controls.

Reinventing government evolved into the e-government initiatives of the early years of the new century. At the same time, government agencies began to adopt the knowledge management practices being adopted by knowledge industries. In just a few years it became increasingly apparent that the information technology industry was driving knowledge management. IT was recognized as only one aspect of KM; other components include people, systems, and organizational cultures. Federal agencies were required by the Enterprise Architecture Act of 2002 to complete self-assessments of their IT uses and perceived needs. The goal of the assessments was to reduce IT costs by the greater use of common standards and collaboration whenever possible. By 2005, most of the building blocks for KM were readily available or already in place.

Several reasons for the apparent differences in the way the private and public sector function include: basic environmental factors, the ways in which sector organizations interact with their environments and with their stakeholders, and differences in organizational structures and processes. Because public organizations are insulated from market pressures, they are not as influenced by rewards and punishments exercised by market controls.

2

KM: A Self-Regulating Social System

> *Useful knowledge is not a "thing" that can be managed*
> *like other assets, as a self-contained entity. Nor does it*
> *just float free in cyberspace. . . . Only when information*
> *is used by people does it become knowledge.*
> (Wenger, McDermott, and Snyder 2002)

Businesses and government departments and agencies spend billions of dollars each year for purchases of information and communications technology and knowledge management (KM) equipment, materials, and consulting. One information and technology services executive estimated in 2005 that for the public and private sectors combined, IT and KM purchases together made up an annual U.S. market in excess of $12 billion. Much of this money is spent on the technology parts and pieces that together produce *knowledge management systems* (KMS). But technical mechanisms are only part of the story; KM is more than technology. It is a social system in which the needs and dictates of the people for whom KM is designed remain paramount.

The phrase *social system* is used in this chapter to collectively refer to a complex set of interacting parts and pieces that together make a knowledge management system. Some authors have referred to these same components as *conditions for success,* as *the fundamental components of KM,* and by other labels. Alluding to the pieces as integral components in a system helps prospective users of KM understand that it is not just another monolithic management theory, but is instead a set of tools, procedures, and activities, held together by a unifying philosophy. That philosophy is *sharing knowledge for public sector innovation.* Also, the KM systems that are employed in government departments and agencies are not composed of a predetermined set of static rules and regulations. Rather, they represent a dynamic evolving transformation process, one that has still to achieve its full potential.

Chapter Objectives

This chapter serves as an overview of the next six chapters in the book. The underlying principle is a model of the social system I refer to as the *total knowledge management system*. The salient objectives for this chapter include the following:

- To initiate the process of looking at knowledge management not as an unrelated collection of unrelated technologies and organizational policies and procedures, but as an integrated system composed of five essential subsystems.
- To introduce readers to the proposition that knowledge management systems have the power to transform government agencies into learning organizations.
- To help readers visualize the information technology component of KM as being more a key subsystem of tools and process for data transformation, and less an end in itself.
- To help readers see how the well-known set of steps in the knowledge creation/combination process relate to and interact with the remaining components of the total KM system.
- To review for those not familiar with the tools and processes of KM the several key activities that contribute to and result from changing attitudes of workers from knowledge hoarding to knowledge sharing.
- To reinforce in readers' memories the importance of developing a supportive and collaborative culture for successful implementation of KM.
- To introduce readers to the concepts of organizational learning and to show how the technical and social processes of KM contribute to achieving the goal of transformation from a bureaucracy to a learning organization.
- To introduce readers to the proposition that successful implementation of a knowledge management system may generate a significant contribution to the use of generative learning along with the more commonly encountered adaptive learning.

Organizations Are Not Machines

It is important to note that the use of the terms *mechanisms* and *systems* in this discussion is in no way intended to imply that organizations are like machines, regardless of how well-oiled and smoothly functioning they might be. Such a conclusion runs counter to the basic tenets of knowledge management. Rather, organizations such as government agencies are living *social organisms*—entities that grow, evolve, and eventually die. The science of complexity theory extends this concept to suggest that organizations such as government agencies and departments are actually self-regulating and self-organizing organisms. As such, they are similar to ecosystems in which the living components—in this case, human beings—learn and evolve from contact with forces present in their internal and external environments. A primary objective of knowledge management is to create an organizational environment in which the collection and transfer of knowledge insure that, as much as is possible, organizations change in ways that better meet the needs and expectations of their relevant stakeholders.

As it is used in this discussion, the term *mechanism* is defined as *a collection of moving parts that work together to perform a complete function or purpose.* Such a collection of working parts is typically referred to as a *system.* A system has been defined as being composed of a set of interrelated components such that neither the properties of the component nor those of the system itself can be altered without fundamentally changing the system (National Defense University 2005). Systems can be any of several different types, from simple mechanical systems with predetermined motions of levers and pulleys such as an automobile engine, to complex social organizations, such as government agencies, that are established to accomplish specific objectives. Research on the *systems concept* focuses on the interactive processes between system components and subsystems, and the interactions of the system, its components, and its subsystems with its environment.

The term *mechanism* also refers to the structure or arrangement of the parts of a system *or mechanical device.* In this sense, the word is used as a metaphor for the architecture of the social system (that is, the enterprise architecture). The architecture of the social system defines the way people, technology, and knowledge resources are organized to form a knowledge management system. Government departments and agencies use KM systems, either as a whole or in their various parts, as components in the larger system of management practices employed to achieve agency goals and objectives.

The Knowledge Management Systems Model

This chapter proceeds upon the premise that KM is a dynamic, evolving set of interacting existing and new tools, practices, and procedures that employ technology and social interactions in the delivery of public services. The model of the knowledge management systems displayed in Figure 2.1 illustrates how the combined concepts, mechanisms, and processes of a KM system interact to shape an organizational culture that values knowledge creation and knowledge sharing. Together, these mechanisms, process, and subsystems may be considered a total knowledge management system.

26

Figure 2.1 Fundamental Mechanisms, Processes, and Payoffs in a Public-Sector Knowledge Management System

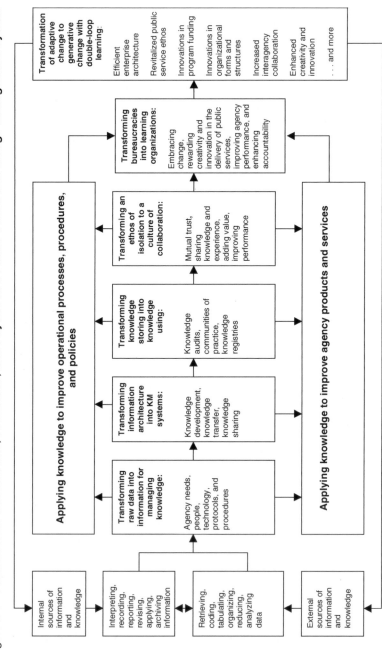

Figure 2.2   **How KM Subsystems Interact to Produce Learning and Generative Change**

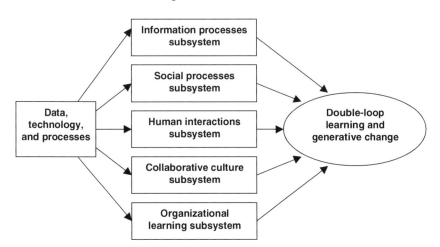

This model of the KM system should be viewed as a living, dynamic system in which new, innovative tools, goals, approaches, and other elements are being added almost daily. Parts of what was new in KM one year are likely to be supplanted or replaced in the next. As KM concepts continue to evolve and change their focus, they are eventually replaced by improved ideas and processes as our knowledge about knowledge also grows. KM is, indeed, an evolving discipline.

1. Many authors researching and writing in the KM field of inquiry seem to have their particular favorite lists of basic elements for knowledge management. However, exposure to a wide variety of government KM applications and a broad reading in the KM literature suggest that five chief subsystems—each with a varying set of parts or components—come together to make up the fundamental building blocks of KM. Moreover, there seems to be significant agreement that a chief outcome of successful implementation of a KM system is the type of agency transformation mandated by recent presidential initiatives. These five subsystems and the transformation outcome incorporated into this model represent a realistic consensus of views on what should be included in the still-evolving KM discipline. Figure 2.2 illustrates the way in which the five KM subsystems collectively contribute to the payoffs occurring from transforming adaptive change to change that is generative.

2. An information technology–based *information processes subsystem* of hardware and software tools facilitates the transformation of data to infor-

mation, and of information to knowledge. This subsystem also supports the ultimate goal of knowledge eventually enabling individual and organizational learning. The processes in this subsystem revolve around designing and investing in the agency-wide enterprise technology architecture needed for supporting an agency-wide knowledge management system. Together, these are the fundamental building blocks of all KM systems: information needs of the agency, its people, its technology, its processes, and its culture.

3. In a *social processes subsystem,* knowledge sharing and distribution are enabled and promoted. This subsystem is a product of the agency's investment in the technology. However, its more important elements include the social components of its operations. These ultimately result in formation of the informal, self-regulating communities of practice that form the heart of the next subsystem. The chief components of this subsystem reflect earlier thinking on the cycle of learning. The four social processes include socialization, internalization, combining, and externalizing (or sharing).

4. A *human interactions subsystem* makes it possible to support and value knowledge creating, collecting, and sharing. With information and communications technology serving as the underlying support platform, three key actions illustrate the types of mechanisms and processes that take place at this stage of the system: knowledge audits, communities of practice, and knowledge registries; many others could be included.

5. A *collaborative culture subsystem* includes all the KM applications designed to improve the products and services provided by an agency. It also includes knowledge applications designed to improve the agency's internal processes, procedures, and policies, as well as its service delivery mechanisms. The product and delivery applications are shaped by the agency's enterprise architecture, people, mission, and culture. The product of this subsystem is the sought-after *culture of collaboration* that nurtures employee willingness to share their knowledge for the good of the organization. This, in turn, facilitates the creation of new knowledge that, in application, adds even greater value to the agency's delivered services. This subsystem has as one of its fundamental goals the transformation of the often-encountered ethos of self-before-others into a culture of collaboration and unselfish service before self. It is, then, the essence of the culture change that is needed for successful implementation of KM into a public organization.

6. An *organizational learning subsystem* makes it possible for a government agency or department to transform itself from the traditional hierarchical, bureaucratic structure thought for decades to be the public service ideal, to become an organization that learns from its mistakes and successes. Learning organizations can exist only when experience and knowledge are consistently and extensively shared, valued, and promoted. Thus, they are products

of an organizational culture in which hierarchical, bureaucratic structures are transformed into flat, team-driven, collaborative organizations of empowered individuals. A consistent problem with stopping the system at this point is that the change processes that agencies adopt are reactive rather than proactive. Reactive change is adaptive change, whereas proactive change is generative change.

7. This is the apex of the total knowledge management system idea: an organizational culture in which adaptive change is transformed into generative change. In the generative organization, creativity and innovation are not only tolerated, they are celebrated. They are the products of the interchange that occurs as a result of the interaction among these salient KMS subsystems. This culture change is the benefit received when agency leaders support and reward innovation and creativity, regardless of the outcome of that innovation. Adaptive change happens when organizations evolve to the point where managers and staff search out ways to react to changes in their environment. However, generative change is the organizational characteristic that makes it possible for agencies to make changes to their operational systems before problems occur; it produces and promotes the continuous improvement process, and enables the management transformation process that results in innovative solutions to agency problems.

The Information Processes Subsystem

The need to manage large amounts of data, to transform that data into the type and amount of information needed by decision makers, is one of the earliest drivers of the knowledge management discipline. One thing that government does well and does often is to collect data. This data ranges from the Census of Population, which takes place every ten years, to the Census of Industry, which occurs every five years, to the annual collection of agricultural production, trade statistics, and tax receipts—and much more in between. All this raw data is meaningless until it is coded, transformed, shaped into graphic communications forms, evaluated and interpreted, recorded and published, and eventually filed for future reference—only then does it become information. This information is one kind of input needed by a knowledge management system. It remains processed data until it is put to some use by people somewhere. Then it becomes knowledge, the kind known as *explicit knowledge.* Explicit knowledge is what is found in reports and manuals, films, radio scripts, charts and graphs, and speeches and books.

The second type of knowledge is fundamentally different from explicit knowledge. Called *tacit knowledge,* it often skips the information stage because it is knowledge that exists in the minds of human beings. It is knowledge gained from experience, from doing and acting. It is difficult if not impossible to convert tacit knowledge to explicit knowledge. A written report of an event is not the same thing as being there or experiencing the activity by taking part in its production or delivery.

Two of the key questions underlying the "hard" or technology-driven side of KM are, How do you convert raw data into information? And, once that the data are information, how is that information converted into usable knowledge? These are questions that revolve around the concepts of knowledge creation and conversion. Knowledge creation occurs when people use what they know or have learned to perform what for them is a creative or innovative task. For example, electricians learn to handle electricity from what happens when they try to handle a live or "hot" line. The shock they receive is the lesson; they then know that to avoid a shock, one must turn off a breaker or switch so that the line is no longer "hot." Once learned, such knowledge is seldom forgotten. Clearly, knowledge is created by human experience, which can be from doing; or, it can be learned by reading about a phenomenon, by watching a film or video, or from listening to a narrative—someone telling a story about their experience.

The Social Processes Subsystem

In the social processes subsystem, knowledge collection, distribution, and sharing are enabled and promoted. This subsystem is a product of the agency's investment in the technology, of course. However, the more important elements are the social processes that put technology to work.

The four social processes are *socialization, internalization, combining,* and *externalizing* (Nonaka and Takeuchi 1995). These ultimately result in formation of the informal, self-regulating *communities of practice* that form the heart of the human interactions subsystem. These components have evolved from earlier thinking on learning theory and the learning or knowledge cycle, including the work of Kurt Lewin, John Dewey, and Jean Piaget (Blessing and Wallace 2000).

Converting Information into Knowledge

Information does not become knowledge until it is used by someone. The conversion of information into knowledge entails a vastly different process than converting data into information. Although IT tools may be used in the process, they are secondary to the rule of human interaction. Nonaka and Takeuchi (1995) explained this as a process of converting tacit knowledge into explicit knowledge, and vice versa. They identified four modes of knowledge conversion. Each of the conversion processes has been given a label. For example, converting tacit knowledge into more explicit knowledge occurs through a process of *socialization*. Converting tacit knowledge to explicit knowledge occurs in a process of *internalization*—the process that transforms explicit knowledge into tacit knowledge. When new explicit knowledge is combined with existing explicit knowledge, a process of *combination* is involved.

Tacit vs. Explicit Knowledge

The distinctions between the two types of knowledge found in organizations—explicit and tacit—have been thoroughly critiqued by the authors of many papers and books that touch upon KM, beginning with the authors some consider to be KM's intellectual pioneers—Michael Polanyi in 1958, Ikujiro Nonaka and Hirotaka Takeuchi in 1995, and Karl-Erik Svieby in 1997, for example (Saint-Onge and Wallace 2003, Ash and Cohendet, 2004). Therefore, that distinction is only briefly reviewed here. The foundation stones of the discipline were set when the distinction was made between knowledge that is tacit (implicit) and knowledge that is explicit (Polanyi 1958). Table 2.1 compares the two forms of knowledge on several key characteristics.

Tacit knowledge exists in the minds of the holders, who for our purposes are the men and women in government with the skills and understanding that can come only with education and years of experience in public service. Tacit knowledge is difficult to express in its full form; the type of knowledge learned on the job cannot be written in books or learned at the computer.

Some people believe that tacit knowledge is inexpressible (Tiwana 2001). Explicit knowledge, on the other hand, represents knowledge that can be stored in books, pamphlets, manuals, drawings, and databases and on hard drives or computer discs. Because of this characteristic, explicit knowledge is considered as knowledge that can be codified—that is, knowledge that can be written in books and/or recorded in other media.

A list of the tools used in knowledge management systems includes the mechanisms and technology of collecting, storing, retrieving, organizing, transforming, and distributing knowledge. It is generally understood that these tools are what make it possible to process explicit knowledge, but that they are less appropriate for managing implicit knowledge.

Data conversion or transformation is both a mechanical and a mental process. Modern desktop and laptop computers and software programs are capable of quietly processing and organizing reams of data in a very short period. Of course, they have to be told what to do, how to go about the organizing, and in what form to present the results of their processing. That is a technical task relatively easily

Table 2.1

A Comparison of Tacit and Explicit Knowledge

Characteristic	Tacit knowledge	Explicit knowledge
Nature	Personal, context specific	May be codified, written
Formality	Hard to formalize, codify, record, code, or express	Is formalized through the process of explanation or interpretation of tacit knowledge
Location	In the minds of workers	Manuals, reports, drawings, databases, e-communications, charts, films, etc.
Conversion process	Conversion to explicit knowledge occurs in social processes, including externalization in stories, etc.	Converted back to tacit knowledge through personal understanding, absorption, or remembering
IT influence	Difficult for IT to play a role in tacit knowledge; sharing is personal and takes place in social situations	Fully supportable by IT and ICT
Medium	Needs a rich communications environment, a culture of sharing and trust	Can be transferred through normal communications media

Source: Tiwana 2001, 39.

learned by humans. Thus, the transformation of raw data into information occurs when humans impose a structure on the data according to an organizing structure that has meaning for those persons who will use the data.

The Human Interactions Subsystem

One way to approach the task of understanding the basic components of knowledge is to begin by reviewing some of the key activities or beliefs that are encapsulated in most if not all KM systems. Each of the activities helps facilitate the development of an organizational culture in which knowledge is collected, valued, and transferred. Among the more important activities are knowledge audits, communities of practice, and knowledge registries.

Beginning with a Knowledge Audit

The information audit is one of the first steps to be taken when establishing a knowledge management system. Knowledge audits have been recognized since the early 1990s as a way of identifying and cataloging an organization's information needs and knowledge assets, and determining how closely these needs and assets are aligned (Griffiths 2005). Government organizations at all levels need to conduct information audits regularly so that they know what they know. In addition, agencies need to have an understanding of the knowledge existing in the organization and of the context in which that knowledge and experience must be applied in the conduct of the agency's business. Closing the gaps between knowledge needs and information available helps the organization accomplish its program objectives.

Peter Griffiths (2005), head of the information services unit at the UK Home Office, has suggested that the audit also be used in the creation and publication of such new information items as:

- Descriptive documents spelling out how information is currently managed in an agency.
- Formal statements of information requirements by an organization or its component units.
- Statements of the availability of information resources within the agency—as well as any restrictions on use, security, licensing, etc.
- Analyses of the differences between needs and availability statements.
- Recommendations for provision of additional resources or changes in information-management practices, technology use, or information sources.
- Case data for supporting recommended changes.

The information audit achieves these tasks by first looking at the organization's information needs, then conducting an inventory of the information assets of the organization. The capstone process involves determining—only by working hand in glove with the organization's leadership—how closely the two elements of the knowledge management system align.

The skills and resources required for conducting a meaningful information audit are dauntingly large for many government agencies. The audit team must ensure that the audit focuses explicitly on the needs of the sponsoring organization and have the full support of senior-level management to smooth over operating-level objections that are likely to arise over the time and effort required to complete an audit. The team must possess the skills and knowledge to be able to make such meaningful tasks and interpretations as:

- Establishing how the present and future roles of information and knowledge are needed for adding value to the organization, agency, or department.

- Determining how knowledge supports the organization's present and future objectives, either directly or by helping workers who support operations designed to achieve those objectives.
- Assessing the scope and identifying the location and source of the information required by the organization, while at the same time relating that information to the knowledge that already exists in the organization, or that which is in other ways generated internally.

Growing a Community of Practice

Communities of practice have become one of the principle mechanisms driving the transformation of data into information and information into knowledge. Communities are also what make a culture of knowledge sharing the characteristic that helps define learning organizations. Communities of practice are groups of people with like interests, knowledge, concerns, skills, and training who come together in some social situation, such as an informal meeting or conference, to share what they know and what they do not know. The purpose of such sessions is to learn from each other. The sharing of knowledge helps all members of the community to learn, including the individual doing the sharing. Learning by sharing is similar to learning by doing; it may not result in the tacit knowledge of a skill that is forged through years or decades on a job, but it does help avoid repeating the learning failures that may have occurred in the past (Ash and Cohendet 2004).

A community of practice may be defined as a tightly knit group of members of an organization who are engaged in a shared practice (Wasko and Faraj 2005). The members know each other and work together. They usually meet face to face, and are continually engaged in negotiating, communicating, and coordinating with each other directly. Interacting in this way, communities of practice are able to perform the following functions for organizations (Snyder and Briggs 2003):

- They husband and develop the knowledge assets of organizations.
- They operate as "social learning systems," where practitioners connect to solve problems, share ideas, set standards, and develop informal relationships with peers and stakeholders.
- They complement the information-transmitting activities of formal units in organizations that have the primary purpose of delivering a product or service.
- They bridge formal organizational boundaries, thus increasing the collective store of knowledge, skills, and professional trust and reciprocity.

In some agencies *communities of interest* may be used as a synonym for communities of practice. However, although their fundamental goals are similar, their functions and organizational benefits are structurally and operationally quite different. A community of interest is typically a formal grouping, such as a work team or a department or unit, with a vested interest in the delivery of the service, while a community of practice is more commonly an informal group of persons, often widely dispersed geographically, who share a passionate interest in the topic, product, or service.

Although the procedures and processes involved in moving a community of interest to a community of practice (CoP) are discussed in detail in a later chapter, before continuing it is important to have an understanding of how the CoP can build on and utilize the information technology tools deployed in conducting an information audit and building a knowledge registry. This can be achieved by examining a case history of an early CoP formed in the Federal Highway Administration.

Mike Burk is a knowledge management professional at the U.S. Department of Transportation's Highway Administration (FHWA). As the administration's senior knowledge officer, he directed creation of one of the earliest and most often cited "best practices" models of a community of practice in the federal government (Snyder and Briggs 2003).

The FHWA recognized that an informal community of practice was forming with federal, state, and local highway and safety personnel using the Internet to share knowledge on the use of highway "rumble strips." Rumble strips are the serrated bands installed along the outer edge of highway paving that produce a loud rumble noise when driven over. They are designed to let drivers know they are about to drive off the highway, and are particularly useful for alerting drowsy drivers before they have an accident. The knowledge-sharing activities of this CoP are supported by the Web site http://safety.fhwa.dot.gov/roadway_dept/rumble/index. The site was created and maintained in a collaborative effort by the knowledge manager for the FHWA's New York division, a FHWA marketing specialist, several highway safety engineers, and an outside consultant. Anyone with an interest in highway construction and safety can access the site for reports from states that have installed the devices, descriptions of the various types available, word on some of their drawbacks, and a short video on the various types of strips and how they are installed.

Forming and Maintaining a Knowledge Registry

Although it is commonly recognized that knowledge resides in the minds of individuals, knowledge sharing takes place in the context of two or more individuals in social settings. These can be as small as two people chatting over a cup of coffee, or as large as a community of professionals with hundreds and even thousands of members. More than one community can exist in an agency or subunit. When personal contact is impossible, or when a knowledge seeker does not know where in the organization knowledge is stored or who holds the needed knowledge, a place where it is possible to quickly look up the source is needed. In practice, these locations are referred to as "virtual yellow pages," or by their more formal name, knowledge registries.

The process-based mission assurance (PBMA) knowledge management system was formed in 1998 by NASA's Office of Safety and Mission Assurance to enable senior managers, program executives, and program and project managers to find critical managerial, scientific, engineering, and technical skills to support NASA's mission. One of the ways that the PBMA knowledge management system makes this possible is through development and regular maintenance of its knowledge registry. The registry serves as a knowledge locator, identifying where in the agency to find expertise on safety and mission assurance and technology. Other tools are also used in the application of knowledge management, as are tools and processes not necessarily considered to be KM components. More will be discussed later.

The PBMA unit of NASA reported in 2005 that it served more than 340 separate communities of practice; those communities, in turn, served the unit's more than 7,200 staff members and their outside stakeholders.

A Collaborative Culture Subsystem

Every organization has its own organizational culture and climate (Schein 1992, McNabb and Sepic 1995). The role of the culture of an organization has also achieved key importance in the literature of knowledge management. Knowledge accumulation and transfer occurs best at the point of contact where an organization's communities of practice interact with—and strive to interpret—the work environment. Contact in this instance does not have to be face-to-face. Rather, it can and does occur more often today as informal messaging via electronic communication processes. Contact may take place in formal work settings and informal social sessions. Formal settings—such as meetings and conferences—produce the type of knowledge that is typically explicit and nonthreatening to the participants. Typically, it is of lesser value than the contact that occurs in informal settings.

Sharing of knowledge in the formal, organizational structure way is invaluable, of course, but it is often not the knowledge that results in innovative solutions to thorny, often nagging, problems of practice. Informal situations, however, are often the milieus where new insights and creative problem solving occur. It is in informal settings, where people know and respect each other for their individual intellectual abilities and contributions, that creativity and innovation thrive. Accordingly,

> [T]he process of creating, accumulating, and distributing knowledge . . . is achieved through the functioning of informal groups of people, or autonomous "communities" acting under conditions of voluntary exchange and respect of the social norms that are defined within each group. (Ash and Cohendet 2004, 9)

None of this sharing can take place if the organizational culture does not support the mechanisms of knowledge management. To be successful, a senior-level administrator must champion the activity both within the organization and without. Different performance measurements apply, particularly when comparing public-sector KM initiatives with the same tools and practices applied in the private sector. In government, the profit motive is usually not a limiting factor, whereas earnings and profits are salient concerns in business. The willingness to go to bat for the people and programs during budget negotiations, as well as a vociferously supportive attitude of senior management, help shape an organization's internal environment. They are also among the chief factors that make successful adoption of KM possible.

It is impossible to overemphasize the importance of a positive, collaborative culture. People who share work interests or practices are held together by a common bond of purpose and skills and typically have the same desire for successfully accomplishing the organization's mission. Their skills range from learning by doing, leading relevant conversations, identifying best practices and exemplars, managing arguments and disagreements, and providing mutual support and recognition for participants.

Implementing a knowledge management system or any of its components begins with preparing the organizational culture to accept the KM way of sharing information. This does not mean designing and carrying out a costly and often ineffective program to completely transform the culture of the organization. Federal Highway Administration chief knowledge officer Mike Burk explained what he found to be effective in his organization:

> To implement knowledge management, how much does an organization need to change its culture? Some people believe that a wholesale transformation is required in the way people work and act, but this is largely a myth. The fact is that successful knowledge management programs work with organizational cultures and behaviors, not against them. (Burk 1999)

It is clear that some aspects of a corporate culture can interfere with a knowledge management system. For example, some members of the organization will remain proprietary about their knowledge, believing that the possession of that knowledge places them in a position of power, where others must come to them for help. They fear a loss of control if others gain access to their department's knowledge. Others may not see any personal benefit accruing from sharing their knowledge. Burk concluded that such problems can be addressed by appropriate use of communication about KM and its benefits for everyone in the organization. Formal recognition and reward of individuals who go out of their way to share knowledge is another way of promoting acceptance of the KM program.

The Organizational Learning Subsystem

Government organizations learn by following a process of developing, collecting, and processing the knowledge, experience, and skills that their people need to perform their tasks. However, it has been suggested that government agencies can improve the quality of this learning by developing innovative solutions to old and new problems—and making changes to the system before circumstances become problems (Lawrence 1998).

Organizations learn from interactions with their environment. These interactions occur when the organization develops *collaborative networks* with internal and external stakeholder groups. These networks make it possible to benefit from the knowledge, capabilities, and experiences of those individuals and groups. This collaborative learning is a reflection of the strong bond that exists between the principles and practices of knowledge management and the learning organization outcomes. This bond is increasingly recognized in public-sector organizations around the globe. In the Central American country of El Salvador, for example, a study partially financed by the World Bank strongly endorsed developing KM systems to enable organizational learning to take place in both the public and the private sectors (*Conectándonos al Futuro de El Salvador* 1999).

What are the chief components of an organizational learning subsystem? The first two elements of organizational learning—what Peter Senge refers to as "disciplines"—are inherently personal. One is the knowledge or *personal mastery* held by the people in an agency—what is sometimes referred to as the *intellectual capital* of an organization (Senge 1990; McElyea 2002). The second is the *mental models* that shape and frame the way people think, learn, and react to environmental stimuli.

The next three components are a reflection of the influence placed upon individuals in their interactions with other people in their social organizations. The first of these three social factors is the *shared vision* of the individuals in the agency. This forms the basis for the shared concern, or passion, over the mission. It is also the basis for the commitment individuals share toward the agency, their unit, and their fellow workers. In another circumstance, it might have been referred to as *loyalty to the cause;* Senge refers to it as "shared vision" (9). It involves identifying the "shared pictures of the future" that result in genuine commitment and voluntary enrollment in serving rather than simply complying with a directive from management.

The second of the three organizational elements is *team learning,* which Senge describes as beginning with dialogue and ending with thinking together. Team learning is about aligning team members' efforts and collaboration. The final element in this subsystem is an echo of the approach taken in this text: *systems thinking*—Senge's "fifth discipline." This makes it possible for all the other elements to function in the organization and its people. It "integrates the disciplines, fusing them into a coherent body of theory and practice" (12).

Double-Learning at the Forest Service

The U.S. Forest Service, once one of the federal government's most admired agencies, is an example of an agency that has been forced in reaction to public pressure to evolve from its traditional, often hidebound role as the guardian of the nation's forests to become instead a conservation organization with many missions and many stakeholders. A white paper produced in May of 2000 described the agency as a "learning organization" (Apple 2000). Clearly, the Forest Service has learned and has changed. However, that change may have been more reactive (adaptive) than proactive (generative).

Beginning in the late 1960s, the Forest Service came under intense pressure and criticism for focusing too much on managing the development of the commodity value of forest products, especially timber and grazing, and for not paying enough attention to such values as wildlife, wilderness, and recreation. It was also being criticized for not responding to shifting societal demands on the non-revenue values. Passage of the National Environmental Policy Act in 1969 forced the service to change; new ways to operate, new missions, and more and more vocal stakeholder groups had to be dealt with. For the Forest Service, the path to becoming a learning organization began with changing employees' visions of themselves from seeing themselves as the forestry experts to viewing themselves as stewards of the nation's trust.

Change for the Forest Service meant developing the capacity to (1) change in response to experience, (2) monitor their operations more closely, (3) identify the environmental impact of their operations, and (4) begin to listen to their clients for clues to the adequacy of their performance. The Forest Service developed the ability to accept and implement adaptive change by reacting outside pressures.

Generative Change in Canada's PSC

The Public Service Commission of Canada (PSC) is an independent agency responsible for preserving and promoting the values of competence, nonpartisanship, and representativeness among the members of Canada's professional public service. In this role, it is also a key participant in the implementation of the Public Service Modernization Act and, particularly, the Public Service Employment Act, which came into force in 2005. The PSC has also long shown an interest in the concepts of knowledge management and learning organizations. Eton Lawrence (1998), a member of the PSC's policy research and communications branch, quoted a 1998 Privy Council report to the prime minister regarding which areas of the Canadian government needed further improvement:

> In human resources management, the goal is to become a learning- and knowledge-based organization, one able to provide people with the breadth of knowledge and experience necessary to advise and serve in a modern global government.

Lawrence went on to add that, although that this trend is seen in both the public and the private sectors as more or less inevitable, the real challenge government agencies face is how to go about actually transforming an agency into a learning organization. One of the first answers to this conundrum is not simply relying on adaptive learning, but also incorporating generative learning. Generative learning is what happens when people and organizations learn how to go beyond reacting to environmental pressures, to be able to anticipate potential problems—and opportunities—before they occur. Lawrence described this skill as learning that is more deliberative, reflective, and anticipatory. Organizations, to be successful, must learn how to employ both types of learning.

Conclusion

This chapter introduced a model of a vision of a total knowledge management system. The components or subsystems that make up the system include:

- A technology-based *information processes subsystem* that collects, codifies, and records data according to agency needs, in forms that people want and need, according to protocols and procedures set forth by the federal government's enterprise architecture initiative.
- A *social processes subsystem* that transfers and transforms information into knowledge through the processes of socialization, internalization, combining, and externalization.
- A *human interactions subsystem* that employs such tools as knowledge audits, communities of practice, and knowledge registries, among others, in order to begin the transition from a culture of knowledge hoarding to one of knowledge sharing.
- A *collaborative culture subsystem* that makes it the norm for all the experiences and knowledge of all members of a community of interest to be freely shared and employed when and where they are needed for carrying out the mission of the agency.
- An *organizational learning subsystem* that enables the transformation of agency focus solely on the essential single-loop, adaptive change process to also value and implement the more rewarding processes of double-loop, generative learning.

A number of domestic and international public-sector case examples were used to illustrate how the various components discussed in the chapter are implemented in actual agencies and departments.

Part 2

Transforming Government with KM

3

The Technology and Processes Subsystem

Information consists of facts and data that are organized to describe a particular situation or condition. Knowledge is subsequently applied to interpret the available information about a particular situation and to decide how to manage it. Knowledge consists of facts, truths, and beliefs, perspectives and concepts, judgments and expectations, methodologies and know-how. Knowledge is accumulated and integrated and held over long periods to be available to be applied to handle specific situations and problems. . . . We use knowledge to determine what a particular situation means.

(Wiig 1994, xiv–vx)

A fundamental purpose of knowledge management is to give all members of an organization the power that can be gained from shared and reusable knowledge. Designing a system for knowledge to be shared in an organization requires establishing the best combination of people, information, processes, and technology. In the public sector, knowledge management systems must enable the organization to develop and maintain the ability to (1) identify relevant information that is needed for completion of the agency's mission, (2) strengthen interagency collaborations, and (3) store, organize, and catalog everyday and invaluable knowledge so that it can be used in the near and distant future.

To avoid being blinded by the exorbitant claims often touted for KM, the public sector system designer must also keep in mind that not everyone believes that KM is the wave of the future in either the private or the public sector. Rather, KM has good intentions, but in the harsh glare of reality, it is only as good as the people who design and use it.

Not everyone believes that KM is worth the time and money required for its implementation. Some critics are even harsher in their opinion of the discipline. One critic (Fuller 2002, 32), for example, has offered the opinion that KM portends the end of knowledge in science and practice, as well as signaling the final disintegration of the university, among other calamities. As if this weren't enough, he went on to claim that, "Knowledge management updates the spirit that led to the burning of the Library of Alexandria and the stigmatizing of universities during the Scientific and Industrial Revolutions."

Adjusting for the obvious hyperbole in Fuller's comments, there is no denying the fact that the knowledge management discipline does contain many controversial features, misconceptions, and contending theories. Perhaps after reading this book, the stress that some readers may suffer from those controversies may be alleviated—and they may sleep more soundly knowing that the nation's libraries and universities are safe, at least for another generation.

Chapter Objectives

This chapter has been framed on a set of objectives that are designed to help readers:

- Recognize that, although opinions differ on the number and categories of fundamental components that go together to constitute a knowledge management program and/or the KM discipline, it is possible to see a consensus on five basic components.
- Know and understand the basic processes that make it possible for a knowledge management system to achieve its goals and objectives.
- Begin to understand the contributing, but not dominant, role that technology plays in the knowledge management concept.
- Understand the importance of integrating information and communications technologies with knowledge management systems procedures.
- Gain a brief understanding of the potential that mobile and wireless technologies have for influencing all agency delivery systems, as well as their knowledge management systems.
- Begin to see how performance measurement, one of the key components of KM, functions to improve performance and enhance accountability.

The Chief Components of KM

A government manager wishing to implement a knowledge management program will wish to begin by knowing which of the litany of components and processes are critical for success. One way to do this is to study what ele-

Table 3.1

Five-Model Comparison of Perceived Critical KM Components

	KM 4 pillars	European model	**KM 4 enablers**	KMAT model	Navy Dept.
Technology	√	√	√	√	√
Leadership	√	√		√	
Culture		√	√	√	√
Measurement		√	√	√	
Process		√		√	√
Organization	√	√			
Infrastructure			√		
Learning	√				√
Content					√

Source: Girard 2005.

ments leaders of other successful KM systems have identified as crucial for a successful implementation. John P. Girard reported on the results of just such a study in 2005. He surveyed 2,650 Canadian public-sector middle managers to identify what characteristics they felt were crucial for KM. Girard found that, with only minor variation, the majority of the respondents gave similar importance rankings to a list of items found in five different KM models. He compared the rankings in four theoretical models and one experience-based model developed by the U.S. Navy. Over all, these nine components were mentioned in the models: technology, leadership, culture, measurement, process, organization, infrastructure, learning, and content.

The four theoretical models were (1) the popular *four pillars* model developed by Stankosky at George Washington University, (2) a model based on research with European managers exclusively, (3) a *four exemplars* model based on a large-sample study by the American Productivity and Quality Center, and (4) a model based on findings of a study that employed the Knowledge Management Assessment Tool (KMAT). The Department of the Navy's (DON) model was the experience-based example studied. Table 3.1 summarizes the salient components listed in each model.

Five of the constructs clearly stand out in this five-model comparison as the most important for successful implementation of KM. They are technology, culture, leadership, measurement, and process. With very little modification, the factors are clearly as applicable in the public sector as they are in industry. Therefore, they constitute the fundamental components in all KM and KM systems applications. Technology and measurement are discussed in this chapter; culture and leadership are often considered to be mutually supporting factors in a larger construct and are, therefore, discussed together in a later chapter. Process is important enough to merit a chapter of its own; it constitutes the substance and content presented in the next chapter.

The nearly universal agreement that technology plays and will continue to play a dominant role in KM applications justifies including it first in this treatment of the processes that constitute the foundation stones of KM. Technology is approached from several different points: technology collectively, information technology (IT), and information and communications technology (ICT). All refer in the broadest sense to the concept of computer-enabled collection and transmission of data, information, and knowledge.

The Role of Technology in KM

The term *technology* is often used by government planners, managers, and administrators as a synonym for either information technology (IT) or information and communications technology (ICT), or for both. However, IT is generally considered to refer to computer-aided hardware and software used in the collection, storage, codification, and reporting of data and information. ICT, on the other hand, includes the computer-aided tools of IT and the variety of means for communicating information and knowledge both internally and externally. In the past decade or so, ICT has produced a number of new tools for knowledge management, including the Internet, intranet and groupware applications, mobile communication devices and systems, and many others (Sydänmaanlakka 2002). The label *information and communications technology* may include a number of subcategories, such as knowledge-providing technology, production technology, and innovation-development technology (Sundbo 2004).

The federal government is attempting to bring a measure of coordination and control to the technology side of knowledge management systems by implementing what is known as the enterprise architecture initiative. *Enterprise architecture* is the term used to mean information technology architecture that encompasses the entire organization, not just its component parts. *Information architecture* was first used in the 1980s to refer to an enterprise-wide model for all data creation and movement in an organization (McGee and Prusak 1993). Initially, the model attempted to account for and accommodate all of an enterprise's relevant entities with a use for data, including customers, products, employees, and all their data relationships. Although the original effort failed, it was reborn in today's enterprise architecture initiative. As incorporated into that initiative, the goal of the information architecture model is to develop a "map" of the organization's data needs, and then to construct an information system based on this map.

Implementing the information and communications technology architecture component of a knowledge management system begins with aligning the system with the agency's knowledge needs. Designing an agency's information technology architecture entails organizing the agency's entire knowledge and information technology resources to carry out the mission of the organization. There are two key parts to designing information technology systems architecture: information system architecture and technology system architecture. Although they are often considered as two almost identical versions of the same concept, significant differences exist. Information architecture deals with the logical flow of information within an agency, whereas technology architecture deals with the physical organization of the technical equipment and staff (Gardner 2000).

Information architecture is built from the sources and destinations of information and knowledge in the organization and the connections between the two that create a channel between sources and users. The computers, terminal, monitors, controlling software, etc. that transform data to information, and the storage locations and data repositories, where data and information are kept until needed, are all parts of the technology architecture. Sources and destinations are the information creators and users who determine the beginning and ending condition of the information. The condition, or state, of the information then influences the scale and scope of the ICT "problem." This refers to designing answers to the management question: How can the volume of information be delivered wherever in the world it is needed, in a form that is recognizable and useful, in a timely manner, and with an acceptable level of accuracy, openness, and security? The technology answer to this question results in establishing the performance specifications for information technology architecture. These performance specifications are, therefore, simply a differently worded expression of the communications problem.

It is generally accepted today that the technology architecture should be driven by the agency's information architecture—it must be user-needs driven, not entirely data or technology driven, as Gardner (2000) has suggested. This supports the contention of knowledge management systems designers and government knowledge users that the information handled by technology systems is far more valuable than the system itself. "The information is the asset; the system is the means to exploit it" (Gardner 2000, 142). In the final analysis, the fundamental point of the government's technology architecture initiative is to specify what equipment and staff goes where, and how much of each is needed.

Despite growing agreement with this idea, the communications and technology problem is, apparently, not going away. In a front-page article in the industry journal *KMWorld,* Jonathan Spira identified what he saw as a symptom of this disease still infecting this conflict in ideas—the wrong thinking that still characterizes many competing KM systems suppliers:

> It isn't any news to anyone reading this that [the two industry giants] have been fighting over the knowledge sharing and collaboration . . . space for many years. Despite the time that has passed, they have not begun to recognize the challenges ahead. The reason: They don't seem to understand what collaboration and knowledge sharing are; their products reflect a lack of perception about the needs of knowledge/information workers and how they work—and how they use the software they have been given. (Spira 2005, 1)

The solution Spira proposed was for collaborative enterprise knowledge software competitors to develop new systems that are designed from the beginning for knowledge and information work, which keeps knowledge workers focused on their tasks. Spira added emphasis to his proposed solution with the reminder that collaboration and sharing within and across agencies and knowledge sharing are "less a question of technology than of systems that facilitate people working together."

Key it Processes in KM

Designing a knowledge management system for a government agency requires consideration of the major processes that together make up what is now recognized as the knowledge management discipline. Alavi and Leidner (2001) concluded that there are five key processes extant in KM: knowledge creation, knowledge storage, knowledge and retrieval, knowledge transfer, and knowledge application. Each of these processes is supported by one or more ICT technologies, and each contributes to one or more knowledge application tasks. The processes and supporting technologies are displayed in Table 3.2.

Among the many ICT tools found in the creation, retrieval, and transfer processes in public-sector KM systems are data mining software, e-learning tools, electronic bulletin boards, intranets, knowledge repositories and directories, databases, discussion forums revolving around communities of practice, and others. Missing in the Alavi and Leidner list were Web-based systems. Where knowledge is applied, such tools as expert systems and workflow systems can be found.

Knowledge management systems are the logical culmination of a management system that uses ICT to facilitate the capture, combination, and application processes of knowledge within the organization. It is important to recall,

Table 3.2

Knowledge Management Process and Supporting ICT Tools

Knowledge management processes	Supporting information and communications technologies	What the information technologies enable	Example platform technologies
Knowledge creation	Data mining, e-learning tools	The creation and combination of new sources of knowledge; just-in-time learning	Knowledge "yellow pages"; stories, dialogues, and discussions
Knowledge storage and retrieval	Electronic bulletin boards, knowledge repositories, and databases	Support of individual and organizational memory; intergroup knowledge access	Groupware and communication technologies
Knowledge combination and transfer	Electronic bulletin boards, discussion forums, knowledge directories	More extensive internal networks and communication channels, and faster access to knowledge sources	Intranets; communities of practice
Knowledge application and reuse	Expert systems, workflow systems	Knowledge applied across time and space; faster application of new knowledge	Knowledge management systems

Sources: Butler et al. 2003; Alavi and Leidner 2001.

however, that no single technology constitutes a knowledge management system (Alavi and Leidner 2001). Rather, three technology tools are found in most successful implementations. The first is a system for coding and sharing of best practices in public and private organizations. The second is the creation and religious maintenance of an organizational knowledge directory. The third is the creation of formal and informal knowledge networks. In order to learn from others, knowledge workers must have free and open access to communication with others with similar interest and focus in the practice.

Integrating Technology Architecture

The preceding chapters discussed how knowledge management systems have evolved from governments' attempts that began more than fifty years ago to integrate their information technology applications. The federal enterprise architecture initiative of the early years of the twenty-first century is one of the government's latest efforts to bring structure, rationality, and commonality to the many different information and communications technologies in use today—and to do so while meeting mandates to improve their performance and their accountability.

IT, and more recently information and communications technology (ICT), has a long history of failures to atone for. Better integration and planning, such as that taking place under the federal enterprise architecture initiative, is bringing order to the disorder that once reigned.

One of the reasons for this disorder in IT and ICT applications has long been the inability of organizations to collect and share information across agency boundaries. Employing enterprise architecture is the first step in designing a KM system that results in a true knowledge-sharing environment in which the system is adapted to support real enterprise processes and the operational needs of the organization. In the past, components of a knowledge management system were often added piecemeal, as knowledge needs became apparent and as technology became available. Thus, adding such increasingly rich and powerful technology as Web sites and Web services, Internet open access, intranets, taxonomies, portals, data warehouses, search engines, collaboration schemes, links to external information providers, and many other agency-specific software systems often led to what Malafsky (2005) has described as KM programs' becoming "mired in [technological] complexity." This chapter is an attempt to bring some meaningful sense of order to the complexity that characterizes much of KM.

When applied appropriately, ICT enables transformations and innovation in such features of public programs as policy formation, administration, and the delivery of program services. More importantly, ICT gives government administrators the power to pick up the pace of innovation in their agencies. The ability that ICTs give managers to improve agency efficiency and effectiveness has long been a justifying principle upon which ICT programs were implemented. For example, there is no question that without ICTs e-government would not be possible.

To help agencies avoid the pitfalls and disorder that often accompanied earlier applications of ICTs, the Australian Public Service Commission proposed a list of twelve fundamental principles to guide information architecture planning and acquisitions in government agencies (APSC 2002). A selected list of those guiding principles is included here:

- Reduce integration complexity and enable integration and interoperability.
- Take a holistic approach, ensuring that government information can be accessed and applied to improve decision making within and across agencies.
- Design the system to be business event-driven (i.e., to accomplish specific tasks).

- All information must have defined sources who will act as stewards of the information. Authorized information must be accessible and available for reuse.
- ICT systems must comply with government security, confidentiality, and privacy laws and policies. This protection must include avoiding improper denial of service, intentional and accidental modification of the data, and unauthorized access.
- Priority on ICT purchases should be given to products adhering to proven industry standards and open architecture.
- To the maximum extent possible, ICT architecture should enable and support the accessibility of government information and services to citizens, businesses, and other federal government agencies and state and local governments.
- The *total cost of ownership* (TCO) principle should shape ICT planning. TCO includes considering costs and benefits across government for hardware and software technologies; planning must balance development, support, and disaster recovery and system retirement costs against the costs of flexibility, scalability, ease of use, and support over the life cycle of the technology or application.

Finally, the suggestions for developing a strategy for implementing knowledge management systems by Australian KM consultant James Robertson (2004) add further emphasis to the recommendations of the Australian government agency. Robertson asserted that to be successful, a KM strategy must begin by identifying the key needs and issues within the organization. It must also provide a framework for dealing with these needs and issues. However, even with a detailed strategy, a high-level champion, and the appropriate building blocks of ICT technology in place, there is still a high probability that a newly installed KMS will fail. One study reported failure rates for private-sector KMS programs that exceed 80 percent (Butler et al. 2003). Most likely, a key reason for these high failure rates was the lack of commitment by senior-level management to stay the course. Failure rates are nearly as high in the public sector, where KM implementations enjoy knowing that they have the support of executive-branch operational transformation mandates behind their KM efforts.

Where Is KM Technology Headed?

The industry journal *CIO Decisions* reported the results of a 2005 survey of the opinions of 300 senior IT decision makers on what role they envisioned for IT in the future. The answers to that question are a reflection of the first directional trend that KM technology is experiencing: IT appears to be playing a smaller role in government KM systems.

The chief information officer (CIO) sample was divided roughly fifty-fifty in its answers to the question of where they believed KM technology is headed. Half believed that IT's role is diminishing, with the other half responding more optimistically. Half of the optimistic portion strongly believed that IT is definitely not going to be given a smaller role. Rather, they predicted that the resources committed to IT will increase. They were also convinced that IT professionals (such as the CIOs surveyed) will continue to have a voice in shaping the future of their organizations. Most of the remaining optimistic respondents (approximately 20 percent of the total) were convinced that the resources directed to IT would continue to grow, but at a slower pace than in the recent past (May 2005).

The sample was also evenly split demographically, with 150 respondents working in small companies and 150 in large companies. All of the roughly 25 percent of the total who believed that IT will continue to dominate the future were employed in high-performing, large companies. However, only 35 percent of the large-company half were optimistic about IT's future role. On the other hand, fully 65 percent of the small-company respondents were optimistic about the future of IT.

Other studies also indicate that IT and ICT will be taking a much smaller role in knowledge management than it did during the early development years of KM's evolution. As noted, throughout most of the 1990s, nearly all government KM initiatives were driven by outside technology vendors or consultants. Since 2002, however, the enterprise architecture and management transformation initiatives may have influenced an unplanned cooperative approach to IT and KM in the federal government. This symbiotic relationship between IT and KM was described by Bryan Gladstone (2000, 1):

> After two decades working with electronic information and communications technologies, managers are recognizing that success is not about getting people to work with IT, but about helping people to work with other people. Knowledge management is explicitly about how people learn and share together in organizations. As such, it is the only way to ensure that all our expensive investments in information handling and communications actually prove worthwhile.

The second major trend in KM technology is the growing demand for collaboration capability in KM communications hardware and software. These are, in fact, some of the most far-reaching developments in technologies affecting knowledge management. They fall into two broad categories: software that supports collaboration and cross-agency information identification, collection, and sharing; and communications tools and systems that support users' needs for information as they are on the move. In many ways, these trends come together to support tools that facilitate information finding in a variety of ways.

In 2005, public-sector knowledge management system designers could choose from more than thirty separate software products dealing with one or more aspects of collaboration. These included programs for document management, workflow systems, information portals, Web conferencing, and more (Harney 2005). Few of the available systems are all-inclusive in what they can do for the user; most provide only one or a few of the different capabilities incorporated under the umbrella application of collaborative business knowledge (CBK). One of the few systems with an application designed specifically for KM is constructed on three separate modules: collaboration, business process management, and KM. The KM module does search and automatic categorization across all modules and features, and tells users accessing certain documents what similar documents they might like to examine.

Collaborative business (enterprise) knowledge system designers follow three cardinal rules in developing these solutions (Spira 2005): First, all applications must take place in one environment—the "one environment rule." Second, there must be friction-free knowledge sharing—that is, people sharing knowledge and information without having to think about how they do the sharing. And, third, workers are able to communicate and collaborate contextually (i.e, sharing documents and whiteboarding).

Marcelline Saunders, product manager for search and KM for the Canadian systems integrator Hummingbird Ltd., identified collaboration suites as one of the three chief trends in information and communications technology in 2005 (Saunders 2005). The other trends included mobility (m-government) and instant messaging. Collaborations refer to the process and procedures that make it possible for people to easily communicate with other workers both within and without their own organizations—that is, to be able to cross artificial information boundaries as needed. Government workers need to share information within their own agency, across agencies, across national boundaries, and with such organizations as businesses and nongovernmental organizations (NGOs). Saunders identified a solution to the need for collaboration as one consisting of a single component that fits into existing and planned information architecture, is part of a managed desktop tool set, has community support, guarantees privacy, and involves local formal (teams) and informal (communities of practice) groups.

Dr. Bob Lewis of Lockheed Martin, a speaker at the 2005 Washington, DC,

KM conference, also identified collaboration systems as one of the important product directions that information-finding technology is taking (Lewis 2005). One of the evolving collaboration technologies identified by Lewis includes a new and more powerful and directed search engine that can build a search based on the user's previous searches and what other organization members searching the same topic have found. Lewis also touched on the ultimate collaboration tool, the collaborative "system of systems," which is an innovative product that facilitates interfacing between systems, thereby allowing communications between separate communities of practice, for example.

Collaboration is the chief ingredient for enabling vertical and horizontal cross-boundary data integration among government agencies. According to a National Association of State Chief Information Officers' 2005 research brief, state and federal agencies must find better ways to break down existing information silos and facilitate greater data integration. This is particularly important in areas of public safety, disaster relief, and homeland security (NASCIO 2005).

Data integration is a third trend shaping government's implementation of KM and the information architecture that facilitates knowledge collection and sharing. Integration is the tools and processes necessary to provide for electronic sharing of information between two or more databases or systems (NASCIO 2005). The electronic sharing utilizes a standard message format, such as extensible markup language (XML). XML has become the standard in the federal, state, and local levels of government for data sharing and information exchange. The movement of information occurs in several different ways. First, it occurs by extracting relevant data from each source and storing it centrally. A second model operates by retrieving data from each source (in the de facto net) on an as-needed basis. Actual data sharing occurs in one of two ways: for information or intelligence gathering, it is usually accessed by a query. Or, it is exchanged between sources for use in a specific application. Finally, integration is the process of sharing data across organizations and domains, within an established enterprise, and based on standard formats.

Advances in Mobile Technology

Mobile technology is a fourth trend affecting KM and IT. Many federal workers are highly mobile and widely dispersed across the country. Law enforcement, emergency services agencies, inspection agencies (such as those in food system, customs, case workers, transportation, labor, and health), remote workers (such as parks, environmental protection, and resource management), and the staffs of elected officials are all candidates for greater use of mobile technology. These thousands of workers must have access to the most current policies and procedures, manuals, forms, and regulations. They need to be connected to home-agency and outside databases, have access to department intranets and portals, and have the ability to communicate and collaborate in real time. Field workers often have an even greater need to be kept informed than do home office support personnel.

In 2005, instant messaging (IM) was well on the way to becoming a fifth trend in information and communications technology, although it was still evolving as an application in government technology. If IM is adopted in government to the extent that it has been in the private sector, it is expected to ultimately take some of the pressure off the large and growing use of e-mail. E-mail is deeply engrained as the medium of choice for internal communications. As such, many agency managers report serious overloading of their e-mail message boxes. Some workers spend up to three or more hours each workday reading and responding to e-mails, many of which need not have been sent in the first place. Instant messaging will have to be integrated into existing e-mail systems, or it, too, may contribute to information overload.

From E-Government to M-Government

After the wholesale movement toward Web-based communications systems, the adoption of wireless communications technology may be the most significant of the current trends in emerging technology for KM. In the public sector, this trend toward mobile communications is called *m-government*. M-government is defined as programs and activities designed to provide information and communication services to public employees through wireless communication networks and the use of portable communications devices. The services provided to public employees also improve the ability of other stakeholders—citizens, businesses, nonprofit organizations, other governments, and legislative bodies—to access government services. M-government is facilitated by two directions in technology. The first is *wireless technology*; the second is *mobile technology*. Although the terms are similar and often used synonymously, there are subtle differences.

Wireless technology is broader in scope than mobile technology. Most wireless devices are mobile. However, mobile devices are not all wireless. A desktop PC is not a mobile device, but it can be connected wirelessly to a local area network (LAN) for Internet access. Mobile technology, on the other hand, consists of the portable devices that government workers can carry and use for communication. They include mobile (cell) phones, laptop computers, personal digital assistants (PDAs), pocket computers, pagers, wearable computers, and related equipment and supporting systems (Moon 2004).

Although the adoption of mobile technologies in areas of government services other than public safety has been relatively slow until now, many believe that once certain concerns over security are resolved, growth in their adoption will be dramatic. Most governments believe that mobile technologies can greatly improve the efficiency, effectiveness, responsiveness, and accountability in the management of such reaction and prevention programs as natural disasters, fire suppression, law enforcement, and homeland security.

Among the barriers limiting far greater m-government implementation are issues relating to security and privacy, accessibility, and impacts of other public services. For greater adoption by governments, mobile technologies must not only guarantee the security of communications, they must also be able to operate across many different platforms or architectures—in what is known as "interoperability." Two types of interoperability have been identified: operational and technical. Operational interoperability refers to the different agency networks that collect, organize, and disseminate information. Technical interoperability refers to hardware and software compatibility. For mobile technologies to work in government they must:

- Be part of a comprehensive infrastructure that supports effective information sharing,
- Be secure and guarantee privacy,
- Overcome barriers of ambiguity about statutory authority,
- Be open to public scrutiny and trust,
- Overcome problems of lack of experience among users,
- Be hardware and software compatible,
- Be guided by agreed-upon data-sharing standards and limitations,
- Be introduced within a culture that values and rewards information sharing,
- Finally, an infrastructure for knowledge management must be in place (Moon 2004, 11)

In 2003, three best-practices examples of m-government applications at the state level included California, Virginia, and New York. Each of these programs was described in a 2004 research report sponsored by the IBM Center for the Business of Government, and carried out by Professor M. Jae Moon of Texas A&M and a group of A&M graduate students. The examples are summarized in the following paragraphs.

California, long a pioneer in both e-government and m-government, retains the practice of keeping funding for new wireless technology within each department or agency, without any central departmental control. Virginia and New York have each taken the route of centralized ICT management, which has allowed them to introduce what Moon (19) described as "innovative, strategic, specific m-government plans in a more proactive and effective way."

In one of the nation's earliest applications of mobile technology, California introduced a wireless program known as "My California on the Go" in 2001. It was introduced as a way for citizens to receive instant wireless updates on energy warnings, traffic jams, state lottery results, press releases, and emergency information from the governor's office. Anyone with a PDA, pager, or cell phone could access the information.

Virginia has the reputation for having been the first state to introduce such services as online, real-time customer service assistance and online driver's license renewals, among others. Continuing its tradition of leadership in e-government, Virginia launched a wireless state portal, "My Mobile Virginia." This was the first program in the nation to make government services available via wireless and mobile devices. Most of the services are for citizens, although some are for state employees. Downloadable information services include emergency weather information, terrorism threats, legislative information, lobbyist information, election information, tax information, and information for tourists. What may have been the most important governmental reform related to technology planning in the state was the establishment in 2003 of the Virginia Information Technology Agency (VITA). This agency oversees ICT planning for the entire state government.

The State of New York had moved much earlier to coordinate ICT at the state level, when the Office for Technology (OFT) was established in 1996. New York introduced the Statewide Wireless Network (SWN) in 2000. The primary objective of the SWN is to increase and improve inter- and intrastate agency communications. However, it is also enabling a better working relationship between state agencies and local government offices. New York has also adopted additional mobile technologies. For example, the New York Division of Parole adopted a wireless program to facilitate better communication among the more than 1,200 parole officers and 45,000 parolees. Parole officers were issued handheld computers—"WorkPads"—linked to a mainframe at agency headquarters. While in the field, officers were able to immediately request more help and attain additional information. Their knowledge level was thereby greatly enhanced.

Performance Measurment and KM

Like organizations in the private sector, governments must measure their performance progress in a variety of activity categories. Government agencies are today subject to performance analysis that is as rigorous as any-thing in business or industry. Moreover, government managers must establish specific goals and objectives and report the organization's progress toward accomplishing the objectives. Broadly speaking, there are three main reasons for managers to measure their performance and value their assets (Bahra 2001).

The first reason is because measuring performance provides benchmarks against which to measure future positive or negative change. Second, measurement serves as a motivator for management by stimulating management focus on what is important. Third, measurement is a rationale for having made the investment, which in time will have an impact on justifying future investments. Both the public and the private sector are today employing return-on-investment (ROI) metrics.

Benefits and Pitfalls

A recent study on the use of performance measurements in state governments found that the evidence clearly supports the belief that performance measurement can have an important and influential effect on the management of public programs (Melkers and Willoughby 2004). The benefits occurred more in the area of managing state agency programs than for the program budgeting process. Although not specifically mentioning the items, two of the study findings pertained closely to ICT and knowledge management. First, the use of performance measurement in the states has improved both the substance and the quality of communication between and among executive agencies, agencies, the state budge office, and legislators and their staffs. Second, the effects of this improved communication extend beyond state government. Communication with the public about government performance has improved, and many former problems in reporting to external stakeholders have been resolved.

The chief difficulty in measuring knowledge management investments is that they are often intangible or provide results at some unknown future date. Also, appropriately attributing cost data is often difficult. If measurements are accepted as necessary, a way must be found to surmount these problems; one such method for measuring knowledge management investments has been developed by researchers at the UK Cranfield School of Management. Researchers Karin Breu, David Grimshaw, and Andrew Myers (2000) asked industry leaders across the UK to identify the knowledge-based benefits they had received from IT and KM. Factors and their components are presented in Table 3.3.

The items are grouped into five composite benefit factors: innovation and

Table 3.3

Benefit Factors and Their Constituent Components

Factor	Representative Constituent Components
Innovation and growth	• New products/services • Research and development • New [program] opportunities • Developing new constituencies • Capability to innovate • Organizational responsiveness • Organizational integration • Organizational flexibility • Sharing of ideas and knowledge • Organizational learning • Speed of decision making
Customer focus	• Customer/client retention • Customer service provided • Meeting customer/client needs • Product/service quality
Supplier network	• Supply chain efficiency • Integration of logistics • Supplier relationships • Sustaining existing markets • Time to market of new products/services
Internal quality	• Process innovation • Capability for change • Operational efficiency • Project management • Product/services management • Staff morale • Quality of decision making

Source: Cranfield School of Management (UK). Modified from Bahra 2001, p. 97.

growth, organizational responsiveness, customer (or client) focus, supplier network, and an internal quality factor. Each factor includes five or more identifiable and measurable characteristics (Bahra 2001); each is described below in more detail.

Innovation and Growth: This component describes the benefits to the organization that arise from a culture and philosophy that encourage new products and services, including approaches to the delivery of those services. It also values higher output from research and development efforts, seeking out and exploiting new business opportunities, and enhancing the creative and innovative capability of the organization.

Organizational Responsiveness: This component includes success at reducing or eliminating geographic barriers and achieving organizational integration and flexibility. In this way, agencies seek ways to become what is often referred to as "lean and mean," "quick on the feet," and welcoming of change. The organizational culture is one in which the sharing of ideas and organizational learning is honored. A key metric often employed is improving the speed of decision making.

Customer Focus: Until recently, losing customers was not a concern of public agencies. However, with outsourcing and privatization, it has become of some concern to agencies. Therefore, achieving continuous improvements in such externally focused activities as customer retention, meeting customer needs, and maintaining product and service quality are important components of a system of performance measurements.

Supplier Network: These are the benefits an organization gains through common standards achieved through closer collaboration with other value-chain organizations and agencies. It may also mean establishing programs for involving suppliers in product and service design. In state and local governments, for example, this is increasingly being accomplished by greater use of design-build-operate public works contracts. Integrating logistics and improving supplier relationships are also included in this factor.

Internal Quality: These are the measurable benefits that occur as a result of process innovation, being open to change, enhancing organizational efficiency, and better management of projects. In addition, it includes the human resources benefits of better employee morale, improved retention, and higher-quality decision making.

Results of the UK survey quantified progress by using planning period percentage objectives for each factor. Respondents were also to state their actual results. By comparing achieved versus targeted results, agency administrators are then able to identify areas where additional performance efforts are needed.

Conclusion

Designing an effective and far-reaching public sector knowledge management system requires the best combination of people, information, processes, and technology. Public-sector knowledge management systems must be designed so that the agency personnel are able to (1) identify relevant information that is needed for completion of the agency's mission, (2) strengthen interagency collaborations, and (3) store, organize, and catalog everyday and invaluable knowledge so that it can be used in the near and distant future.

A survey of Canadian public-sector managers found that, with only minor variation, the majority of the respondents gave similar importance rankings to items found in five different KM models. Nine components may be considered to be fundamental components in all KM and KM systems applications: technology, leadership, culture, measurement, process, organization, infrastructure, learning, and content.

Implementing the information and communications technology architecture component of a KMS begins with aligning the system with the agency's knowledge needs. Design ing the information technology architecture entails organizing the agency's knowledge and information technology resources to carry out the mission of the organization. There are two key parts to designing information technology systems architecture: information system architecture and technology system architecture.

Three trends are evident in the changing role of IT in supporting knowledge management: a diminishing role for ICT, a growing need for integration and collaboration, and acceleration in the use of wireless and mobile technology by government agencies.

The use of performance measurements in the fifty state governments supports the belief that performance measurement can have an important and influential effect on the management of public programs.

4

Knowledge Processes and Policy Directives

*One of the most fundamental implications emerging from the science
of complexity is that order naturally emerges in systems, no matter
how simple, complex, nonlinear, or chaotic the system is. Natural
order evolves through self-organization.*
(Lewin 1999, 215)

Government agencies and departments, like all organizations, produce new
strategies, structures, and processes from interaction with their external and
internal environments. This evolutionary process is reflected in the phenomenon known as *organizational learning.* Organizational learning is ethic free;
it can be either good or bad. Members of an organization will tend to act in
ways they are expected to act. Two factors help shape organizational learning: leadership and organizational culture. These two concepts are used by
senior managers in their efforts to influence the direction that organizational
learning will take. Public-sector managers, administrators, and workers develop behavior patterns from cues they receive from information and experience. Some of that learning comes from higher-level managers in the form of
a clearly identified vision and ethic; more learning comes from workers'
interactions with their peers and their experiences carrying out their occupational tasks. Knowledge management facilitates both types of learning.

Organizational behavior is also learned. Knowledge that is shared, combined, and applied in new situations helps shape the organizational learning
process by capturing the best practices of the organization and the identified
exemplar models they are encouraged to emulate.

Governments everywhere are promoting learning and knowledge building in individuals and organizations. Knowledge management systems and
the monitoring of best-practices model performances are among the tools
used in this process. The federal government has been involved in a con-

tinuing process of transforming the way it operates since the early 1990s. Although the labels and processes may change, the direction of the desired changes has not: Government is trying to become more responsive to market pressures.

This chapter examines two related processes that are shaping public management in the first decade of the twenty-first century: the primacy of collaboration in knowledge creation, sharing, and use; and management policy directives that are driving the transformation of government. Collaboration is a fundamental tenet of knowledge management; government transformation is encapsulated in the e-government and the President's Management Agenda initiatives.

Chapter Objectives

Objectives for this chapter include helping readers to achieve the following:

- Gain an understanding of the mechanisms and interactions involved in the processes that help make knowledge management systems possible.
- Become aware of some of the tools and processes involved in creating, capturing, and sharing knowledge in public-sector organizations.
- Be able to define and understand how such social interactions as collaboration and integration are facilitating knowledge sharing in government agencies.
- Understand the relationship that exists between e-government and knowledge management.
- Understand how the federal government's enterprise architecture initiative and the President's Management Agenda are shaping present and future government operations, including knowledge management.

Social and Policy Influences on KM

For an organization to achieve its inherent potential, its existing knowledge must be identified, collected, organized, and shared; in brief, the existing knowledge must be put to work. When workers in government agencies put their knowledge to work, both they and the agency learn from the experience. That learning occurs as a result of and during a series of logical action processes. This chapter focuses on three major themes related to knowledge management in the public sector. First, it briefly reviews fundamental social interactions that characterize human activity in knowledge management systems. Second, it looks at how government is selectively adopting, shaping, and reacting to information and communications technologies, concepts, and practices in collaborative efforts to achieve its operational objectives. Third, it examines management directives that are shaping the way that government is organized, functions, and delivers services, information, and knowledge across government agencies and to outside stakeholders.

The first force shaping learning and knowledge creation in the public sector relates to the processes individuals and government organizations go through as they react to events in their environment. These are the social actions and behaviors that individuals and organizations follow in the process of learning. Learning activity, in turn, facilitates the key KM activities of creating, developing, combining, and sharing of knowledge. Creative solutions to old and new problems and innovation are produced by the application of that knowledge. A primary process of a successful knowledge management system that is enabled by these interactive activities is cross-agency and cross-government collaboration and integration.

The second force shaping the internal and external operations of government—including knowledge management—is discussed under a framework established by the federal government's enterprise architecture initiative. This program facilitates the horizontal and vertical collaboration and integration sought for federal, state, and local governments by establishing common standards and guidelines for all information technology applications.

The third influence shaping the public sector has to do with changes taking place in the way that government is thought about, the way it operates, and the paths that reformers believe it should be taking. These concepts are reviewed in the framework of the primary policy directives driving government transformation: the President's Management Agenda and the e-government initiative.

Interactive Social Processes

Three interactive social processes contribute to this major subsystem: knowledge development, knowledge transfer, and knowledge sharing. These processes and examples of the activities and tools with which they are associated are displayed in the model shown in Figure 4.1.

When organizations invest in the technologies necessary to promote these knowledge creation, development, and learning processes they facilitate knowledge sharing and distribution. The effectiveness of these learning processes is a product of the agency's investment in its information and communications technology. However, the more important elements of this subsystem are not the technology but the social interactions that technology makes possible. Available technology may give birth to the informal, self-regulating communities of practice that are at the heart of knowledge management applications.

Figure 4.1   **Mechanisms Facilitating Knowledge Management and Agency Collaboration**

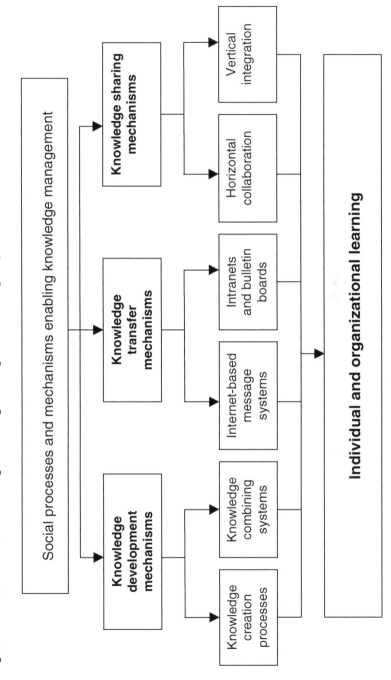

Each of these mechanisms hosts at least two separate but related procedures. For example, the two primary components of the knowledge development mechanism are knowledge creation and knowledge combining. Together, they contribute to individual and organizational learning.

Knowledge creation is a product of science and experience. Learning follows experimentation. Researchers in individual and organizational learning have studied the phenomenon extensively. They have concluded that in humans, learning usually takes place in a closed circle of steps called the learning cycle.

Building on the cycle of adult learning proposed by Kurt Lewin (1946), David Kolb (1984) provided a model of the learning cycle that is used to describe the process people go through in learning. The model identifies four stages, which follow from each other: concrete experience, reflective observation, abstract conceptualization, and active experimentation. Concrete experience knows something by being acquainted with it—by doing and experiencing—as opposed to the more theoretical "knowing about" something (which is represented by abstract conceptualization). Reflecting observation is more passive than concrete experience, which involves observing and thinking about something. Active experimentation is learning by doing.

A similar cycle of learning has also been suggested for knowledge applications in organizational learning, which follow these four social interactions: socialization, externalization, combination, and internalization (Nonaka and Takeuchi 1995). Many believe this process to be one of the fundamental subsystems in all knowledge management systems. Socialization refers to personal knowledge that is generated in social situations such as the workplace. Externalization refers to individuals' absorbing the new knowledge and communicating it to others. Combination is the process of putting bits and pieces of existing knowledge together to create new knowledge or new applications for existing knowledge. Internalization is the process of acceptance and even "taking ownership" of the newly formed knowledge.

Two components that illustrate the processes contained in the knowledge transfer mechanism are Web-based communications systems and intranets, among a host of other tools and processes. Knowledge transfer is facilitated by information and communications technology. And, two of the key components in the knowledge-sharing mechanism include collaboration and integration, which are key concepts in the government's enterprise architecture initiative. These transactions are facilitated and enhanced through functioning knowledge management systems.

These three mechanisms and their respective components facilitate the collaboration that is being required in government today. Collaboration is the efforts of two or more entities or agencies to accomplish more than the sum of their individual efforts. Collaboration occurs between government agencies, between subdivisions in an agency, between businesses and the government, and between individuals and government. Supporters of collaboration claim that it can lead to better service to the public, lower taxes, better decision making, and greater public participation in government processes. Collaboration in government is not new; there are many examples where government has successfully collaborated with others. Unfortunately, many collaborative opportunities are missed, and others fade due to the high level of effort needed to keep them working successfully (SAP 2001).

E-government has not changed the need for and desirability of collaboration; it just makes it easier to do, more cost effective, easier to monitor, and thus easier to maintain. E-government technology affects government collaboration in three ways. First, it improves communications between agencies, individuals, or groups; second, it can automate the process, as in natural disaster alerts and homeland security warnings; and third, it allows better monitoring of processes, as exemplified in the regular monitoring of agency progress on complying with mandated collaboration programs (U.S. GAO 2003b).

Monitoring Agency Progress with Collaboration

A concern with collaborative programs is whether they are being implemented as originally planned, and whether actual benefits are being realized. This is critical when a program depends on the cooperation of many groups. Congress has required regular updates of the progress that agencies are making in achieving their collaboration objectives. For example, the General Accounting Office issued a report in 2003 on the progress made by four federal agencies (see Table 4.1).

After more than a year of working to achieve their collaboration goals, none of the agencies studied had fully achieved involving all their important stakeholders in their program. For example, the e-payroll initiative managed by the Office of Personnel Management had initiated steps to promote close collaboration with its four selected e-payroll providers (reduced from the original twenty-two providers). However, it had yet to address the concerns of a key stakeholder whose participation will be required to make changes to its payroll processes and procedures. For the Geospatial one-stop initiative, the Interior Department had established a board of directors with broad representation, but had not yet taken steps to ensure that key state and local government stakeholders were involved.

The GSA-sponsored integrated acquisition environment had put a number of tools to work promoting collaboration, but had not yet involved the chief financial officers of their partner agencies. And finally, the business

Table 4.1

Four E-Government Collaboration Efforts Reviewed

Agency/activity	Managing partner	Collaboration goal
E-payroll	Office of Personnel Management	Standardize payroll operations across all federal agencies
Geospatial one-stop	Department of the Interior	Coordinate the collection and maintenance of geospatial data (all data associated with geographic locations)
Integrated acquisition environment	General Services Administration	Improve federal agencies' acquisition of goods and services
Business gateway	Small Business Administration	Reduce the paperwork burden on small businesses and help them find, understand, and comply with federal, state, and local laws and regulations

gateway program of the Small Business Administration had not taken critical steps to enable an effective collaborative decision-making process, and had not reached formal agreements on partner roles and responsibilities.

Award-Winning Examples

It is important to note that, despite such problems, most government agencies are making stellar progress in their efforts to meet the collection of transformation initiatives. For example, two federal agencies and one State of Illinois program were honored for their progress by being named the three best-practices knowledge management agencies of 2005 by the E-Government Institute. The institute annually selects best-in-class programs in three categories:

- *Innovative Use of Technology in a Knowledge Management Solution:* Presented to a project that has used contemporary or leading-edge commercial technology to implement a creative solution to a real business problem.
- *Knowledge Management Initiative Delivering a High Value to a Broad User Community/Supporting Agency Mission:* Presented to a solution that was successfully adopted and used by a larger user community.
- *Initiative or Organization Successfully Using Innovative Knowledge Management Practices:* Presented to an organization or initiative that promoted the practice of KM and information sharing to the benefit of an organization.

The Joint Forces Command's Collaborative Information Environment (CIE) won in the first category, Innovative Use of Technology. The CIE combines information technology with complementary organizational changes and dynamic KM processes to transform future command-and-control operations. CIE is a virtual collection of individuals, organizations, systems, infrastructure, and processes that let users create and share the information needed to plan, execute, and assess joint forces operations, and make decisions better and faster than their adversaries. Using a virtual information warehouse, users can rapidly extract timely, assured, and relevant information needed to accomplish their mission.

The Defense Acquisition University (DAU), Department of Defense, Technology and Logistics Sharing System (AT&L), was honored for achievement in the second category, a high-value KM program. DAU's knowledge systems provide the AT&L workforce and their partners with the tools and resources they need to improve job performance anywhere and at any time. This is done by integrating learning assets and maintaining a continuous presence to the workforce by online communities of practice and knowledge systems that support the AT&L's performance learning model. AT&L's knowledge sharing system is a key component serving as the central gateway for all AT&L resources and information. As the primary reference tool, it provides a link for sharing information and reference assets among a wide range of organizations and disciplines for an integrated, decentralized information system.

The collaboration component of the DAU program is called the Acquisition Community Connection (ACC). The ACC includes publicly accessible knowledge communities whose goal is to connect people with know-how across government and industry. There are more than 10,000—out of a potential of 1.5 million—members of the ACC dispersed across Defense Department services and agencies, private industry, and a combination of federal, state, and local governments.

The award-winning state program is the Knowledge Management Division of the Bureau of Strategic Sourcing and Procurement arm of the State of Illinois central management services agency. This agency won for innovative use of technology and KM processes. The Bureau of Strategic Sourcing and Procurement (BOSSAP) created the knowledge management division to supply five separate outreach portfolios to various procurement staff spread throughout state offices. The KM division provides such services as research, professional development, administration of procurement systems, contract compliance, and a procurement call center. Using a "home-grown" system on a Lotus Notes platform instead of expensive new technology, the division's KM system has helped save more than $100 million out of an estimated $7-

billion budget. According to the awards announcement press release, "The KM division minimizes reinvention and knowledge evaporation, and integrates business functions with related knowledge, thus creating a connected and continual learning environment."

IT Architecture Influences

Political and policy influences are two of the more influential forces acting on public-sector IT and KM in the first decade of the twenty-first century. Together, these influences are shaping knowledge formation and application, and are contributing to continued evolution in information and communications technology. Political and policy decisions are requiring government agencies to achieve three objectives: (1) adopt strategic IT architecture planning that includes provision for knowledge management; (2) transform their operations to coincide with mandated business-based management models and significantly greater cooperation and collaboration across agencies; and (3) design and implement new information acquisition and delivery systems for more and improved e-government programs. The federal enterprise architecture (FEA) initiative is the program developed to achieve the first of these objectives. Business models contained in the President's Management Agenda are being applied for achieving the second of these objectives; and an e-government initiative is facilitating the third.

Bringing Rationality to IT

It became clear in the 1990s that some degree of higher-level coordination and control was needed over the acquisitions and applications of IT systems by agencies; a single organization was proposed for overseeing all IT resources. The federal government's answer was to place information resources management (IRM) under the auspices of the Office of Management and Budget. The OMB's tasks and responsibilities include oversight of planning and budgeting for all federal agency activities associated with acquiring, storing, processing, and distributing data and information.

While the OMB began assisting agencies to increase their coordination and control over their IT, others in government were envisioning a greater role for IT in all levels of government. The dream was to put the lessons learned in the private sector's use of IT to work for similar goals in government—to make government more like business. If government was to be more businesslike, it meant following higher performance standards, more and stronger measurements, and a greater emphasis on—and stricter accountability for—results. That vision became codified in the reinventing government and national performance review initiatives that came out of the Clinton White House.

The adoption of e-government at the federal level became more of a reality in February of 2002, when President George W. Bush included his President's Management Agenda (PMA) in the annual budget submission to Congress. The PMA was offered as a way of getting government to be more focused on citizens and results. Two key components of the PMA were (1) an e-government focus on Internet-based technology in an effort to make it easier for citizens and businesses to interact with government agencies and departments, and (2) a federal enterprise architecture initiative that aimed to transform government to be more like business (U.S. OMB 2005a).

The policy directive in 2002 established the federal enterprise architecture (FEA) process to guide agencies in the analysis of their current and future IT needs. It also proposed the implementation of common practices and systems government-wide. The FEA initiative was developed by the OMB's Office of E-Government and Information Technology, which continues to hold oversight responsibility for FEA. The structure of the FEA is illustrated in Figure 4.2

The term "enterprise architecture" refers to a transformation model that federal agencies are required to implement prior to making new IT purchases. Agencies are required to identify their present and future lines of business, their desired outcomes, the kinds of data they produce and use, and the information technology and service channels through which their products and services are delivered to the public. It consists of five reference models, a set of policies, and instructions for operating procedures. The models include business- and performance-based processes and a framework for cross-agency collaboration, transformation, and improvement.

Integrating KM into the FEA

The FEA program is constructed around five interrelated elements: a performance reference model (PRM), a business reference model (BRM), a services component reference model (SRM), a technical reference model (TRM), and a data reference model (DRM).

Each reference model incorporates a number of different "domains," or business activities, under its umbrella. For example, the services component model covers seven domains: customer services, process automation, business management services, digital asset services, business analytical services, back office services, and support services (U.S. OMB 2005a).

The OMB has also recommended performance measurement categories for each of the reference models in its description of the FEA program. For

74

Figure 4.2 **KM in the Federal Enterprise Architecture Reference Model (FY07)**

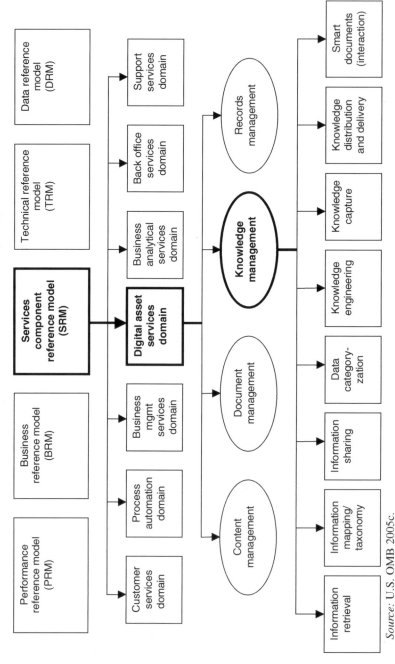

Source: U.S. OMB 2005c.

Table 4.2

KM Capabilities to Transform Information into Meaningful Knowledge

Service component	Defines the set of capabilities that
Information retrieval	Allows access to data and information for use by an organization and its stakeholders
Information mapping/taxonomy	Supports the creation and maintenance of relationships between data entities, naming standards, and categorization
Information sharing	Supports the use of documents and data in a multiuser environment for use by an organization and its stakeholders
Categorization	Allows classification of data and information into specific layers or types to support an organization
Knowledge engineering	Supports the translation of knowledge from an expert into the knowledge base of an expert system
Knowledge capture	Facilitates the collection of data and information
Knowledge distribution and delivery	Supports the transfer of knowledge to the end user
Smart documents	Supports the interaction of information and process (business logic) rules between users of the document; that is, the logic and use of the document is embedded within the document itself and is managed within the document parameters.

Source: U.S. OMB 2005c.

example, seven measurement groupings are included for information and technology management: lifecycle/change management, system development, system maintenance, IT infrastructure maintenance, IT security, record retention, and information management.

Each domain frames a distinct set of "capabilities" or tasks that contribute to achieving the mission of that domain. For example, four capabilities are included in the digital asset services domain: content management, document management, knowledge management, and records management. The eight primary functions or responsibilities that fall under the knowledge management set of capabilities and their definitions are displayed in Table 4.2.

To summarize, the federal government's knowledge management functions and processes are one of the four capabilities in the *digital asset services domain,* which is one of the seven domains included in the *services components reference model* (SRM), which is one of the five reference models that make up the federal enterprise architecture program.

Box 4.1

Enterprise Architecture at the Department of Defense (DoD)

The U.S. Department of Defense Architecture Framework (DODAF) is the department's guiding framework for implementing the five reference models contained in the Federal Enterprise Architecture (FEA) initiative. The framework is built on the assumption that there is no single view of an architecture (business processes, networks, hardware, data management, knowledge management, etc.) that is right for all users. Despite this assumption, DoD IT architecture will use standardized products, components, terms, and definitions wherever possible.

Three fundamental positions guide development and maintenance of DoD's enterprise architecture: an operational view, a technical view, and a systems view. The operational view focuses on user needs by addressing the tasks and activities of concern and the information and knowledge exchanges that are required for DoD to achieve its mission.

Second, the technical view is shaped by a minimal set of time-based standards and rules that govern the implantation, arrangement, interaction, and interdependence of system requirements. And third, the systems view is centered on systems of concern and the connections among them, in keeping with the view of first importance, the operational view.

Source: Malafsky 2005.

Box 4.1, describing the agenda guiding the Department of Defense as it implements the FEA, is typical of the basis for the flexible approach encouraged by the OMB for FEA implementation by federal departments and agencies.

A Bigger Role for KM

The concept of a *knowledge base* is important to cooperative planning processes in all agency operations, including e-government. The term *knowledge base* has traditionally referred to the data produced by the knowledge-acquisition and compilation phases of creating an expert system application. That definition must now be broadened to include every imaginable corporate intellectual, technological, and experiential asset—it refers to

Table 4.3

Additional Services Model (SRM) Domains and Capabilities with KM

Domains	Service component	Capabilities
Business management services:	Organizational management	Workgroup/groupware, network management
Digital asset services:	Content management	Content authoring, content review and approval, content publishing and delivery, syndication management
	Document management	Document imaging, document referencing, document revisions, library/storage, document review and approval, document [format] conversion, indexing, classification
	Records management	Record linking/association, document classification, document retirement, digital rights management
Business analytical services:	Knowledge discovery	Data mining, modeling, simulation
	Reporting	Ad hoc (supports use of reports as needed); standardized/canned (supports use of preconceived or pre-written reports); OLAP (supports analysis of information summarized into multidimensional views and hierarchies)
Back office services:	Data management	Data exchange; data warehouse; data mart (subset of a data warehouse); meta data management (data that describes data); data cleansing, extraction, and transformation (manipulation of data); loading and archiving; data recovery; data classification
Support services:	Collaboration	E-mail, remarks logs, document library, shared calendaring, task management
	Search	Query (records retrieval), precision/recall ranking, classification. pattern matching
	Communication	Real time/chat, instant messaging, audio/video conferencing, community of interest management

Source: U.S. OMB 2004c.

the complete collection of all expertise, experience, and knowledge of all personnel within a public organization.

In keeping with this broadened definition, government managers are beginning to bring other information assets and practices into knowledge management. Elements of knowledge management are spread across several domains of the services components model, as noted in Table 4.3. KM processes and procedures are also found in the business management, business analytical, back office services, and support services domains.

Missing IT Architecture

Table 4.2 does not include the technology domains, service components, or capabilities included in the enterprise architecture initiative. These elements are included in the technical reference model (TRM). Although current thinking in KM places a lesser importance upon technology than occurred in the recent past, most observers recognize that these elements clearly contribute to an effective, well-oiled knowledge management system (McElroy 2003).

The TRM is a component-driven, technical framework for standards and technologies that support and enable delivery of the knowledge management activities in the service components and capabilities. It is also designed to unify existing agency technology and provide e-government guidance by providing a foundation for reuse and standardization of technology and service components government-wide.

The TRM consists of four broad components: service access and delivery, service platform and infrastructure, component framework, and a service interface and integration element. All of these components contribute to successful operation of a KM system, although the following three may be slightly more relevant: service access and delivery, service platform and infrastructure, and the service interface and integration component.

The service access and delivery element manages the collection of access and delivery channels used to leverage the service component. It is also charged with managing adherence to the legislative requirements and mandates affecting IT use. Its responsibilities include:

- Access channels (Web browsers, wireless, collaboration communications, etc.),
- Delivery channels (Internet, intranet, and extranet delivery, peer-to-peer communications, etc.),
- Service requirements (legislative compliance, hosting, user authentication, etc.), and
- Transport (supporting network services, etc.).

The services platform and infrastructure element defines the collection of platforms, hardware, and infrastructure standards that enable component-based architectures and service component reuse. Component-based architectures base their design on categories of business, service, performance, technical, and data elements. Larger lines of business, service, and technol-

Figure 4.3   **Service Interface and Integration Service Areas**

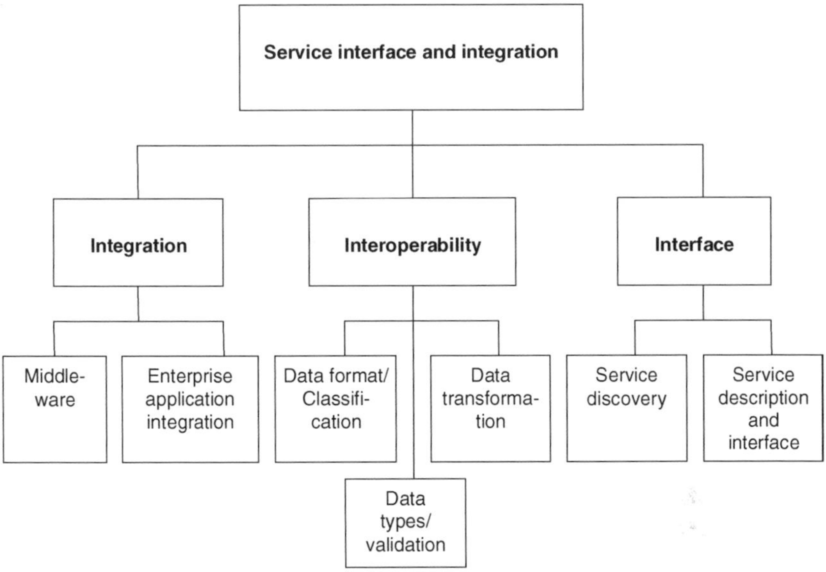

```
                    ┌─────────────────────────────────┐
                    │ Service interface and integration │
                    └─────────────────────────────────┘
          ┌──────────────────────┼──────────────────────┐
   ┌──────────────┐      ┌──────────────┐      ┌──────────────┐
   │ Integration  │      │Interoperability│    │  Interface   │
   └──────────────┘      └──────────────┘      └──────────────┘
     ┌──────┴──────┐      ┌──────┴──────┐      ┌──────┴──────┐
  ┌────────┐ ┌──────────┐ ┌──────────┐ ┌──────────┐ ┌──────────┐ ┌──────────┐
  │Middle- │ │Enterprise│ │Data format/│ │  Data  │ │ Service  │ │ Service  │
  │ ware   │ │application│ │Classifi-  │ │transforma-│ │discovery│ │description│
  │        │ │integration│ │cation     │ │  tion    │ │          │ │   and    │
  └────────┘ └──────────┘ └──────────┘ └──────────┘ └──────────┘ │interface │
                              ┌──────────┐                        └──────────┘
                              │   Data   │
                              │  types/  │
                              │validation│
                              └──────────┘
```

Source: U.S. OMB 2004c.

ogy infrastructures are composed of these "building blocks." The services platform manages the following processes:

- Support platforms,
- Software engineering,
- Delivery servers,
- Database management and storage, and
- Hardware and infrastructure.

The service interface and integration component deals with the discovery, interaction, and communication technologies that join disparate systems and information providers. The three service program activity/process categories included in this domain are presented in Figure 4.3.

One of the functions in this domain of the TRM model that has received significant attention since 9/11 is the capability of legacy systems to integrate outside agency information stovepipes. Integration refers to software that enables elements of distributed applications to interoperate, that is, to be able to share function, content, and communications across agencies and a variety of environments. Service integration is designed to produce platform and location transparency, transaction management, basic messaging between points, and guaranteed message delivery. *Middleware* describes the technologies that enable flexibility, interoperability, and portability of existing infrastructure by linking two otherwise separate applications.

FEA at the Department of the Interior

The U.S. Department of the Interior (DOI) has produced a pilot enterprise architecture application for the recreational facilities operated by department agencies. An earlier version of the data reference model (DRM) of the FEA was used to set the program in motion. The DRM is designed to promote common identification, use, and sharing of data and information across the federal government, a department, or an agency. It does this by standardizing data in three areas: data context, data sharing, and data description.

Interior uses the DRM to share information on its recreational amenities in a way that can be easily interpreted and used by many different users. Data are categorized according to activities performed within the recreational resource, resource management, and tourism activities, thereby supplying requesting agencies with information about recreation areas and activities. An agency with an inquiry can look in the BRM for a function that describes the activity it is seeking. Once the function is identified, the agency can use the federal enterprise architecture management subsystem to identify investments that the DOI supports in the recreation/amenity. This allows the inquiring agency to identify investment needs, and to avoid unnecessary duplication in recreation investments (OMB 2005c).

Management Agenda Influences

A global trend to transform government so that it more closely reflects best practices found in business has been under way since the 1980s. This trend has blurred much of the former distinction that existed between public- and private-sector management. A reflection of this trend is the global movement to move the public administration discipline from its traditional focus to a business-driven approach that is reflected in the proposed new title: new public management (Barzelay 2001, Christensen and Lægreid 2002, Lane 2000), as the following quote explains:

> Since the 1980s, the international tendency in administrative reform has been a neo-liberal one, encompassing managerial thinking and a market

Figure 4.4   **Evolution of Business Models into the President's Management Agenda (PMA) of 2002**

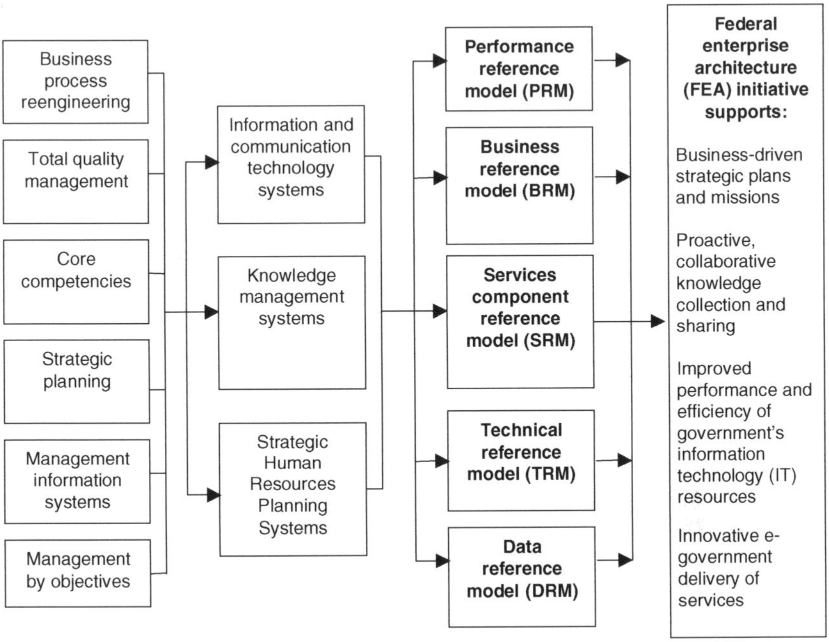

Source: U.S. OMB 2004c.

mentality. The private sector has become the role model, and public administration has come to be seen as a provider of services to citizens who were redefined as clients and consumers. . . . These new administrative doctrines came to be known collectively as new Public Management. (Christensen and Lægreid 2002, 17)

In the United States, new public management concepts are reflected in the business reference models contained in the President's Management Agenda (PMA) and its sister initiative, e-government. Both are reflections of the changes now taking place in government, and knowledge management is an integral component in these transformation initiatives. The PMA focuses on bringing rational planning to IT in government. E-government is putting IT to work by making it easier for citizens to communicate with government agencies. Figure 4.4 illustrates how KM and earlier management concepts contributed to the evolution of the structure and focus of the PMA.

Conclusion

This chapter focused on three major KM themes. First, it examined some of the fundamental social interactions that characterize knowledge management systems. Second, it looked at how government is adopting, shaping, and re-acting to information and communications technologies, concepts, and practices in collaborative efforts to achieve its operational objectives. Third, it examined management directives that are shaping the way that government is organized, functions, and delivers services, information, and knowledge across government agencies and outside stakeholders.

The forces shaping knowledge creation in the public sector include three interactive social processes: knowledge development, knowledge transfer, and knowledge sharing. Also shaping the internal and external operations of government—including knowledge management—is the federal government's enterprise architecture initiative, which is designed to bring about horizontal and vertical collaboration and integration among federal, state, and local governments by establishing common standards and guidelines for all information technology applications.

Changes in the way that government operates and the paths that reformers believe it should follow are influenced by the President's Management Agenda and the e-government initiative.

E-government technology affects government collaboration in three ways: it improves communications between the agencies, individuals, or groups; it can automate the process; and it allows better monitoring of the processes. Collaboration between government agencies, between subdivisions in an agency, between businesses and the government, and between individuals and government is also facilitated by interagency knowledge management initiatives.

Political and policy decisions require government agencies to adopt strategic IT architecture planning that includes provision for knowledge management, to transform their operations to coincide with using business-based management models, and to exercise greater cooperation and collaboration across agencies. Agencies must also design and implement new information acquisition and delivery systems for more and improved e-government programs. The federal enterprise architecture (FEA) initiative, the business models contained in the President's Management Agenda, and an e-government initiative are the policy directives driving the changes.

5

Principles and Processes in Implementing KM

Policy implementation *refers to the connection between the expression of governmental intention and the achievement of results in the world of action . . . [it is] the set of actions induced among those who are required by a public policy to cooperate and perhaps coordinated toward the achievement of the mandate.*
(O'Toole 1996)

The technology-centered approach to knowledge management solutions and implementation has been, arguably, the single most damaging element of knowledge management in practice. It is, perhaps, the single most important reason that the proper approach to knowledge management has not been used by most of those who have so ventured.
(Hylton 2002)

This book is not about the executive and legislative designers of public policy. Rather, it is about the thousands of men and women who are charged with the responsibility of implementing policy. They do this in hundreds of different agencies and smaller units spread throughout the agencies and offices of the federal, state, and local governments. As used in this text, *implementation* refers to the processes agency staff must follow when required by a public policy to cooperate and coordinate their efforts to comply with a mandate (O'Toole 1996). More specifically, it is about how these government workers *manage* the exploitation of an agency's intellectual capital.

Many management processes and procedures, including financial, human resources, and information and communications systems to name but a few, have long been available to assist government workers in the implementation process (Kettl 2002). However, these tools, processes, and procedures may also exercise conflicting influence and control over the way that government programs and initiatives are administered. Because government managers must answer to political pressures, they often do not have the luxury of refusing to implement a management directive or initiative. Examples include the strategic planning, enterprise architecture, President's Management Agenda, and e-government mandates.

In the twenty-first century, managing an agency's knowledge has become one of the most important of all organizational procedures and processes. Information—and the knowledge creation and sharing that information enables—is a basic and necessary factor in the complex process of government transformation. Knowledge management has donned the mantle of a presidential mandate; it is a vital component in the President's Management Agenda. KM principles and systems are essential contributors to the successful implementation of the agenda's transformations, including e-government, as Kettl has noted:

> In the twenty-first century . . . information has become essential. As computerized information technology and e-government spread, and as more government work occurs across organizational boundaries, information offers the most effective bridge [to transformed governance]. Information technology makes possible instantaneous, boundary-free communications, and that communication is necessary for coordinating twenty-first century work. (Kettl 2002, 169)

A measure of influence, guidance, and control over the information and information technology is necessary if government reformers are to be convinced that information and knowledge are put to work effectively and efficiently. Not surprisingly, an excellent way of achieving this guidance and control has been shown to be through the implementation of knowledge management principles. The importance of the implementation process has been emphasized with its elevation to one of two fundamental principles underlying successful KM applications (emphasis added):

1. Top management should guide the development of an overall policy on corporate information and knowledge and enthusiastically support its use throughout the organization.
2. *Appropriate steps should be taken to effectively implement the policy and ensure that it is followed and applied throughout the organization.* (Gaston 1997)

Chapter Objectives

The objectives for this chapter include gaining an understanding of the following knowledge topics:

- What is involved in implementing a KM program?
- What is a *knowledge base,* and how does an agency go about identifying its contents and locations?
- What are some of the fundamental principles and practices involved in implementing KM?
- What is a *knowledge audit,* what does it do, and what steps are involved in conducting one?
- What role does a knowledge repository hold in collecting, storing, and making readily available information about an agency knowledge base?
- When and where should federal government managers develop communities of practice (CoPs) to address program priorities, particularly those that cross boundaries within and outside agencies?
- How can federal, state, and local agencies create and manage such informal action-learning groups as communities of practice? How can they be launched and how can managers help them achieve desired results?

How KM Pays Its Way

Before continuing, it is important to determine what it is about knowledge and knowledge management programs that makes them worth the price of their adoption. Three concepts of knowledge correspond with the idea that investments in knowledge management systems can earn a quick return by contributing to the successful implementation of such important government initiatives as e-government, homeland security, privatization and market-based delivery of government services, collaboration, and performance management (Voss, Roeder, and Marker 2003).

First, the knowledge held by an organization's people and the many interested and involved individuals from outside of the agency constitute what should be recognized and nurtured as an agency's *intellectual capital.* Intellectual capital is the basis for planning and shaping implementation of all public policy.

Many different sources contribute to the intellectual capital in public-sector organizations. The implementation of policy involves the cooperation and collaboration of the many different stakeholders that have a direct and indirect influence on agency performance. These stakeholders' actions range from directives issued by legislative policymakers to the participation of the polity. Intellectual capital refers to an organization's recorded and remembered information, experiences, and human talent—its *knowledge base*. The term *knowledge asset* also suggests a management understanding that information is a critical part of the asset base of the government agency. Without knowledge management systems in place such information and knowledge is typically either improperly or inefficiently warehoused or, too often, simply lost. This has been particularly true in large, physically dispersed public-sector agencies; the problem will be exacerbated with the expected wholesale retirement of baby boom–generation managers. The implementation challenge is to find what knowledge the agency has and how to make it available for continued use.

Second, the combined knowledge management concepts of learning organizations and best-practices process optimization are core elements in the management models being applied in the President's Management Agenda (PMA). The goal of these two concepts is to optimize organization processes with regard to time, costs, and quality through knowledge management. Networks acquire and distribute knowledge across agencies and across organizational functions.

Third, identification and management of an agency's knowledge base is a fundamental concept underlying all processes in e-government. The term *knowledge base* has traditionally referred to the data collected by the knowledge-acquisition and compilation phases of information systems. In the past, a knowledge base was defined as "the absolute collection of all expertise, experience, and knowledge of those within any organization" (Voss, Roeder, and Marker 2003). But that definition must now be broadened to include every imaginable organizational intellectual asset, whether it resides within the agency or with one of the agency's stakeholders. In the context of this contribution, a central goal is to build a knowledge base under the premise of a relevant methodology.

Implementing KM

There are at least two ways to approach the question of what is involved in implementing a KM program. One is to look at the issue sequentially, enumerating a list of steps everyone needs to follow if the implementation is to be successful. One such list proposed that implementation follow a five-step process, as follows (Gaston 1997):

1. Form a knowledge committee to create policies and standards and lead implementation.
2. Appoint a chief knowledge officer.

3. Make supporting announcements within the agency.
4. Make or coordinate needed revisions to related policies, such as:

    a. Information resources management
    b. Strategic information systems planning
    c. Information security
    d. Budget approval processes.

5. Create and implement a knowledge policy.

This list of implementation steps offers good advice to the KM-program planner. However, a major difficulty with the sequential approach is that each implementation is situation and time specific. Therefore, agency managers might be better armed by using the list (or any other author's list) as a guide only and instead focusing on the fundamental processes that are involved in a KM program.

Implementing IM isn't easy, whether it is in government or industry. Far more implementation initiatives fail than succeed. The Knowledge Management Roundtable, a community of practice sponsored by the International Center for Applied Studies in Information Technology at George Mason University, surveyed a sample of business and government KM managers to determine what worked and what did not work. The sample agreed on the top three difficulties that contribute to KM failures (ICASIT 2003):

- KM not being a priority of senior management.
- A lack of a knowledge-sharing culture in the organization.
- Lack of time or priorities of knowledge users.

The study also identified three challenges for people trying to implement KM: showing the business benefits of KM, motivating the workforce to use KM once it is up and running, and keeping top management involved.

Three Basic Processes

Amrit Tiwana (2002) identified three basic processes of knowledge management: knowledge acquisition, knowledge sharing, and knowledge utilization. *Acquisition* is the process of developing and/or creating intellectual capital, including insights, skills, experiences, and relationships. This is typically a chief province of information technology, which employs technology in a variety of ways and with a variety of objectives to capture data and develop databases, and uses such tools as key-word scanners, note-capture tools, and electronic whiteboards in support of knowledge acquisition. Knowledge repositories are a way to categorize and store collected knowledge.

Knowledge sharing is disseminating and making available the collected knowledge of the agency and its staff. Knowledge sharing is enabled through a social process made possible by an organizational culture that honors and rewards sharing activities. There are, of course, many ways to distribute knowledge. Many of these involve the application of information technology tools, such as expert systems, Web portals, and the like. Informal discussions over coffee are another way.

Knowledge utilization is the process of integrating knowledge into the agency. One increasingly important method to accomplish this task is by establishing and promoting greater use of communities of practice. Communities of practice are informal groups of individuals with a common interest in a topic or a program connected in electronic networks to share members' experience, knowledge, and advice.

Fundamental Process at the State Department

The first attempt of the U.S. Department of State to institute a KM program began in 1999 with the Foreign Affairs Systems Integration (FASI) project. Although unsuccessful, the FASI plan was an attempt to acquire a standard system that featured a Web-based portal, applications, and tools for improved interagency communications, information sharing, and knowledge management to support the U.S foreign affairs overseas offices. The program was set up within the department's Bureau of Information Resource Management (IRM). A 2002 review found that the FASI program was not meeting expectations. It was unable to identify system requirements, consider alternatives, ensure interagency commitment, and conduct overseas testing of the system. In 2002, the State Department's newly appointed undersecretary for management formed an information technology review group, led by an outside consultant, to study the department's IT uses and capabilities. According to the director of the e-diplomacy initiative, the task force was charged with putting the Department of State's core business practices and users' requirements "in the driver's seat," and assisting department bureaus to translate those requirements into appropriate information technology (Holmes 2003).

After a wide series of interviews with department employees, the consultant determined that KM is a major part of the Department of State's businesses. As such, he recommended that it not be part of the IRM, but instead be transferred to a central office under the leadership of the under secretary for management, and that the FASI experiment be terminated. A new office, out from under IT management, would help the department to focus its efforts on managing knowledge to accomplish the following and other business issues:

- Capturing the knowledge of foreign service officers (FSOs) to ease the transition of their replacements as they rotate positions at overseas missions every two to three years.
- Safeguarding against potential knowledge losses when about 45 percent of the department's workforce becomes eligible to retire by the end of FY 2006.
- Overcoming current problems with antiquated, inefficient, and incompatible IT systems at overseas posts, which hamper FSOs from getting the information they need, when they need it, to conduct the department's diplomatic mission.
- Improving communications, collaboration, and knowledge exchange across the department's decentralized organizational structure and among the Foreign Service's core political, economic, administrative, consular, and public diplomacy areas.

In June of 2002, the undersecretary for management accepted the recommendations and formally established the office of e-diplomacy. Implementation of KM began immediately. The stated mission of the e-diplomacy office was:

> [T]o enhance the Department's foreign affairs leadership by promoting a knowledge-sharing culture and making new technologies readily available to help provide faster, more effective service to internal and external customers. This mission reflects the commitments of the Secretary and Under Secretary for Management to putting secure and innovative systems at headquarters and overseas missions to support diplomacy in the new century, ensuring that the systems meet business needs, and making better use of the knowledge and experience resident in the Department. (DOS 2003, 5)

The State Department's Office of the Inspector General (OIG) conducted a study of the KM activities of a number of other federal, international, and private-sector organizations in its development of an implementation strategy for the department. The OIG found that five key processes or principles seemed to be present in most of the KM programs they examined. Table 5.1 is an overview of the five principles and some examples of the practices associated with each principle.

Table 5.1

Successful KM Implementation Principles and Practices

Principle 1	Principle 2	Principle 3	Principle 4	Principle 5
Recognizing the benefits of KM to the organization	Ensuring organization-wide support for KM	Appreciating cultural barriers to KM success	Building KM communities	Using information technology in KM
Practices: Understanding the KM concept	*Practices:* Securing executive-level support and sponsorship	*Practices:* Understanding cultural hindrances to KM	*Practices:* Defining and identifying KM communities	*Practices:* Understanding the role of IT
Recognizing the benefits of KM	Designating a focal point for KM	Overcoming cultural barriers	Supporting KM communities	Choosing appropriate technology
Identifying critical business needs as a basis for KM	Providing funding and staff resources		Fostering innovative community activities	Managing and sustaining IT and data
Appreciating different approaches to applying KM	Documenting KM directions			
Managing and measuring KM results				

Source: DOS 2003, p. 10.

KM at the State Department

Since its implementation in 2002, the office of e-diplomacy has used the principles identified by the inspector general to implement several ongoing KM programs. One of its first actions was to establish an intranet to provide information, Internet links, and other resources to aid employees wanting to know more about knowledge-sharing tools and techniques. The KM office also provided software tailored to support classified information exchange and knowledge sharing by department bureaus and missions around the world.

A third early e-diplomacy task was to survey KM initiatives and systems that already existed in the Department of State, with the eventual goal of sharing best practices and coordinating efforts to avoid duplication. The Bureau for Administration, Center for Administrative Innovations (A/CAI) was the most comprehensive KM program found. Beginning in July 2001, A/CAI employed a variety of methods to compile and share information on how to make the department's administrative operations "best-in-class," and to network with other agencies to capture information on effective strategies for improving administrative services.

A fourth e-diplomacy program was overseeing collection of user requirements for developing a State Messaging and Archive Retrieval Toolset. The department planned to replace its outdated telegram and e-mail technology with a secure, state-of-the art, Web-based system for handling all types of documents. The project used KM practices to determine the best approach to system design and implementation. Other KM early activities included participating in designing and implementing an open-source information system, a G8 knowledge management project (Web site), and leading a department-wide collaborative application technology solutions forum.

Measuring E-Diplomacy Program Performance

The Department of State's FY 2005 performance summary identified three key management priorities: one focused on people ("right-sizing"), the second on facilities (embassy security, construction, and maintenance), and the third on systems. The systems priority was constructed around a knowledge management framework. Called the State Messaging and Archive Retrieval Toolset (SMART), the purpose of the program is to develop a simple, secure, and user-driven system to support foreign affairs activities around the world. Designed to replace the department's old cable system, SMART uses a Web-based technology platform that gives users the ability to share information quickly and economically.

Moreover, it gives department managers and the diplomatic community

Table 5.2

Partial Results of 2005 Performance Review on KM and Leadership

Actions being taken	Expected results of actions
• Improving department intranet site to collect, integrate, and share knowledge more efficiently	• The department's institutional knowledge is made available to its own professionals and to other foreign affairs, intelligence, and homeland security agencies
• Strengthening collaboration and information sharing with USAID through a new connection between DOS and USAID	• Special expertise is easier to locate
• Creating a global task force on new diplomacy to exploit technology in new diplomatic and public diplomacy engagement strategies	• Employees are more productive and applications more efficient
• Exploiting key technologies to improve the department's performance worldwide	
• Making greater use of classified and unclassified government networks for information exchange and collaboration	
• Developing the State Messaging and Archive Retrieval Toolset, to provide diplomats and managers with enhanced communications and knowledge management tools	
• Selecting a vendor to develop a solution for a design/demonstration of a messaging solution to be piloted to over 3,000 users in domestic and overseas locations	
• In FY 2005, beginning worldwide deployment of the SMART system	

Source: DOS 2004. FY 2005 Performance Summary.

enhanced communications capabilities and provides the building blocks for great implementation of knowledge management programs and procedures (DOS 2004).

The last item to be rated in the plan was the department's progress on the strategic goal of Management and Organizational Excellence: Knowledge Management and Leadership. Results were contained under four categories:

findings, recommendations, actions being taken, and expected results. The actions being taken and expected results points are displayed in Table 5.2.

Moving Beyond Implementation

The three fundamental concepts of knowledge discussed earlier in the chapter —knowledge as intellectual capital, knowledge as a facilitator of management transformation, and the greatly expanded scope of knowledge—may also be extended to reflect key KM practices. These practices may be seen as answers to the following implementation process questions: What knowledge does the agency have? What knowledge does the agency need? And, how can the agency know that its strategies, program plans, and decision making aren't simply examples of reinventing the wheel? The basic collecting, sharing, and saving activities of knowledge management may provide answers to these questions.

Knowledge audits can tell an agency manager what knowledge is resident in the organization and its people; program planning and performance reviews can help an administrator identify gaps in his or her knowledge; and communities of practice and knowledge repositories can tell a decision maker what previous solutions worked and what did not work. Knowledge audits, communities of practice, and knowledge repositories are discussed in greater detail in the following sections.

Conducting a Knowledge Audit

In the private sector, knowledge management implementation has encountered more problems and been forced to endure a larger failure rate than knowledge management in government. Industry consultant Dr. Ann Hylton and others have pointed to the failure of KM programs in business to begin with a comprehensive audit of the extent and location of the knowledge that exists in the organization. In many of the reported failures, the initial knowledge analysis stopped with locating the knowledge spelled out in documents and other printed sources. The analysts failed to locate, capture, organize, and disseminate the tacit knowledge contained in the minds of the organization's workers (Baxter 2002). The purpose, scope, and focus of a knowledge audit is explained in Box 5.1.

The Australian Government's Information Management Office (AGIMO) has developed a comprehensive checklist of issues and actions that agency managers seeking to adopt KM practices should follow (AGIMO 2004). The first item on the checklist was: *conduct a knowledge audit.* AGIMO defined a knowledge audit as an inventory of available knowledge assets and resources. AGIMO added that the purpose of an audit is to identify and com-

Box 5.1

**So What Is a Knowledge Audit? What Will It
Investigate and Evaluate?**

The knowledge audit (k-audit) is the all-important first major phase, stage, or step of a knowledge management initiative. It is used to provide a sound investigation into the organization's knowledge "health." The k-audit is a discovery, verification, and validation tool, providing fact finding, analysis, interpretation, and reports. It includes a study of corporate information and knowledge policies and practices, and of corporate information and knowledge structure and flow.

The knowledge audit serves to help the audited unit, whether the whole organization or part of it, to determine whether it "knows what it knows" and "knows what it doesn't know" about its existing knowledge state. It will also help it to unearth what it should know to better leverage knowledge for business and competitive advantage. This enlightenment sets the agenda for the knowledge management initiative, program, and implementation.

A complete knowledge audit will evaluate the organization's knowledge environment, its knowledge ecology—primarily the corporate knowledge structure and the enhancing social and behavioral culture of the people within the organization. The k-audit examines knowl-

pare the gap between the ideal or desired state of agency knowledge and the existing knowledge environment. The rationale for conducting an audit is because knowledge gaps can impede innovation, block opportunities for performance improvement, or hamper technology implementations. Knowledge audits may be conducted at the agency, group, section, or team level, or even the level of the entire public service.

The types of questions the Australian Information Management Office recommended be asked in an information audit include the following:

- What knowledge does the organization need to acquire or develop?
- Where are knowledge flows impeded?
- How can knowledge be better shared and organized?
- What knowledge resources are currently in use?
- What are the current and future benchmarks for knowledge use?

edge sources and use: *how* and *why* knowledge is acquired, accessed, disseminated, shared, and used. Most importantly, the knowledge audit investigates the perceptions of knowledge management effectiveness through the knowing eyes of the knowledge people, the true knowledge workers.

The knowledge audit offers a *full and detailed examination, review, assessment, and evaluation* of an organization's knowledge abilities, its existing knowledge assets and resources, *and its knowledge management activities.* It will help the audited unit to determine *what* knowledge is being managed and *how well* it is being managed. The audit helps to make the knowledge in the audited unit visible, understandable, and appreciated.

At the most detailed level, the knowledge audit investigates and evaluates the company's information systems, its processes, and its knowledge-enabling tools and technology. It will examine how well current processes support knowledge capture, storage, access, dissemination, use, and sharing. Ultimately, the knowledge audit will reveal knowledge management strengths, weaknesses, opportunities and threats/risks, knowledge flow, and gaps, using scientific knowledge auditing methods, systems, and analysis tools. The main knowledge-auditing tools are the knowledge survey, the knowledge inventory, and knowledge mapping.

Source: Hylton 2002. Used with permission.

Once a knowledge audit is complete, KM managers turn to ways that the agency's identified knowledge—and the knowledge held by relevant individuals and outside organizations—is nurtured and multiplied. One way this is done is through encouraging the formation of communities of practice.

Forming Communities of Practice

The knowledge base of an organization is typically spread among many different individuals, units, groups, and external stakeholders. A key task of knowledge management is to provide a means for the many diverse knowledge holders to share their knowledge and experience. One of the most powerful and efficient ways this is done is through the mechanisms of an informal community of persons with like concerns or interests. These communities of like-minded individuals, in fact, are often referred to as "the lifeblood of KM programs," and one of the "key building blocks in the organization and management of [agency] innovation and creativity" (AGIMO 2004; Ash and Cohendet 2004).

Two similar but fundamentally different labels are often used interchangeably when referring to these groups: communities of interest and communities of practice. As a result, they are often mistakenly taken for one another. Agencies also use a variety of other terms to describe either or both of these groups, such as learning networks, knowledge communities, competency networks, and others (Wenger, McDermott, and Snyder 2002). However, it is important to remember that the two are different; communities of interest are not communities of practice, although communities of practice may also incorporate communities of interest.

A *community of interest* is a particular type of network that features peer-to-peer collaborative activities to build member skills as well as organizational and societal capabilities. Communities of interest are people who share a common interest in a topic but who do not necessarily depend upon each other's contributions to advance their knowledge. A community of practice, however, is a group of people voluntarily agreeing to work with one another to exchange and share knowledge that is gained from experience and that is often not available in any other form or from any other source. A community of practice is held together by an informal bond of shared purpose and experience; members willingly share the learning and knowledge they have developed through their experience in discussions, stories, examples, arguments, and even disagreements. This sharing is facilitated by group discussions, one-on-one conversations, private reading about new ideas, or watching other knowledge workers disagree over cutting-edge issues (Ash and Cohendet 2004).

How Communities of Practice Facilitate Change

Among the many benefits public-sector managers have identified for communities of practice are these three recommendations for what the federal government can do to spur improvements at the local level on a national scale (Snyder and Briggs 2004):

1. Sponsor and support local communities of practice to achieve outcomes that require ongoing innovation and action-learning. A federal community of practice can serve as a community sponsor, provide strategic focus, make available seed funding, and provide institutional legitimacy. Also, federal community coordinators can help develop a learning agenda for local participants, build the community, and lead outcome-oriented initiatives. The federal agency can also serve as com-

munity champions, provide support staff to bridge formal-unit barriers, coach community initiatives, and liaise with sponsors and stakeholders.
2. Coordinate community goals with agency imperatives and policy mandates. Coordination actions include linking the community's learning agenda with agency objectives; leveraging community capabilities by implementing them in recognized service-delivery systems; and partnering with community of practice members to accelerate the spread of good ideas.
3. Make it possible to leverage the power of the federal government in order to broaden the scope and scale of pilot projects. Leveraging can turn a relatively small investment in infrastructure and senior executive attention into the means for more learning networks and thereby achieve results not otherwise possible.

Leveraging Core Dimensions

The effectiveness of a community of practice depends on strength in three core dimensions: its *domain, community,* and *practice. Domain* refers to the focus and identity of the group. For example, a domain of a community of practice in the homeland security area might be airport security. *Community* refers to the relationships and interactions among the members of the community. The airport security community might involve members of local, state, and federal law enforcement agencies, fire and medical agencies, anti-terrorism agencies, airport management, airlines and support organizations, and others. *Practice* refers to the community's best practices, methods, and learning activities that give members of the community their particular edge. For the airport security example, practice might include a collection of international best practices examples of airport security programs. The binding cord that holds the community together might be a combined commitment to ensuring that the nation has a secure, safe, and efficient air travel system. *Practice* also refers to the special skills of the subgroups of a larger CoP. In airport security, a special interest group within a CoP might be law enforcement personnel; another might be fire fighting professionals; and another might be communications personnel. The dimensions of domain, community, and practice are, of course, highly interrelated. Sample components that help to define each dimension include the following:

1. Domain
   • The domain of a community of practice can be the issues or problems that practitioners battle with or what they consider essential to the task.

- In some cases, it is particularly challenging to set the boundaries for a domain; they can be too narrow or too broad.
- Members typically have a strong interest in the topic and an understanding of how it can contribute to an organization's effectiveness.
- In the political context, legitimacy and attention is given to domain, to the citizens affected by it, and to the practitioners who care about it.

2. Community
- This includes community members at various levels: conveners, core group, and active and peripheral memberships. Leadership by an effective community coordinator and core group is essential.
- Members exhibit feelings of trust, openness, belonging, shared common values and commitment, and commitment to others in the network.

3. Practice
- Practice refers both to methodologies and to skills. It includes the "best practices" exemplars in the domain. These can be contained in documents, or exist as the tacit skills of skilled, knowledgeable staff.
- Practice includes the techniques, methods, stories, tools, and professional attitudes of the members.
- In addition, it includes learning activities engaged to build, share, and apply the practice.

CoPs with State and Local Governments

Snyder and Briggs (2004) determined that at least four types of situations exist in which managers in federal agencies might want to establish communities of practice with state and local governments:

Building new capabilities: Departments or agencies could convene and cultivate a community of stakeholders at the national level in order to provide guidance and leadership for the variety of federal mandates and policy directives or best practices that state and local agencies must or might implement.

Increasing current capability levels: In many cases, the problem is not to build a new capability, but rather to lift an established capability to a new level—or even to simply maintain it at its existing high performance levels. This situation occurs regularly in those agencies in which key personnel are regularly rotated from position to position, or posting to posting, as with military and State Department personnel.

Integrating new capability dimensions: Communities of practice are good for integrating new dimensions into established operations. For example, federal agencies have been mandated to incorporate a variety of e-government capabilities to reduce operational costs and to increase citizen access and convenience. State and local governments are following suit as fast as their intellectual and financial resources allow. As technological advances occur, the CoP might be the best source for disseminating information about such advances in tools, procedures, and policies.

Attracting, retaining, and developing talent: Every agency in the federal government—like organizations nationwide—is faced with a demographic "time bomb" that threatens to see nearly half their employees retire by 2010. One way that communities of practice can build organizational capabilities is by providing professionals a forum for sharing their learning with new or younger staff members. The CoP can also be a forum through which new hires may test ideas and innovations. Possibly most important, it can also be a place for building relationships and gaining a sense of commitment and professional identity with colleagues. The informal sense of belonging among practitioners and associated opportunities for professional development may be the most beneficial capacity that government organizations have that enables them to attract, retain, and develop top talent. The army's very successful CompanyCommand community of practice is an example.

Communities of Practice in Practice

By 2005, there were hundreds if not thousands of communities of practice effectively functioning at the federal, state, and local government levels, and their numbers keep growing every year (O'Hara 2004). These range in size from fewer than five members to the more than 7,000 members of the army's CompanyCommand CoP. And some may be even larger. The smallest community sponsored by the Department of Health and Human Services (DHHS)—the SAS Users' Group—listed just two members. The two largest DHHS communities were the Division of Medicare Operations–Chicago, with 353 members, and the Survey and Certification Website CoP, with 309 members. A typical example at DHHS is the Knowledge Management Integration community of practice, with 38 members. The mission of the group is to integrate KM efforts throughout the department's management services group, while increasing knowledge exchange internally. The integration CoP listed the availability of five recent information libraries: knowledge management courses, DHHS taxonomy, a link to FAA taxonomy, retirement CDs, and an informational brochure for a 2005 KM Fair.

Almost every agency has at least one currently functioning CoP. For example, the DHHS communities of practice home page lists 38 CoPs, the Federal Highway Administration sponsors more than 20 communities, and the Federal Aviation Administration has more than 10 communities. The federal Chief Information Officers (CIO) Council's knowledge management working group has listed these special interest groups (SIGs) within the CoP (KM.gov 2004):

- *Communities of Practice.* This "CoP on CoPs" is a government-wide network of people interested in learning about and sharing experiences in establishing and supporting CoPs as a means to address compelling business needs within their organizations.
- *Knowledge Retention.* This community is sharing information of collecting and archiving knowledge that might be lost due to employee retirements.
- *Taxonomy and Semantics.* This SIG is being formed in response to questions and concerns about taxonomies, thesauri, indexing, topic maps, ontologies, and how the semantic web activities support KM in government. The mission statement of this CoP is displayed in Box 5.2.
- *Technology and KM.gov Content.* This special community SIG assesses technologies claiming to support or enhance knowledge management efforts. KM.gov is the federal government's communications tool (e.g., journals and a Web site). Box 5.3 includes a list of some of the technology tools used in running a community of practice.
- *Policy and Outreach.* The purpose of this group is to educate such stakeholders as the administration, Congress, and other public policy organizations about knowledge management and how it can help the federal government achieve its objectives.

Starting the Company Commanders' CoP

Writing for *Federal Computer Week,* Colleen O'Hara (2004) identified the U.S. Army's CompanyCommand community of practice as possibly the most successful of the many federal government CoPs then in operation. The story of how that community was born was told by two of its founders at the March 2, 2004, meeting of the Knowledge Roundtable in Washington, D.C.

Army majors Nate Allen and Tony Burgess were neighbors and company commanders in the same Brigade at Lanai, Hawaii. The two officers met as often as possible during the evenings to share experiences about what was going on in their companies. They soon concluded that it would be great if other company commanders could easily share their ideas with like-minded leaders across the army. Every captain they spoke with agreed that finding a better way to share their concerns was a great idea. However, at the time, no forum existed that made it possible. And, after com-

Box 5.2

Mission Statement of the KM.gov
Taxonomies and Semantics SIG

The Taxonomies and Semantics SIG is a community of practice whose members have a common interest in both the theory and practice of taxonomies and semantics. As a community of practice, members identify areas of common interest and the SIG provides opportunities to learn and share knowledge. The scope of interest for this SIG potentially is very broad. The SIG does not limit the scope, rather provides boundaries by defining what is meant by "taxonomies" and "semantics."

Taxonomies are defined simply as the structures used to organize information. . . . From an information science perspective . . . taxonomies may take on one or a combination of several types of structures— they may be simple flat structures, hierarchies, network/plex structures, or faceted taxonomies. Each of these kinds of structures serves as a different kind of information management and access purpose. All are critical for supporting today's complex information solutions and are integral components of today's complex information systems.

Semantics are at base the processes that use or create values for taxonomies. Without semantics, taxonomies are simple or elaborate but empty structures. Officially, semantics is a branch of linguistics that deals with the study of meaning, changes in meaning, and the principles that govern the relationship between sentences or words and their meanings. . . . Semantics involves the study of the relationships between signs and symbols. From an information perspective, semantics also involves effective information communication within and across languages, information surrogation, information organization, and discovery.

The SIG supports several types of activities, including informal open lunch discussion sessions, formal speaker and panel programs, online discussions, and knowledge interchange. The SIG also alerts members to educational and training events, conferences, associations, journals in the field, and new books on these topics.

Source: Hsu 2004.

Box 5.3

**Some Technologies Used in Running
Communities of Practice**

- Face-to-face conferences
- Experts' and panel presentations
- Online discussions
- Chat rooms
- "Brown bag" luncheon presentations
- "Water cooler" meeting areas
- In-agency coffee houses
- After-work social events
- Teleconferences
- Special face-to-face meetings
- Special projects
- On-site visits and informal one-to-one interactions
- Federal agency–champion visits to local partner communities
- One-to-one interactions by phone and e-mail
- Intranets
- Web sites [information published for all network members]
- Listservs [information sent to selected external groups and members]

Sources: AGIMO 2004; Lesser and Storck 2001.

pleting their assignments most commanders were transferred to other positions, which left them no way to continue to tap into the collected knowledge after they were gone. More critical, newly appointed company commanders did not have any way to find out how others dealt with similar problems. The rapid growth of the Internet presented a solution to their problem.

By chance, the two ran into a volunteer, Steve Sweitzer, who designed a Web page for them for no charge. In just two months, they had collected a team of officers who contributed their input and time to make the CoP a success. By 2005, membership had grown to more than 7,000. With this growth came an increasingly wider scope for the community. The vision of the CoP became, "Every company-level leader worldwide connected in a vibrant conversation about leading and building combat-ready teams" (O'Hara

2004). Allen and Burgess would like to see every company-level leader in the army—past, present, and future—connected in a conversation about building effective units.

Companycommand..army.mil also supports "ProReading," a professional reading program service for company commanders. This program provides the army's more than 20,000 company-level leaders with "best practices" models of how their fellow officers mesh professional reading with mission accomplishment by showing members how dedicated commanders "made it happen."

The Role of Knowledge Repositories

One of the great advantages of the community of practice system is that the community is able to function as a virtual, living storehouse—or *repository*—of knowledge (Lesser and Storck 2001). As such, it makes it possible for members to reuse the knowledge and experience gained by other members.

Most government communities of practice maintain some form of electronic library as a repository of their collected knowledge. When the knowledge of an organization is collected and organized in relevant, shared categories, it makes it easy for other and newer members of an organization to access and apply the knowledge they need. Such a system is an efficient means of recycling intellectual capital, making it possible for agencies to achieve more with their increasingly limited resources. According to Lesser and Storck, such repositories provide a number of important benefits (2001, 838):

- They provide a common virtual workspace, where members store, organize, and download prior presentations, tools, and other material community members consider valuable.
- The presence of a meta-data system not only allows users to access and use information, it also adds to the credibility of the data by letting the user know the name of the individual who initially developed the information.
- The inclusion in the repository of human interventions, such as content managers or teams, ensures that the collected information remains new and relevant. Content managers can also serve as "traffic cops," able to direct searchers to particularly relevant sources the searcher might otherwise miss.
- Storehouses also provide a mechanism for evaluating the trustworthiness and reciprocity of members by providing a record of who shares what and when.

An example of how a knowledge repository functions within a community of practice framework is NASA's Virtual Research Center (VRC), a Web-based project-management information and knowledge-sharing system implemented in 1997 (NASA 2002). The system uses such knowledge management tools as a document manager, an action item tracker, a calendar, a team directory, a threaded discussion tool, and an activity log. By 2002, the VRC community of practice had more than 3,300 registered members, working on over 175 project teams, and with nearly 15,000 files stored in VCR team libraries.

As NASA continued to grow the community, it initiated such projects as developing ways to incorporate object-oriented software technologies, and become the environment for both knowledge management and collaborative engineering. Resources such as a threaded discussion tool will provide teams the capability to describe their experiences and thought processes. A search engine gives users the capacity to search through seventy-five different repository file formats for keywords.

Conclusion

Three concepts of knowledge support the idea that investments in knowledge management systems can contribute to successful implementation of such important government programs as e-government, homeland security, privatization and market-based delivery of government services, collaboration, and performance management: (1) the knowledge held by an organization's people and individuals from outside of the agency constitute an agency's *intellectual capital.* Intellectual capital refers to an organization's recorded and remembered information, experiences, and human talent; (2) knowledge management concepts of learning organizations and best-practices process are core elements in the President's Management Agenda (PMA). These two concepts optimize organization time, costs, and quality through KM processes; (3) identification and management of an agency's knowledge base underlies all processes in e-government.

The Knowledge Management Roundtable determined that three difficulties contribute to KM failures: KM not being a priority of senior management; lack of a knowledge-sharing in the organization; and lack of time or KM priorities of knowledge users.

Three basic processes of knowledge management are: knowledge acquisition, knowledge sharing, and knowledge utilization. *Acquisition* is the process of developing and/or creating intellectual capital, including insights, skills, experiences, and relationships. *Knowledge sharing* is disseminating and making available the collected knowledge of the agency and its staff. Knowledge sharing is enabled through a social process made possible by an organizational culture that honors and rewards sharing activities. *Knowledge utilization* is the process of integrating knowledge into the agency.

The three fundamental concepts of knowledge—knowledge as intellectual capital, knowledge as a facilitator of management transformation, and the greatly expanded scope of knowledge—may also be extended to reflect key KM practices.

6

Building a Collaborative Learning Culture

Knowledge management is a methodology for capturing the important knowledge within an organization and utilizing it to support the organization's [operating] requirements. . . . When the organizational currency is ideas . . . sophisticated approaches must be employed to foster the creation, evolution and communication of those ideas. The intent is to improve the organizational environment [culture] for valuing, generating, sharing and applying knowledge.
(U.S. Dept. of Defense, KM position announcement [U.S. DOD 2002])

Snyder and Briggs (2003) described the experiences of four different public-sector collaborative programs for community development: Boost4Kids, SafeCities, 21st Century Skills, and the Federal Highway Administration's Rumble Strips Initiative. Their IBM Business of Government–sponsored report focused on the methods the people behind these innovative programs used to develop local networks to build local coalitions, operate after-school programs, link education to job training, trace illegal guns, and improve highway safety. The networks combined a number of different learning activities to develop and share the knowledge needed to grow the coalitions. The underlying concept tying the four programs together was development of a collaborative learning culture based on trust and mutual respect. These programs succeeded because the cultural barriers that often make it impossible for KM to succeed were replaced by a culture of collaboration, trust, and commitment.

Chapter Objectives

Successful implementation of a knowledge management initiative in a public-sector agency is influenced by a number of controllable and uncontrollable factors. Several of these are discussed in this chapter, including organizational culture, climate, operating policies, and leadership. The chapter objectives, therefore, are that readers take away the following benefits from the chapter:

- To gain an understanding of the role of organizational culture, climate, and policies in shaping the success or failure of KM in government agencies.
- To recognize the different paths and destinations that knowledge management can take in an agency, depending upon the state of the culture of the organization.
- To understand the meaning and role of organizational culture, climate, and policies.
- By reading about actual government programs in Canada and the United States, to develop a greater awareness of how culture shapes knowledge capture and sharing.
- To develop an awareness of the role of leadership in KM program adoptions.

Culture in Public-sector Systems

The concept of culture in public-sector knowledge management systems is a point of concern on two distinct planes. One is the political culture that shapes an agency's operating environment and policy focus. This culture is driven by policy formation and emphasis, which is often expressed as mandated executive or legislative initiatives. Political culture is a reflection of political party philosophy and traditions. The distinct polarity that characterizes the polity at the national level as the twenty-first century begins may be even more pronounced at the state and local level, where states and municipal governments can be classified as strongly liberal or conservative.

These opposing philosophies influence the direction of state and local political actions. In the instances where legislatures and the executive represent opposing political philosophies, or where the legislature is evenly divided between parties, it is often difficult to move forward with an ambitious policy agenda (Melkers and Willoughby 2004). For example, for one two-year session at the turn of the twenty-first century, the Washington State House of Representatives was evenly split between the Democratic and Republican parties; opposing party members exhibited little or no willingness to compromise on proposed legislation. As a result, little legislation was enacted and hardly any progress was made on solving pressing social problems. Rather, the session was characterized by acrimonious name calling and blaming the other party for the collapse of the legislative process.

Organizational culture refers to the internal climate in which the members of an agency carry out their daily tasks and responsibilities. Mutual trust and respect, job satisfaction, and commitment to a mission are all reflections of a particular organizational culture, just as are their opposites. Organizational culture is expressed in the phrase "the way we do things around here."

The political culture of an agency can change rather quickly—at least on the surface—with a change of administrations, whereas the organizational culture of an agency is longer lived and harder to change. The results of a study of a local unit of the General Services Administration in 1995 made this point of conventional wisdom clear. The study was carried out to determine whether the culture that existed in the organization at that time was conducive to adoption of a total quality management initiative (McNabb and Sepic 1995). The researchers found that, without the wholehearted support of senior management, most change initiatives tried in that unit would be failures.

Culture and Knowledge Management

For a public-sector KM program to be successful, a number of specific organizational culture conditions must be present. First, there must be a culture of openly sharing information. Members must trust one another to do the right thing when it comes to sharing information (U.S. GAO 2003b). Users of knowledge generated by others must freely give credit where credit is due. And, the agency must support human resources policy that promotes a willingness to learn among members of the agency. Clearly, this involves the social side of KM, not the technology side. One way that governments have initiated the type of culture in which KM has a chance of thriving is by forming "communities of practice." As we saw in the preceding chapter, communities of practice are groups of people who "share a concern, a set of problems, or a passion about a topic, and who deepen their knowledge and expertise in this area by interacting on an ongoing basis" (Wenger, McDermott, and Snyder 2002, 4).

It is important to remember that it is not necessary that the members of a community of practice work in relatively close proximity to one another every day. Rather, the members of the community participate because they value spending time together and what they learn when they do meet. Because they value the relationships, eventually a common bond of mutual understandings and shared standards, work ethics, and aspirations develops. Thus, the members succeed by forging their own subculture within—and despite—the larger organization's broader operating culture. Before proceeding with this discussion, a quick review of some of the research on organizational culture and how it can be a barrier to organizational change of any kind is in order.

Barriers to Organizational Change

Researchers and practitioners now agree that most if not all KM adoption failures—and failures of other such change initiatives—are not failures of management. Rather, they should be attributed to a deeper, more fundamental source: the all-pervasive culture of the organization and the operating climate that culture shapes in an organization (Bock 1999; Knapp and Yu 1999; Rastrogi 2000; Holowetzki 2002). More often than not, managers and administrators become victims of that culture, just as change itself is a victim of the implementation process. Thus, in order to improve the odds of success when attempting to introduce any change into an organization, government managers should first conduct a comprehensive examination of their organization's underlying culture and the operating climate that is created and constantly influenced by that culture. In this way they are able to identify the barriers to success beforehand and plan and implement change strategies before implementing a change.

Culture, Climate, and Change

Together, the organizational characteristics with the greatest power to shape the effectiveness of an agency are culture and climate; their nature dictates the state of acceptance required for acceptance of a knowledge management initiative. If the organization's culture and climate refuse to accept change, such initiatives as KM will fail, regardless of the desires and plans of the organization's managers. Staff members are more likely to go through the motions of reacting to the change, but without any real substantive modification taking place.

Organizational change refers to the process of altering people's actions, reactions, and interactions in such a way as to move the organization's existing state to some future desired state (Pettigrew 1990). The only way to bring about change that lasts—that is, to bring about an organization-wide acceptance of knowledge management as the new way of operating—is for management to develop a working environment in which employees are able to operate more effectively within the new environment. Pettigrew terms this "influencing the conditions that determine the interpretation of situations and the regulation of ideas." Thus, the organization's culture and/or its climate must be modified, or the processes, policies, or technologies to be changed must be modified to match the dictates of the organization's culture and climate; otherwise, organizations will resist knowledge management in whatever form it appears.

Organizations are supposed to provide employees a recognized, stable way of dealing with the problems of their environment (J.Q. Wilson 1989). Implementation of change initiatives may become even more difficult when the organization is a public agency, as managers of such agencies are forced to use as incentives for adoption rewards that are largely nonmaterial. Bringing the knowledge management way of operating into such an organization has been shown to be a "long-term, complex process of cultural reform that requires unprecedented technical competence and may take as long as ten years to complete, if at all" (Wollner 1992).

Culture in the Public Sector

The use of KM in government agencies has become an important tool in the effort to "reinvent government" by giving public service managers new freedom to manage their resources as they manage their operations. Advocates for organizational transformation at the municipal, state, and federal levels of government are using KM initiatives to help bring about long-desired change. These "change advocates" note that organized and clearly directed process-action teams—groups of workers who share a common interest in a work task or job—often experience dramatic success in improving their customer service processes. This is particularly true when the teams use customer requirements as a baseline against which change is measured. Agencies that have employed KM have reported such positive changes as reductions in operating costs, general process improvements, and less management time spent in "putting out fires" with more time for planning, together with the overall benefit of improved employee morale (Cummins and Stonebraker 1989, Curda 1993).

Regretfully, the progress seen in agency operations through the use of KM has not been consistent, or long lasting. When such programs have been a success, they have usually followed a progression similar to what Eskildson (1994) described as a "bottoms up" transformation process. In such situations, organizations empower personnel in a process of setting specific goals for enhancing customer-valued benefits in the beginning years of the program. This process then infuses the goals throughout the overall culture of the organization. However, incomplete employee empowerment has been found to be a major cause of disappointing results with implementing KM in public agencies. Because empowerment is founded on trust rather than control, major supervisory retraining may be required before the process succeeds. Training managerial and supervisory members in the use of basic knowledge-sharing techniques and processes can readily be achieved; the really difficult task is changing basic attitudes regarding trust.

To successfully implement a long-lasting knowledge-sharing culture within a public agency requires leaders who are cultural change agents, not old-style managers who believe in autocratic controls founded predominantly for controlling costs. The new public manager as change agent is one who views the KM approach as a set of attitudes and behaviors of everyone in the organization, as well as those served by the agency. These expectations are, of course, shaped by the culture and climate of an organization as well as management's policies. To help foster understanding of how these forces affect acceptance of change by an organization, a model of the forces involved in the process follows (Figure 6.1).

What Is Organizational Culture?

All organizations have their own individual and unique cultures (Schein 1992; Wilson 1989). Because the organization's culture dictates what behaviors are acceptable, it also establishes the ways in which problems are addressed within the group, spells out how relationships are defined and supported, and establishes the manner in which work is done. Figure 6.1 illustrates two different cultures.

Once a culture is established, not only does it affect everyone within the organization, it is extremely difficult to change. As Wilson (1989) has noted, "Culture is to an organization what personality is to an individual. Like human culture generally, it is passed on from one generation to the next. It changes slowly, if at all."

By its influence on the behaviors and attitudes of an agency's personnel and the leadership styles of its senior managers, culture creates a specific climate of operations within the organization. A direct product of the interaction of the organization's culture, climate, and people is a set of processes and procedures that both legitimize and direct the work of the organization. Together, the operating processes and procedures are expressed as the policies that guide the organization's actions. The effective integration of culture, climate, and policies, then, is what determines the relative ability of the organization to carry out its mission, as well as its ability to accept and integrate change (Schein 1992). Two standard performance measurements of this condition of final integration have been employee achievement on relevant metrics, such as contributing to a community of practice, and job satisfaction.

The performance outcomes of job satisfaction and job performance also have an influence on an organization's readiness to accept the organizational culture that knowledge management requires. Employees and managers who are comfortable and secure in their jobs (have high job satisfaction), and are rated high in job performance, will most likely have the appropriate attitudes toward implementing the KM initiative.

Figure 6.1 Organizational Factors Affecting the Culture of an Organization

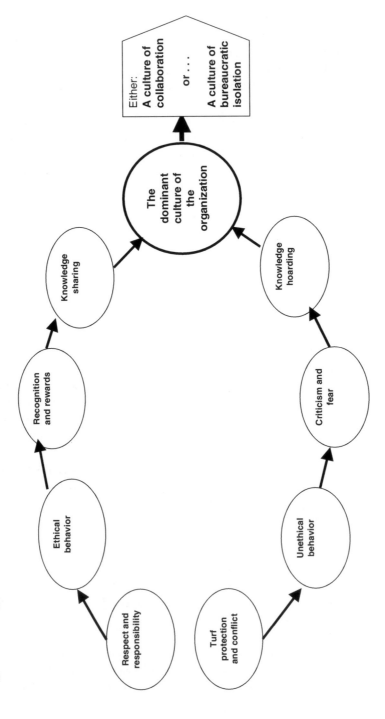

Whenever a major change of any type is proposed for implementation, whether it is a change in the basic information technology employed, in basic operating procedures, or in processes for the resolution of conflict, a state of anxiety often develops among the members of the organization. This state of anxiety is sometimes referred to as stress, and high levels of stress are a significant barrier to change. When stress is high, often performance is lowered and job satisfaction reduced. In the end, agency product or service quality suffers—along with customer/client satisfaction (Sepic and McNabb 1992).

The established culture of an organization is also shaped by a set of learned consequences of the behaviors of members of the agency. Changing the existing culture can be done only when employees learn new sets of accepted behaviors. To change these learned habits, existing perceptions must be "undercut" while the new culture is reinforced (Thompson and Luthans 1990). The workplace environment must be closely managed to ensure that only the new culture is supported.

Dimensions of Organizational Culture

An organization's culture shapes all of its actions, operations, and relationships in an organization is its culture. Schein (1992, 7) has defined culture as the "pattern of basic assumptions that the group learned as it solved its problems of external adaptation and internal integration, which has worked well enough to be considered valid and, therefore, to be taught to new members as the correct way to perceive, think and feel in relation to these problems." Thus, culture sets both the limits (constraints) and the direction of movement of behavior within the organization: Culture dictates acceptance of all organizational change.

An organization's culture is expressed in three levels of human behavior and cognition: what is created or produced, what is valued, and what are the group's basic beliefs or assumptions. Included in what is produced is the level and way of using technology in the group, together with other patterns of behavior among and between group members. Technology refers not just to a type or level of hardware, or technologies—computers, for example—but rather to what J.Q. Wilson (1989) has called a "set of tactics" that employees use to do their tasks. Thus, technology in this sense should be considered the method or means of doing the job that seems easiest and most attractive to the doers at the time. Knowledge collection and sharing procedures and practices are part of the technology of KM.

A problem sometimes cited with the study of culture in organizations has been the failure of researchers to state and rigorously test hypotheses about culture (Wilson 1989). As a result, it has been argued that culture is no more than a "mushy word used to dignify the hunches and intuitions of soft-headed writers who produce journalism in the guise of scholarship." Wilson refuted this criticism, stating that although organizational culture is admittedly a vague concept, it is, indeed, no less real than concepts such as national culture or human personality (McNabb and Sepic 1995).

Sepic and McNabb (1992) tested a number of different scales to measure characteristics of organizational culture in a large and diverse government agency. They found that these five constructs as factors contributed to organizational culture: its basic organizational structure, technology, role clarity, social support, and human interaction. In a content analysis survey of the literature describing KM implementation problems, Holowetzki (2002) later identified six cultural factors affecting knowledge management implementation success: information systems, organizational structure, reward systems, processes, people, and leadership. The relevance of these two studies for KM lies in the recognition that organizational culture is a multifaceted construct, and that any benchmarking study should therefore include a number of different components.

Dimensions of Organizational Climate

The climate of an organization emerges from the interaction of people and its basic underlying culture. Often incorrectly used as a synonym for culture (Schein 1992; Turnipseed 1988), climate instead must be considered to be a reflection of the agency's culture and a reflection that is distorted by the qualities and abilities of the people in the group.

Organizational climate has been defined as a "concept reflecting the content and strength of the prevalent values, norms, attitudes, behaviors and feelings" of the people within an organization (Payne 1971); as the level and form of organizational support, openness within the organization, its supervisory style, conflict between members, and autonomy and quality of relationships (Lewicki et al. 1996); and as the norms, feelings, and attitudes—in a word, the "atmosphere"—prevailing in an organization (Dastmalchian, Blyton, and Adamson 1991).

Measurements of the climate of a government organization may be used as a barometer of employee satisfaction and management effectiveness; thus, if the climate of an organization is "good," it exerts a strong force on the behavior of the organization's members (Turnipseed 1988). Of course, if the climate is "bad," an equally powerful but opposite force is exerted on members' behavior. In further support of this thesis, Reichers and Schneider (1990) identified structure, rewards, and warmth and support as the fundamental dimensions of organizational climate.

From the work of Reichers and Schneider (1990) and Dastmalchian, Blyton, and Adamson (1991), McNabb and Sepic (1995) evaluated four measures of organizational climate in a study of a branch of the General Services Administration. They included (1) the social environment, (2) internal communication, (3) role conflict, and (4) supervisory support. Kopelman, Brief, and Guzzo (1990) earlier concluded that a considerable body of evidence indicates that these dimensions of climate are, in fact, associated with job satisfaction; they also determined that is impossible to precisely identify which particular dimension of climate is or is not consistently related to satisfaction.

Culture and Organizational Policies

Human resources researchers have suggested a wide variety of organizational programs and policies that reflect an organization's basic culture. For example, two constructs identified by McNabb and Sepic (1995) were, first, the attitudes toward training and staff development programs in the organization, and, second, the organization's intrinsic and extrinsic rewards system. Thompson and Luthans (1990) noted that simply announcing what is desired behavior—that is, articulating what type of culture the agency must adopt—is not enough for that culture to be accepted. The policies and practices that managers establish and follow must be consistent with the desired change. That is, if managers desire a climate of trust for their agency, they must trust their employees. If they desire that employees share their knowledge and experience, they must consistently do the same themselves. The problem, however, is generally not with setting an example. Rather it is with coming up with the appropriate incentives for motivating the desired behavior in employees.

Financial incentives are often used as a motivator in the private sector. However, there is little opportunity for managers in government agencies to gain acceptance of new concepts based on the distribution of monetary rewards. The rewards that are available for use by the agency's managers are largely nonmaterial; they fall into such categories as (1) enhancing a sense of purpose or duty within the organization, (2) status that is derived from individual recognition, and (3) membership benefits that come from being a part of an organization that is highly regarded by its members, the publics it serves, and society at large. As limited as these factors—purpose, status, and solidarity—may seem at first glance, they are the fundamental building blocks needed for development of a sense of mission that is commonly shared within the organization. An example of how these factors interact to shape an open and receptive KM culture in a variety of related agencies in Canada follows.

Shaping a Collaborative Culture

Managers must ensure that culture, climate, and policies are in harmony as the first step in laying groundwork for implanting a KM program. The public-sector cases that follow highlight some of the actions taken by management to build a culture of collaboration among a diverse body of regulatory and inspection agencies. The Canadian government's regulatory and inspection community has members representing a variety of federal and provincial government agencies. The community began developing a plan for increasing interorganizational collaboration in 2002, not long after the September 11, 2001, terrorist attack in the United States. Some of the reasons given in support of expanding collaboration among community agencies were (R/IS 2003):

- Different members of the regulatory and inspection communities often serve the same clients, resulting in costly duplication;
- Improved cooperation enhances knowledge sharing and yields improved performance, in terms of both timeliness and outcomes;
- Complementary resources and expertise can be shared, and redundancies kept to a minimum; and
- Interorganizational training can contribute to closer working relationships and create synergies between organizations.

A number of federal inspectors attending the conference at which the plan was broached shared their experiences in situations where such collaboration contributed to more effective outcomes. Inspired by the examples, the Regulatory/Inspection Secretariat (oversight office) began to collect case material and work on the plan to foster a collaborative culture within the regulatory/inspection community. The program to inculcate a broadly based and deeply rooted culture of collaboration was complicated by a number of social and cultural challenges that had come to light during the study of successful cases. Several examples of collaborative government programs in Canada are included in Box 6.1.

Collaboration requires a strong and enduring organizational commitment. Improving cross-agency collaboration requires strong support and direction from senior management and commitment at all levels of the agency. A culture of collaboration is more than the intent and motivation of individual workers; it requires a supportive culture that is shaped by the organizational, political, and legal environment. A culture of collaboration requires investments in financial and human resources, and an effort to identify, collect, and formalize best practices.

Box 6.1

Three Examples of a Culture of Collaboration in the Canadian Government

The Task Force on the Coordination of Federal Activities in the Regions conducted twenty-one case studies to learn from past experiences ways to improve the design and management of horizontal collaborative initiatives. One of these programs studied was the Canadian Maritime Network (Canmarnet). This network was launched by the Department of National Defense in 1994 to gather and share maritime information among federal departments. Other federal agencies participating in the net include Fisheries and Oceans Canada, Citizenship and Immigration, the Royal Canadian Mounted Police, and the Canada Border Services Agency. Canmarnet provides a computerized picture of where offshore maritime vessels are located, the names of the vessels, their destinations, crew lists, and blueprints. Positional information on each offshore vessel is sent to federal departments and agencies daily. The system allows departments to picture normal shipping patterns, and identify any irregularities. The shared information is valuable for such federal government efforts as security, fisheries management, drug control, maritime shipping, immigration, and others.

The Canadian Border Services Agency was established to coordinate key activities shared among three different agencies: the Canada Customs and Revenue Agency; the Intelligence, Interdiction, and Enforcement arm of Citizenship and Immigration Canada; and the Import Inspection at Ports of Entry unit of the Canadian Food Inspection Agency. Using an Automated Targeting System, all imports were put under control of the Canada Border Services Agency, with an agreement between agencies for investigators from other agencies to investigate or provide advice on targeted shipments.

Transport of Dangerous Goods inspectors at Transport Canada collaborate with other departments such as Health Canada, the Canadian Food Inspection Agency, Environment Canada, Natural Resources Canada, and U.S. authorities. This collaboration includes sharing information with other organizations to minimize the risk of jeopardizing other inspections or operations that may already be planned or under way. Failure to share intentions could disrupt a criminal investigation, destroy evidence, or put citizens' health or the environment at risk.

Source: RI/S 2003.

Organizations working together must find common ground for collaboration that is consistent with their respective organizational mandates, jurisdictions, and approaches. Each agency in a collaborative system has its own culture, climate, and policies; each has developed its own distinct approach to problem solution. Although managers tend to have a common understanding of the costs and penalties associated with risk, they also recognize that risk factors and risk assessments vary between agencies. In most collaborative situations, one member typically must take a lead role, thus assuming a disproportionately large share of the risk inherent in the program. Other agencies participate in varying degrees and with varying levels of risk. However, for the collaboration to succeed, partners must have a common understanding on what the program is to achieve, on their individual roles and jurisdictions, and on the approach to be taken. Working at cross purposes means a quick death to efforts to form a culture of collaboration.

Organizations must generate motivation for collaborative work among individuals. This motivation is developed and maintained on a continual basis. This can be done by cultivating such important values as openness to change and diversity within each organization and the greater collaborative team. Primary and secondary partners must be encouraged to buy into the mission of the collaborative activity, the approaches taken, and the shared responsibilities. The key to making this happen lies in the leadership exercised by the lead agency. Organizations in the community must be motivated to share complementary resources, including training, expertise, and equipment. Leadership is discussed in somewhat greater detail later in this chapter.

All members of the collaborative team must be encouraged to accept diversity in cultures and work approaches. Diversity in the workplace commonly refers to ethnic and demographic differences. However, in collaborative task environments it also includes diversity in organizational cultures and approaches. Certainly, it means dealing with the need to coordinate missions, rewards, and support policies.

Collaboration means addressing multiple challenges related to communication within and between organizations. Results of the case studies emphasized that continual and effective communication is necessary for building relationships across organizations—and for maintaining the relationships in the face of constant change. Communication across units is not easy; organizations have their own cultures and their own ways of communication. In some agencies, the most effective medium is by informal "grapevine" communication. In others, formal top-down communications are the norm.

The very nature of collaborative networks necessitates the sharing of knowledge. Sharing past experiences and lessons learned is a primary objective of a culture of collaboration. This often requires establishing a special multi-format and multimedia communications channel. Thus, collecting and sharing the stories of members of an organization or community of interest has become an important activity in public-sector knowledge management.

Saving the Great Lakes

Joint effort on ways to restore the source of fully 20 percent of the world's fresh water is collaboration on a grand scale, indeed. Such a program began May 18, 2004, when President George W. Bush signed Executive Order 13340 establishing the Great Lakes Interagency Task Force (GLTF). The task force was formally launched in December of 2004 as the Great Lakes Regional Collaboration of National Significance (GLRC). With the U.S. Environmental Protection Agency (EPA) as its lead agency, the task force brings together ten U.S. cabinet and agency chiefs to coordinate restoration of the Great Lakes. Together, the ten agencies administer more than 140 federal programs that fund and manage restoration efforts in the United States alone. Since Canada also borders on each of the lakes, Canadian organizations, including Environment Canada and the Province of Ontario, are involved as well. Eight strategy teams, each focusing on a different issue, began work in January 2005 to develop recommendations for action. The first draft of the Action Plan was released in July of 2005 (EPA 2005d).

According to an EPA administrator, the guiding principle of the collaboration follows a key tenet of successful collaborations: a single agency must serve as the leading agency. This means projects must be characterized by central coordination, local control. For the Great Lakes effort, "Policies, priorities and plans will be centrally coordinated; programs, projects and people will be locally controlled" (EPA 2005c). To ensure that the task force complies with an earlier presidential order for employing best practices, the EPA is also responsible for developing a set of principles for successful collaboration that will be used by all agencies involved. Box 6.2 lists the collaborative and coordination responsibilities assigned to the GLTF.

The key cultural directive shaping the new task force was the president's directive that the EPA work with each of the states and cities bordering the lakes and streams to establish a regional collaborative effort. The regional collaboration includes federal agencies, Great Lakes governors, Great Lakes mayors, Great Lakes tribes, and members of the Great Lakes states congressional delegation—working together to restore and protect the Great Lakes ecosystem (EPA 2005a). Although the task force is moving ahead with its mission, it must be kept in mind that cultural changes implemented by external mandate tend to have a short life span.

Box 6.2

Great Lakes Interagency Task Force Collaborative Actions

The following ten objectives for the task force were spelled out in a May 18, 2004, statement announcing the establishment of the collaborative initiative:

1. Help convene and establish a process for collaboration among the members of the task force and the members of the working group established [by the order], with the Great Lakes states, local communities, tribes, regional bodies, and other interests in the region regarding policies, strategies, plans, programs, projects, activities, and priorities for the Great Lakes system.

2. Collaborate with Canada and its provinces and with the binational bodies involved in the Great Lakes region regarding policies, strategies, projects, and priorities for the Great Lakes system.

3. Coordinate the development of consistent federal policies, strategies, projects, and priorities for addressing the restoration and protection of the system and assisting in the appropriate management of the . . . system.

4. Develop outcome-based goals for the system relying upon existing data and science-based indicators of water quality and related environmental factors, [focusing] on such outcomes as cleaner water, sustainable fisheries, and biodiversity of the system.

5. Exchange information regarding policies, strategies, projects, and activities of the agencies represented on the task force.

6. Work to coordinate government action associated with the Great Lakes system.

7. Ensure coordinated federal scientific and other research associated with the Great Lakes system.

8. Ensure coordinated government development and implementation of the Great Lakes portion of the Global Earth Observation System of Systems.

9. Provide assistance and support to agencies represented on the task force.

10. Submit a report to the president in 2005 and thereafter as appropriate summarizing the activities of the task force and providing any recommendations that would advance the policy set forth in Section 1.

Source: EPA 2005b.

To achieve the full potential contained in a public-sector knowledge management system, some person of higher-level responsibility must be willing to come forth as the program's sponsor. Without powerful sponsorship, it is likely that the program will wither on the vine—fulfilling the prophecy that "KM is just another management fad, bound to fly in the face of all other such fads." A significant gap exists between what managers learn about leadership and how leadership is implemented in organizations (Parikh 2005). Indeed, a "crisis of leadership" may exist at the managerial and supervisory implementation levels in both the private and the public sectors.

Leadership in federal government knowledge management programs can take the form of either an internal champion or a sponsor or sponsors; government agencies can benefit from both types of leaders (Wenger, McDermott, and Snyder 2002). A champion is a high-level administrator who has a strong faith in the ability of KM to do what it purports to do for the agency. That faith takes the form of strongly supporting the initiative in highest-level budget negotiations, including providing the KM program leaders enough slack to show that KM has long-term benefits. Moreover, a champion makes sure the program gains high visibility, both within the agency and among other government agencies. In all other organizational paths and ways, he or she clears the way for the agency's KM players—such as members of communities of practice—to perform their actions without fear of seeing the program cut out from beneath them.

Sponsors, on the other hand, are also willing to work to achieve financial support for the KM program, but tend to be less unfailingly enthusiastic about what KM can do for the organization. Sponsors are also less willing to wait long periods for payoffs from KM activities, and more likely to demand performance appraisals and early evidence of successes.

Leadership has a variety of roles and responsibilities in public-sector organizations, among which are the following (Anantatmula 2005):

- Responsibility for strategic planning and systems thinking.
- Allocating the best mix of resources, including but not limited to technology.
- Supporting an organizational culture that honors learning and knowledge sharing.
- Fostering an organizational climate that rewards risk taking, open discussions, and team learning.

KM Leadership at the Department of Defense

First published in 2002, a white paper for the U.S. Department of Defense Comptroller's i-Center emphasized the leadership role of the chief information officer (CIO) in government knowledge programs. Seeing a need for greater leadership in information and knowledge management and technology, Congress passed the Clinger-Cohen Act of 1996, by which the position of CIO was mandated for executive departments and agencies. CIOs were to be responsible for building credible organizations and developing knowledge management capabilities to meet mission needs (U.S. DOD 2002). The Defense Department paper closed with a list of leadership principles for managing information and knowledge functions in all government organizations (Box 6.3).

The establishing act further defined the role of leadership in an organizational culture in its guidelines by warning that in their knowledge management roles, government CIOs should ensure that the KM organizational structure they adopted was consistent with the business, technical, and cultural contexts of their units. For example, one agency might need a CIO who operates as a change agent, while another might need an operations specialist, and another might need a CIO who could play the role of oversight and policy manager. Moreover, the Defense Department added that the CIO position, once established in an agency, needed to be evolutionary rather than static—the position needed to change as the role and scope of technology in government also changes.

It was also recognized that a number of differences exist between the roles and responsibilities of public-sector and private-sector CIOs. For example, government CIOs are constrained in their actions by organizational characteristics typical of government, including little flexibility in financial reward systems and dispersed organizational structures. Some of the challenges facing CIO and chief knowledge officer (CKO) leaders include the following:

Focus on policy limitations: Agency heads are political appointees who are often more focused on policy issues than operational issues, which can make it difficult for the agency or department head to obtain the senior-level support that is critical for the implementation of knowledge management and information technology supporting KM into an agency's business processes.

Personnel decision limitations: Government managers' decisions regarding personnel are often constrained due to work rules or organizational factors. Information and knowledge management job descriptions might not match the evolved occupations. Also, training funds are often limited due to budget considerations.

Differences in job duty limitations: Duties that are typically a private-sector CIO's may not fall under a government CIO's direction at all. For example, some government CIOs are responsible for policy and oversight functions as well as their operational responsibilities.

Box 6.3

Leadership Guidelines for Government CIOs and CKOs

- Recognize the role of knowledge and information management in creating value and the leadership role the manager must assume in order to maximize the full potential of both.
- Position the CIO and CKO for success. They must be recognized as full participants on the management leadership team, and be given the managerial and technical skills required to meet the business needs of the agency.
- Ensure the credibility of the organization. The officers must have the commitment of line management as well as agency top management, and must accomplish quick, high-impact, and visible successes balanced with longer-term strategies. The officers must learn from partnering with successful leaders in the external knowledge and management communities.
- Measure success and demonstrate results. Technical measures must be balanced with business measures. The officers must continually work to achieve a steady flow of feedback between performance measures and business process.
- Organize knowledge and information resources to meet business needs. The officers must have a clear understanding of their responsibilities to meet business needs.
- Be flexible enough to adopt change when it occurs. KM is an evolutionary process.
- Develop the human capital of knowledge and information management. The officers must identify the skills needed to implement knowledge management in line with business needs, develop innovative ways to attract and retain talent, and provide the training tools and methods workers need to perform their duties.

Source: U.S. DOD 2002.

Differences in funding limitations: The public sector faces different funding challenges than do organizations in the private sector. Legislative mandates may force extensive modifications to systems, and IT and KM funds may be contained within the appropriations for a specific program, such as homeland security or e-government. If part of the agency's discretionary spending, they are more subject to volatile changes in the federal budget.

Following long-term investment strategies is also difficult because agencies put together funding requests from eighteen to twenty-four months in advance of funding availability.

Conclusion

Implementation of a knowledge management initiative is influenced by a number of controllable and uncontrollable factors, including organizational culture, climate, operating policies, and leadership. The concept of culture in public-sector knowledge management systems is shaped by two factors: (1) the political culture that shapes an agency's operating environment and policy focus, and (2) the organizational culture. The political culture of an agency can change rather quickly, whereas the organizational culture of an agency is longer lived and harder to change. Mutual trust and respect, job satisfaction, and commitment to a mission are all reflections of organizational culture. A number of specific organizational culture conditions must be present when adopting KM in a public-sector organization. These include: A willingness to openly share information, members' trust of one another to do the right thing when it comes to sharing information, freely giving credit where credit is due, and a human resources policy that promotes a willingness to learn among agency staff.

The climate of an organization emerges from the interaction of people and its basic underlying culture. Often incorrectly used as a synonym for culture, climate instead must be considered to be a reflection of the agency's culture and a reflection that is distorted by the qualities and abilities of the people in the group. Organizational climate consists of the values, norms, attitudes, behaviors, and feelings of the people within an organization. Leadership in federal government knowledge management programs can take many forms. It typically includes existence of an internal champion. A champion is typically a high-level administrator who has a strong faith in the ability of KM to do what it is designed to do for the agency. This entails strongly supporting the initiative in highest-level budget negotiations and giving program leaders enough slack to show that KM has long-term benefits. A champion also makes sure the program receives high visibility within the agency and among other government agencies.

7

KM and Organizational Learning

> *Useful knowledge is not a "thing" that can be managed like*
> *other assets, as a self-contained entity. Nor does it just*
> *float free in cyberspace. . . . Only when information is*
> *used by people does it become knowledge.*
> (Wegner, McDermott, and Snyder 2002)

> *Learning is primarily about the acquisition of*
> *information and knowledge.*
> (Canadian Centre for Management Development 1999)

Organizational learning occurs because individual members of the organization learn. This does not mean that individual learning guarantees organizational learning. Rather, it means that no organizational learning occurs unless
individuals learn. Government agencies encourage individual learning in a
number of ways, including training and management development, communities of practice, intranets, and, increasingly, such Web-based communications as e-mail. Collectively, these and other information-sharing tools are
part of the discipline known as knowledge management; they help enable
learning when they are part of a comprehensive social system designed specifically to husband and exploit knowledge.

   Throughout this book, the point has consistently been made that information is not knowledge. However, Delong (2004) rightfully warned that it is
often difficult to differentiate between the two because knowledge and information are overlapping constructs, and that their relative relevance is established by situational factors. He added,

> Information is data that is structured so that it is transferable, but its imme-
> diate value depends on the potential user's ability to sort, interpret, and

integrate it with their own experience. Knowledge goes a step further and implies the combining of information with the user's own experiences to create the capacity for action. (DeLong 2004, 22)

Information can be readily managed with technology, which does a good job of collecting, acquiring, and storing data and making it available as information. Government organizations spend billions annually investing in information technology for just this purpose. Knowledge, on the other hand, is information that someone has put to work. This is achieved when one or more persons in an organization identify or share knowledge about an issue, a problem, or a solution, and then add what they have learned. The application of their existing knowledge can be combined with the new knowledge in synergistic, innovative, and creative ways. Combining new with existing knowledge results in learning.

The same can be said for organizations. With the right attitudes of managers and administrators, agencies can learn in the same way that individuals learn. Stories abound of government agencies from around the world that have been transformed into learning organizations. This chapter looks at what is known about the linkages between knowledge and learning, including some of the stories of KM and learning organizations in other nations.

Chapter Objectives

Learning objectives for this chapter include helping readers develop an awareness and understanding of the following concepts associated with learning organizations:

- An understanding of the meaning of learning organizations.
- An awareness of the links between knowledge management and learning.
- Recognition of the processes involved in an organization's transformation to a learning organization.
- An understanding of the differences between organizational learning and learning organizations.
- An awareness of the global interest in the benefits accruing from learning organizations.

What Is a Learning Organization?

An organization that learns is one that is quick to identify, digest, and apply the lessons learned in its interactions with its environments. For public-sector

Figure 7.1 **A Model of the Knowledge Management and Organizational Learning System**

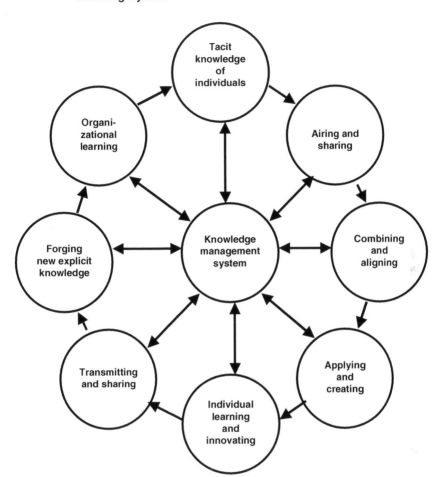

organizations, this involves developing innovative solutions to the constantly changing legal, political, economic, and social environment.

For knowledge to facilitate organizational learning, leadership in the organization must form and maintain a culture that honors and rewards the entire process. Figure 7.1 illustrates the interconnected system in which knowledge management facilitates both individual and organizational learning. The idea of a systems concept is a fundamental component of the learning organization initiative proposed by Peter Senge (1990). In this model, the agency's knowledge management system (KMS) is the keystone of the organizational learning system. All the remaining elements are connected through their inclusion in the KMS. Both tacit and explicit knowledge play key roles in the system, but cannot contribute significantly to organizational learning unless they are coordinated and guided.

Definitions of a Learning Organization

Four early definitions of what constitutes a learning organization are presented in Box 7.1, beginning with Senge's (1990) conceptualization. These are not the only definitions, of course, but they appear often enough in the literature to merit their inclusion with the Senge concept.

Information, Knowledge, and Learning

People learn, begin to understand, and build knowledge through a process that has been boiled down to four easy-to-understand steps (Phillips 1976). First, they define and frame problems on the basis of their prior experience and the knowledge that is already available to them. Problems can be as large as determining how to transform a government department or agency to be more focused on citizens and results, as mandated in the President's Management Agenda (PMA). A key component in the mechanism for making this transformation happen was expanding the role of electronic government. Or, they can be as small as determining a way to personally use less paper, as mandated by the Government Paperwork Elimination Act of 1998.

Second, they seek out, locate, and collect the information they consider essential for dealing with the problems. Information comes from many sources; some is obtained from external sources such as published reports, advice from consultants, and, increasingly, documents and research reports taken from the Internet. Other information comes from internal sources, such as memos, directives, and guidelines distributed by senior management; the experiences and knowledge of other workers in the unit may be one of the most valuable, if often underrated, sources.

Third, individuals analyze and interpret the data they have collected. This is done following clearly defined rules, traditions, and biases. Data are interpreted in accordance with the past experience of the interpreter. Too often, the problem is approached with a preconceived solution in hand. The fourth step is the codification and reporting of the conclusions gathered from the learning process. Knowledge management systems are involved in each of these processes.

Government workers depend on information to do their jobs, and to add to the internal storehouse of knowledge pertaining to the world in which they must function. Often, they examine the results of scientific research as a way

Box 7.1

Four Descriptions of Learning Organizations

A learning organization is one in which people continually expand the capacity to create the results they desire, and where new expanding patterns of thinking are nurtured, where collective aspirations are set free, and where members of the organization are continually learning together to see the whole. (Senge 1990, 3)

A learning [organization] is one with a vision of what it might achieve. Learning to achieve the possible is not a product simply of training individuals. It only happens when learning takes place in the entire organization. The learning [organization] is an organization in which the learning of all its members is facilitated, and one that continuously transforms itself. (Pedler, Burgoyne, and Boydel 1991, 1)

In learning organizations, there is total employee involvement in a collaborative, collective, accountable change that is directed towards achieving the shared values or principles of the members of the organization. (Watkins and Marsick 1992, 118)

An organization can be said to be learning when it acquires information (knowledge, understanding, know-how, techniques, or practices of any kind and by whatever means). (Argyris and Schön 1996, 3)

of collecting information. It is important to note, however, that science, knowledge, and learning are not the same. Learning is what humans do when they internalize and remember information. Nobody likes to know that they have just reinvented the wheel.

In a more formal definition, knowledge has been described as "the set of statements which, to the exclusion of all other statements, denote or describe objects and may be declared true or false." Science, on the other hand, should be considered a "subset of learning. It is composed of denotative statements, but imposes two supplementary conditions on their acceptability: the objects to which they refer must be available for repeated access [to enable replication] . . . and it must be possible to decide whether or not a given statement pertains to the language judged relevant by the experts" (Lyotard 1984, 18).

Clearly, not all knowledge is scientific knowledge. Much of people's knowl-

Box 7.2

A California City's Transformation to a Learning Organization

The expectations and needs that must be served by city government continue to change as urban populations continue to grow, city neighborhoods get older, and the community reflects the greater diversity that characterizes much of California. These changes demand a more customized approach to service delivery, rather than the "one-size-fits-all" model of the past.

The City of Fremont team, composed of the city council, the city manager, and staff have been working together to create a learning organization with a wide range of initiatives to meet changing needs. Elements of this process include:

• Development of a strategic plan that integrates the mission, vision, and values of the organization.
• Promoting shared responsibility for problem identification and solution development.
• Engaging the community in dialogue and collaborative problem solving utilizing tools such as interest-based negotiations and program performance measurement.
• Fostering economic health through a community-wide economic development strategy.
• Creating opportunities to partner with others, from governmental agencies and businesses to nonprofit groups, neighborhoods, and individuals.
• Opportunities for continuous training and technological improvements.

Source: City of Fremont 2002.

edge comes from experiences, human beliefs, human values, and social interaction, not scientific experimentation. This type of knowledge is often called *common sense.* It is most often shared in organizations by narrative—that is, in conversations between two or more workers. When narrative sharing is facilitated in government agencies, the opportunity arises for the organization to transform itself into a *learning organization.* Box 7.2 describes the knowledge products that Fremont, a California city near San Francisco, expects will result from its efforts to transform itself into a learning organization.

Figure 7.2   **A Model of Single-Loop Learning**

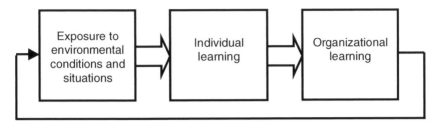

Organizational Learning and Learning Organizations

Organizational learning begins with exposure to an external stimulus. As individuals respond to the stimulus, they learn from the experience and their future behavior is in some way modified. If the responses of the individuals involved result in a more successful way of dealing with the ramifications of the stimulus, the individual adaptations can bring about an adaptation in the organization as well. These adaptations in individuals are what is meant by *single-loop* or *adaptive* learning. The adaptations that occur in organizations are described by the term *organizational learning.*

It is important to note that the adaptation is reactive rather than proactive. Exposure to an external stimulus and individual learning are necessary antecedents for the process of organizational learning. However, they do not turn the organization into a learning organization. That only occurs when the culture of the organization is such that individuals in an organization seek and carry out adaptations prior to the impact of the environmental stimulus (Figure 7.2).

Single-loop learning can and usually does have a positive effect on an agency. When individuals learn by gaining knowledge—whatever the source—it becomes possible for them to make improvements to processes or services or products, or both. This is what is meant by innovation. Knowledgeable members of the agency no longer have to repeat past mistakes.

The new knowledge gained by members of the organization has the power to benefit the agency, provided the agency remains receptive to adaptive change. And when an agency further evolves into a learning organization, it learns not only how to avoid past mistakes, but, more importantly, how to profit from what it has learned by taking advantage of what its members have learned.

How Learning Organizations Evolve

Clearly, individual and organizational learning are different. But what about organizational learning and learning organizations—are they the same? Mark Smith (2001) suggested that the distinction between the concepts of organizational learning and learning organizations rests on the product of the learning process—what results from learning. Perhaps the most valuable product of learning is an ability to adapt to change.

Organizational learning is the term used to describe the processes involved during the learning that takes place by individuals and the collective learning that occurs within organizations; it is based upon a foundation of learning theory, and is often used to describe the processes and results of employee training and management development. Promoting the concept in an agency begins by dealing with the processes needed to bring about a fundamental change in the culture of the organization, transforming it from a reactive to a proactive organization. Smith added that organizational learning is the activity and the process by which an agency eventually becomes a learning organization.

Government agencies can evolve into learning organizations only when learning is integrated into the fundamental fibers of the agency's strategic and operational plans. One of the early government agencies to embrace KM, an intergovernmental planning committee in Alberta, Canada, was able to make this connection an integral component of the province's human resources strategy (HRDC 2003). The council's knowledge management framework was established to help the province reach its future goals by "sustaining and improving operations and service delivery, sharing knowledge to learn from the past, and by leveraging collective expertise to optimize the future for all Albertans." Table 7.1 displays elements of the Alberta guide to KM.

Measuring Organizational Learning in Brazil and Poland

A team of researchers from the Management Department at the University of Brasilia conducted a study to evaluate the extent of organizational learning in an agency of the Brazilian government. Learning in the private sector is considered a way of changing and developing competencies that organizations need in the competitive environment of the knowledge economy. In the public sector, however, this movement for change is driven by transformations reflected in the new public management (Guimaraes et al. 2001).

The study report defined organizational learning in the private sector as a process of organizational change that is intended to achieve high-quality production standards and customer standards. It is based on a framework closely

Table 7.1

Alberta, Canada, Knowledge Management and Learning Organization Framework

Guide elements	Planning focus			
	Planned strategic approach	Enhanced learning environment	Intentional knowledge sharing	Optimizing values
Program	Knowledge management is integrated into day-to-day operations	Learning and development are structured into all roles as major areas of accountability	Knowledge transfer is a priority throughout the organizations and is to occur with no boundaries	Collaborative networks and communities of practice and supporting technology are established to access department/agency/unit memory
Strategies	• Foster new relationships	• Create an expectation for questioning and learning	• Incorporate knowledge reference and retrieval mechanisms into information and knowledge management systems	• Develop internal benchmarking indicators
	• Leverage agency and functional expertise • Promote best practices sharing	• Capitalize on lessons learned	• Facilitate intentional cross-boundary sharing • Identify expertise areas • Develop knowledge repositories	• Conduct knowledge audit
Enabling factors	• Link to long-term objectives	• Create a partnership culture that encourages learning and collaboration	• Integrate into business processes	• Document lessons learned
	• Merge KM with agency and operational strategies	• Emphasize high personal responsibility and teamwork	• Identify critical core knowledge and gaps	• Benchmark best practices/processes
		• Value openness, questioning, and exploring	• Link knowledge sharing and learning to performance	• Leverage databases and information
Chief results	Strategic partnerships and opportunities	Learning organization	Systematic approach to knowledge sharing	Document and share knowledge

Source: HRDC 2003.

linked to innovation, human knowledge, communication, and commitment. These same elements apply to public-sector management by their ability to effect changes in agency members' values, strategies, and beliefs—in a word, the *culture* of the organization.

Their research instrument included questions on five fundamental organizational learning factors: shared vision, systemic vision, mental models, knowledge sharing, and an environment of learning stimulation. They found that less than half of the agency respondents were able to state the organization's objectives and targets, that many workers did not know what went on in other units of the organization, and that lower-level respondents identified the absence of an environment of participation in organizational decision making, but that there was open and easy access to higher-level managers.

The agency workers also perceived that informality and openness of relationships were encouraged. However, there was also a clear respect for authority in decision making and a feeling of obedience in following imposed rules. Both formal and informal means of communication existed. Although no organizational orientation for learning about successful practices from other organizations existed, the informal networks of knowledge sharing among employees were relatively effective. Finally, the researchers concluded that the agency did have some characteristics of a learning organization, but that these corresponded to incremental (single-loop) learning and not transformational (double-loop) learning.

Marcin Sakowicz (2002) found the organizational learning status of a Polish municipal government agency to be somewhat farther along than Guimaraes and his team found in the Brazilian agency. Sakowicz analyzed a municipal administration office in Czestochowa, a city of 250,000 inhabitants located in southern Poland. The study asked whether city officials upgraded their skills and knowledge on a regular basis; whether local authorities provided information to other agencies and citizens; to what extent use of information and communications technology improved knowledge sharing; and how officials used tacit knowledge.

Results from more than 350 survey instruments revealed that only a few departments have identified schemes, strategies, or plans for sharing internal information and knowledge. However, sharing does take place through various informal means such as face-to-face discussions, mentoring, and staff development. Sakowicz concluded that local government in Poland is still in an early phase of putting knowledge and information sharing ahead of modernization of its structure and functions. Moreover, he deemed it doubtful that really effective knowledge management at the local level existed in Poland at the time of his study.

Figure 7.3 **The APHIS Organizational Learning Cycle**

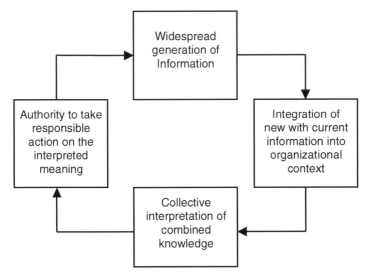

Source: USDA 2004.

Organizational Learning at the Department of Agriculture

A basic concept underlying the idea of organizational learning is what is known as the *organizational learning cycle.* This concept emerged from earlier work in learning theory. One interpretation of the organizational learning cycle was included in a training manual prepared by the U.S. Department of Agriculture's Animal and Plant Health Inspection Service (APHIS). The APHIS four-step closed-loop model included four activities: information generation, integration of the information into the organization, interpretation, and action taken on the interpreted meaning. The APHIS model is presented in Figure 7.3.

The Inspection Service looks upon lifelong learning as the only way to remain competitive in the agency's environment, adding that employees need to invest in their own growth; APHIS can help, but the ultimate responsibility rests on the employees' shoulders.

APHIS identified a list of nearly a dozen characteristics held in common by learning organizations that should be emulated by the service. The list is included here because of its applicability to any agency wishing to evolve toward status as a learning organization. Learning organizations use these activities and strategies in their constant striving to refine their mission and transform themselves for the better:

- Learning organizations consider strategic planning and policy making a learning process; they view management decisions as experiments, not edicts.
- They encourage all stakeholders of the agency—employees, customers, suppliers, collaborators, and other stakeholders—to participate in major policy decisions.
- They use information and communications technology to inform and empower the workforce.
- Accounting and control systems are structured to assist learning.
- Learning organizations focus on pleasing internal customers through constant interdepartmental communications and promoting awareness of overall agency needs.
- They explore new and meaningful ways to reward people for ideas and actions contributing to innovation and agency growth.
- They possess an organizational structure that invents opportunities for individual and agency development.
- They rely on boundary workers—that is, all organizational members who contact external customers, clients, suppliers, stakeholders, and collaborators—for information.
- Learning organizations are those that learn from other agencies through joint training, investments, research and development, job exchanges, and benchmarking.
- They foster a learning climate by encouraging questions, feedback, experimentation, diversity, and a passion for continuous improvement.
- Finally, learning organizations provide self-development resources and facilities to all members, encouraging all workers to take responsibility for their own personal growth and learning.

Learning at the U.S. Corps of Engineers

Writing in the preface of an employees' guide on how to become a learning organization, the commander of the U.S. Army Corps of Engineers (USACE), Lieutenant General Robert B. Flowers, began with why it was important for the Corps to transform itself into a learning organization:

> For over two hundred years, the Army Corps of Engineers has faithfully served the needs of the Army and the Nation. In order to continue this tradition of distinguished service in an increasingly dynamic environment, we must transform the Corps into an organization that continuously and systematically learns. This will ultimately allow us to best achieve our Vision of being the world's premier public engineer-

ing organization responding to our Nation's needs in peace and war. Organizational learning must be embedded in all that we do. We can no longer afford to simply brief each other about what we already know; instead, we must create learning dialogues in our team of teams. (USACE 2003, 3)

The guide, *Learning Organization Doctrine: Roadmap for Transformation,* was structured into three sections (USACE 2003); significant portions of that report are included in the following section.

The first portion of the learning organization report provided a definition of what is meant by a learning organization and described the roles of systematic learning, culture, and leadership in achieving learning organization status. The second section included a detailed discussion of the roles of leadership and management in learning organizations. The third outlined the assumptions and processes involved in the Corps' transformation process. Portions of each of the sections are included here as a case example of the steps public-sector agencies are taking on their paths to becoming learning organizations.

Section 1: The Learning Organization

Why Become a Learning Organization?

The Corps of Engineers is more than 225 years old, and to adapt for the future, it must continuously learn from its work today. Today the rate of change is greater than ever, thus making it even more important the Corps adapt to changing conditions as they occur. Accordingly, the Corps must learn faster than ever before. A new approach to the services it provides and to learning are also necessary. In this way, it will evolve with the needs of the nation, while also improving its competence as an organization. The cultural changes prevalent today require an understanding of all the components of the Corps. A strategy for change must take a holistic approach to align these dynamics to the desired end state.

Narrowly focused new initiatives, such as responding to the latest trend or management fad, will likely not yield enduring and widespread change. Initiatives focused solely on organizational structure will have limited success without aligning the other dynamics within the culture. The Corps must integrate many initiatives, or confusion will impede change. Since 1988, attempts to institutionalize project management as the business process have been frustrating because management did not always view the change holistically. Rather, it focused on the system and structure, doing little to change the skills and attitudes the people needed, the style of leadership, or other elements of its culture.

USACE'S Definition of a Learning Organization

A learning organization systematically learns from its experience of what works and what does not work. The goal of learning is increased innovation, effectiveness, and performance. A learning organization is a nonthreatening, empowering culture where leadership, management, and the workforce focus on continuously developing organizational competence. Box 7.3 is a technical learning example based on recent USACE experience.

The goal of strategic learning is to create the ideal future of the Corps of Engineers in interaction with all its stakeholders. Operational and technical learning comes from the process of designing and delivering products, services, and solutions to complex problems in dialogue with customers. This journey is critical to the future of the Corps. Changes in context and in the social, economic, and governmental environment in which it serves the nation and the army require continuous development of organizational competence. Learning from past and present will prepare the Corps for an uncertain future and will create an organization that values investments in learning, an attribute that attracts and will help retain fresh talent in the ranks of the organization.

The historical and social context of the early years of the twenty-first century dramatically affects how the U.S. Army Corps of Engineers serves the army and the nation. The following Corps realities characterize this context:

Economic and Political Realities

- Increased competition for business in a global economy
- Increased scrutiny from Congress, the Office of Management and Budget (OMB), the media, and interest groups
- Drive to outsource "nongovernmental" work
- More diverse kinds of work; increasing workload (do more with less)

Work Realities

- More multi-stakeholder planning and collaboration (e.g., watersheds)
- Increased responsibilities as stewards of the environment
- New skills, thinking, and tools needed to be a knowledge-based organization
- More rapid pace of work; flexibility needed for continuous change

Box 7.3

From Khobar Towers to Pentagon Renovation

An example of how a project made use of technical learning occurred when the Corps sent a team to study what aspects of the construction of Khobar Towers in Saudi Arabia contributed to the loss of life when terrorists bombed it. By studying what did not work well there, Corps engineers were able to come up with innovative solutions that were later incorporated as best practices into the initial stages of renovation of the Pentagon.

That renovated side was attacked on 9/11/01, and those renovations resulted in a reduction in the loss of lives. Future renovations will continue to employ these innovative best practices. As a secondary benefit, the national television show *60 Minutes II* featured this example of the learning organization in action, thus educating the public about the Corps' commitment to continuous learning.

Talent Realities

- Losing experienced senior people; too few mid-level replacements
- More competition for young talent
- New values and approaches for the workforce

These elements of the new environment of the Corps reflect part of the change in the mode of production from manufacturing to knowledge and service. The manufacturing era required bureaucratic stovepipes of experts to mass produce standardized products. This logic resulted in efficient procedures, work that was fragmented into specialized compartments, and a hierarchical organization. However, the knowledge/service mode of production defining the post-Katrina era requires that bureaucratic think be replaced. This requires interactive teamwork, strategic alliances, integration of knowledge, and coproduction of solutions with customers.

In order to adapt, the Corps is continuing it evolution into a learning organization, one that is centered on these new strategic values. Today's employees are self-developing free agents who want to learn continuously. They want to acquire marketable skills, as well as attain advanced degrees and certificates to show for their learning.

According to the Corps's learning organization report, a potential fit exists between the need to create an interactive organization designed for the knowledge/service mode of production and the needs of today's employees. Creating that fit is the challenge for leadership in this era. Leaders must design the right organization and lead it in the right way. Becoming a learning organization will enable the Corps to adapt to the knowledge/service mode of production. It will also help the Corps attract young self-developers needed for the future. Only an organization that is constantly learning will attract and retain new employees to guarantee the Corps service to the nation.

In times of transformation from the old to the new, people search for the best way to organize work and motivate people in new situations. This began in the early 1980s and has continued to this day.

Sources of Learning

Organizational and individual learning have a variety of sources, including strategy, operations, and technology. Strategic learning comes from continuous dialogue about values and goals with customers, stakeholders, and partners. Operational and technical learning come from the process of designing and delivering products and solutions in dialogue with customers.

Organizational learning also comes from identifying best practices, which can be found both inside and outside the Corps. The goal for the Corps is not to copy the best practices, but to innovate something better adapted to the needs of the Corps. Similarly, members learn from cases drawn from the agency's own experience—both positive and negative—thus leading to answers to such questions as: Why did one strategy succeed and another fail? What could be done differently next time? Why did a particular initiative or operation, which had such support and resources, not produce the hoped for for results? Why did another initiative or operation succeed? What lessons can be applied to improve the Corps as a whole?

The report went on to explain that learning for the Corps of Engineers occurs every day all over the world. Individuals learn. Work groups learn. Project teams learn. Senior strategic leaders learn. A learning organization makes use of these lessons for the whole organization. Training, on the other hand, is about *individual* competence. A learning organization understands the difference between individual competence and organizational competence, and connects them. Even the best training, however, does not make a learning organization. As strategic, operational, and technical learning occur, Corps leaders must bring this learning into meetings and the centers of decision making.

This learning must also be entered into a knowledge management system that filters, distills, and integrates it so that information is turned into knowledge. The Corps must then turn this knowledge into wisdom for use throughout the organization, especially for leaders who must shape culture, policy, decisions, and planning. Knowledge management networks, techniques, and tools alone, however, will not automatically generate the sought-for higher performance, productivity, and effectiveness. Learning must be standardized so that it drives how initiatives are planned and developed, how all elements of the culture are aligned with the mission, and how decisions are made.

The learning organization is initially difficult to understand because it is a systemic concept. People often think about learning as occurring in classes taught in school; learning is considered separate from work. Learning is not "real work" in the craft or manufacturing mode of thinking. Real work in these modes produces deliverables. Some even say that learning takes time away from getting the job done; instead of learning, we could be "doing."

This way of thinking does not portray learning as inherently a part of work. The knowledge/service mode of learning empowers people to improve their effectiveness systematically by making better products and providing better services. Learning is one of the essential keys to productivity in knowledge work. If we are not continuously and systematically learning, others are, and they will reach the goals we are aspiring to reach before we do.

Taking a historical perspective gives an insight into the relationships of learning and work. The purpose and process of learning change. New tools, technology, processes of work, and organizations require new ways of learning. Each changed context sets new purposes for learning. For example, with computers and the Internet, people can learn quickly from colleagues around the globe about their organizational innovations—if the culture and systems are there to empower that to happen, and if they are motivated to learn.

Integrating New Knowledge into the Corps

The Corps is integrating new knowledge into its institutional memory and centers of decision making. Moreover, leaders are taking responsibility for ensuring that learning from projects, initiatives, and organizational strategies is accessible across USACE. The knowledge management system is not just the network that stores the information. It consists primarily of the communities of practice, the experts in each type of work; these experts must filter, condense, and integrate the learning. Technology is considered merely a tool.

The USACE Learning Network integrates leadership, business and communications, and technical learning. The Network consists of three interrelated parts, each with a different but important function. The first part, communities of educational resources, expands the training function by customizing courses and training events to the needs of individuals and groups. Partnerships with universities and firms allows the codesign of on-site customized offerings, distance learning (e-learning), and traditional courses. Internal Corps experts also function as educators, trainers, and mentors.

The second part of the Learning Network, communities of practice, consists of people who share a work practice, competence, or kind of knowledge. The communities of practice filter, distill, and integrate learning from all over the Corps.

The third part of the Learning Network is the Web-based system accessible from anywhere that serves as the communications infrastructure for the communities. The popular word "network" suggests that the Learning Network is a Web-based system. But without the people who use the network, the communication system is no more than a collection of electronic pipes. The Learning Network can be useful as a tool of a learning organization only if both the "people" and the "pipes" are active and working. The people and the pipes develop concurrently through the collaboration of all leaders building the communities and the Web-based system.

The Learning Network encourages virtual sharing and consulting internally based on the latest knowledge and best practices. It also facilitates assessment of individual and group learning and development needs, coaching and mentoring, and the integration of learning into the work process. All these elements of the Learning Network help ensure that learning is readily available to all Corps employees for planning, decision making, and increasing organizational effectiveness.

Section 2: Leadership in Organizational Learning

The Corps of Engineers has identified five dimensions of leadership that affect the transition to a learning organization. These dimensions are strategy, direction, drive, management, and relationships. The Corps' explanation of each dimension is presented in the following pages.

The Strategy Dimension

Learning organizations require leaders who are strategic thinkers. These leaders explain how the organization creates value for its customers and helps them succeed. This value equation is the foundation of the organization's strategic logic. They are visionaries who mobilize all the resources of the organization toward the ideal future. Their focus is global and long term, oriented to the success of the whole social system of the Corps.

The Direction Dimension

The leader with direction talent knows that it is inefficient for everyone to work hard when the direction for the work is unclear. This leader knows how to ask questions of teams and other leaders to make the need for clear direction obvious. This leader does not fear sounding stupid for asking what others have failed to ask: "What is the goal for this activity?" "What are we trying to accomplish?" This leader may also question the stated goal and is not afraid to go against the conventional wisdom of what the purpose is. This leader knows that this courage to ask, and to clarify direction, is extremely valuable to the Corps. The direction dimension is shaped from the interaction of five key activities:

- Creating a motivating culture
- Honest communication
- Focus
- Conceptual thinking
- Stimulating creativity

Creation of a motivating culture indicates the strength of a leader who understands that the motivation of the workforce affects the value created for the customers. Therefore, leaders make the effort to understand what motivates their workforce. Leaders must give staff members what they need to perform well. They provide the workforce with clear mandates, operating principles, resources, authority, knowledge, and tools so they can fulfill their responsibilities. They also give employees responsibilities that bring out the best of their talents. They recognize and reward them in ways they value.

Honest communication comes from a leader who is straight talking and who believes that the best policy is to let people know now what they will likely find out later. This leader tells the good *and* bad news, saying it in a way that does not cause harm to the person or the Corps. This leader knows what to say, when to say it, what forum to use, and what person or persons to say it to.

The Drive Dimension

The leader with drive knows that his or her success comes from engaging the aspirations of teams of talented people and guiding their efforts toward Corps objectives. This leader knows that others must be empowered and knows that drive to accomplish outcomes is a team effort. This leader knows that to make the meeting effective, its outcomes must help make the Corps work better, not just make the team feel good that it did its job.

The drive dimension has two mutually supporting elements: entrepreneurial implementation and innovating systems. Entrepreneurial implementation means boldness and creativity consistent with the shared values and strategy of the Corps. Operational leaders assess local conditions, as well as human and material resource capabilities, and devise what works with their teams. Innovating systems means that leaders efficiently seek the goal, not the beaten path.

The Management Dimension

The management dimension exists in a leader who plans effectively and makes optimal use of resources. This leader recognizes that management is a series of functions to distribute among the members of a team. This leader does not feel he has to be in charge all the time and is comfortable sharing management responsibilities. This leader is comfortable letting the team, when oriented with its mandate, operating principles, and expectations, manage themselves as much as possible. This dimension incorporates five activities. The learning organization manager:

- Coordinates people and work
- Creates accountability for learning and measures results
- Integrates knowledge
- Empowers workers and stakeholders
- Includes learning in projects and meetings

The Relationship Dimension

Organizations in the knowledge/service economy thrive on relationships. Therefore, they seek to identify the values and goals of everyone with a stake in the success of the organization. The leader in these organizations creates relationships by being honest and transparent in forging shared strategy with all internal and external stakeholders. The relationship dimension has four activity responsibilities, which result in the following benefits:

- Developing leadership and talent
- Coaching younger and new workers
- Creating team collaboration and improves productivity
- Developing solutions to help customers succeed, working with them as part of the team, "coproduce" desired outcomes.

Section 3: Creating a Learning Organization

The success of a learning organization improves when leaders empower individuals to use their strengths to help customers succeed. People are more willing to develop and perform when learning builds on their strengths. The Corps remains strong in some leadership strengths, but believes that it needs to continue to develop those strengths. As an engineering organization, the Corps has achieved operational excellence throughout its history.

With retirements, transfers, voluntary departures, and new military personal entering the Corps, new leaders may be assigned to vacated positions. The challenge for the Corps is to select the right person for the position, based not on technical proficiency alone, but also on competence and character as a leader.

Improving Training

Individuals learn every day, everywhere in the Corps. Nonetheless, improving training and increasing individual learning alone do not result in a learning organization. The organization as a whole must continuously become more competent and successful in its missions for the learning organization to become real.

Conclusion

An organization that learns is quick to identify, digest, and apply lessons learned in its interactions with the environment. Public-sector organizations must develop innovative solutions to their changing legal, political, economic, and social environments. For knowledge to contribute to organizational learning, managers and administrators must establish and support a culture that honors and rewards the people who facilitate the learning process.

People understand and build knowledge in four steps: (1) they define and frame problems on the basis of their prior experience and the knowledge that is already available to them; (2) they seek out, locate, and collect the information they consider essential for dealing with the problems; (3) they code and analyze collected data; and (4) data are coded, interpreted, and reported as the conclusions gained during a learning process. Knowledge management systems are involved in each of these processes.

The activities and experiences of the U.S. Department of Agriculture and Corps of Engineers are examples of public-sector efforts to transform their agencies into learning organizations.

Part 3

KM Systems in the Public Sector

8

KM and Innovation in Government

*When [public] organizations innovate, they do not simply process
information, from the outside in, in order to solve existing problems
and adapt to a changing environment. They actually create new
knowledge and information, from the inside out, in order to redefine
both problems and solutions and, in the process, to re-create their
environment.*
(Nonaka and Takeuchi 1995, 47)

*The essence of the IT revolution is not in the IT itself; rather, it is in the
substantial changes of traditional boundaries in tasks and activities.*
(Kusunoki 2004, 310)

Innovation is the process of creating something different; it occurs with the conversion of existing knowledge and ideas into a new benefit, such as new or improved processes or services. A related tern is *invention,* which implies something
entirely new, while innovation can also mean new uses for old or existing tools,
materials, and/or processes. A primary goal of knowledge management in the
public sector is to induce innovation and invention in government agencies.

The innovation process in the public sector includes the search for and
application of new technologies within organizations, new and improved ways
of delivering government services, and new or untried management processes
and systems (Edvinsson et al. 2004). This chapter examines a variety of different public-service organizations in order to identify exemplary models of
innovation management.

Chapter Objectives

Objectives for this chapter are both general and specific. General objectives
refer to information about the constructs and influencers of innovation and

creativity in organizations. Specific objectives relate to the illustrative public-sector cases included. The cases describe the experiences of government administrators in introducing innovative approaches and new technology as tools to improve managing and decision making. The key objectives for this chapter include the following:

- To help readers develop an understanding of the scope and processes of innovation in organizations—and particularly in public-sector departments, agencies, and units—by showing how information, knowledge, and innovation work together to produce learning organizations in which innovation and creativity are the norm, rather than the exception.
- To help readers learn how to identify the issues and problems associated with managing innovation and creativity in public organizations.
- To help readers understand how innovation in procedures, processes, and delivery systems is introduced and managed in government.
- To help readers begin to think about how they might enhance innovative thinking and actions in their organizations.
- To help readers, by reading about how other government entities have introduced innovative ways of accomplishing their mission, to see that innovation can take place in every agency, regardless of what it is, what it does, or who it serves.

Innovation in Organizations

Until the late 1980s and early 1990s, most of the emphasis on managing innovation in organizations focused on changing and improving processes in the manufacturing sector. Manufacturers produce tangible products—"things" that can be touched, carried, consumed, or held. The development, manufacture, and distribution of manufactured goods normally follow a readily definable process. The steps in this process—often referred to as either the *supply chain* or the *value chain*—help make the manufacturing process open to innovation at every link in the chain.

As a group, manufacturers are able to identify and quantify the payoffs they can expect from a specific innovation adoption. Manufacturers of technology products particularly recognize the absolute need for maintaining a healthy flow of new products.

These private-sector managers often use cost-benefit analysis to weigh the expected payoffs against the projected cost of the innovation over its lifetime. They then make their decisions to innovate on the basis of the expected value of the benefit to accrue from that innovation. Peter Senge explained why innovation is more likely to take place in the private sector:

Gradually, I came to realize why business is the locus of innovation in an open society. Despite whatever hold past thinking may have on the business mind, business has a freedom to experiment missing in the public sector and, often, in nonprofit organizations. It also has a clear "bottom line," so that experiments can be evaluated, at least in principle, by objective criteria. (Senge 1990, 15)

Fewer opportunities for implementing innovation in products or processes have surfaced in government and in the service sector in general. Governments provide intangible "products" and services that are typically produced as they are provided to citizens/consumers; this restricts the number of available opportunities for innovation in the delivery chain. As a result, much of the innovation in government has focused on introducing relatively minor, low-cost, and low-risk adjustments or gradual upgrades to existing services or processes (Altshuler and Behn 1997). Far less attention has been devoted to planning and implementing innovation in processes on the more far-reaching, jurisdiction-wide, strategic level. Holley, Dufner, and Reed (2002), for example, found that only two of the fifty states—Utah and Washington—were engaging in statewide need evaluation for strategic information systems planning.

With the advent of the "reinventing government" program under President Clinton and Vice President Gore, innovation was accelerated in government, albeit still at a somewhat slower pace than in industry. Public services are not fabricated from raw materials or parts; they are, as the name implies, *services* rather than products. Government services are intangible, and are typically not "created" until provided. And, although citizens could and did complain when the services failed to meet their expectations, there was no one to listen to and act upon those complaints. Thus, there was little internal need seen for innovation in delivery of the services because there was no external force—such as the market for businesses—driving change.

Until the global government reform movement of the 1990s, government managers and administrators had little opportunity—let alone incentive—to innovate. Today, however, government agencies, departments, and units find themselves in the position of either innovating or being forced to explain "why not" to an active and knowledgeable electorate and legislative oversight bodies. In the first decade of the twenty-first century, a culture that rewards innovation in the way governments work and public-sector managers think became common throughout the world, at all levels of government, from federal departments to the smallest local special service district.

However, it should also be noted that, just as is the case with business and industry, many government innovations do not always achieve the high objectives that are set out for them. Missing the objective target is what happened in Tacoma, Washington, for example, when city leaders and department employees decided to take on a major reorganization of the city's information technology and knowledge management systems. A city-sponsored survey of what can be expected in the way of returns from the costly investment in innovation reported that full returns on the investment may not appear for at least eight to ten years. Meanwhile, the cost of implementing the new system continues to rise.

What Is "Innovation"?

Innovation is creating and applying new or distinctive ways of producing, distributing, and/or delivering products, services, or ideas from producers to users. It is also the design and implementation of new and distinctive organizational structures and processes. It may mean creating or inventing entirely new products or services, developing new components, or creatively experimenting with new combinations of components or materials. Innovation can occur at any step in the value chain: production, delivery, maintenance, and resupply of goods and services.

Because innovation requires the application of both new and existing knowledge as well as implicit and explicit knowledge, organizations have learned that if they wish to be innovative, they must manage knowledge as a critical resource. It may, in fact, be the most important resource an organization has. However, knowledge is stored in the minds of the members of the organization, not in computers or databases.

Managers and administrators of government departments, agencies, and units are responsible for promoting more than one kind of innovation. Sundbo (2001, 17–18) has identified a taxonomy that includes six distinctive forms of innovation:

1. Product innovation: developing or inventing a new public service or product.
2. Process innovation: new management approaches, production methods, or processes.
3. Organizational innovation: designing new forms of public organizations, structures, or management models, including collaborations, networks, or virtual organizations, to name a few.
4. Distribution innovation: a new way of delivering or distributing public services or products.
5. Market innovation: new forms of promoting or marketing public services, initiatives, or programs; it may also include different

Figure 8.1 **How Learning and Knowledge Shape an Organizational Learning System**

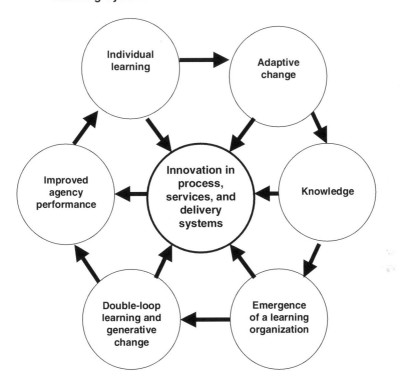

relationships with other public organizations or public/private combinations.

6. Raw material and/or components innovation: use of new materials and other resources in the production or delivery of public services, including alternative fuels and sustainable resources.

Figure 8.1 illustrates the connections of learning, knowledge, change, and innovation in an organizational learning system.

Public-sector innovation may also focus on several different aspects of the public-sector value chain, although most public administrators today overwhelmingly equate innovation with technology. However, an innovation need not result in a change in technology. Rather, it may instead involve different combinations or processes using existing technology. From public management's point of view, however, behavioral innovation may be far more important in the long run. Behavioral innovation may mean new strategies,

new ways of learning and sharing, and new ways of reacting to such environmental changes as increased diversity in the workplace.

Why Governments Innovate

Governments, like manufacturing, service, and distribution organizations,
have been forced to move away from the long history of Industrial-Age management thinking that characterized the traditional, hierarchical bureaucracies that existed in the public sector. Government has found that it must change
in order to cope with an Information-Age environment. City, county, state,
and federal government agencies and departments have been forced to morph
into networked organizations that collaborate with other agencies to take
advantage of and learn from all the information and expertise available inside and outside of their organizations. And managers and administrators
have had to change they way they function as well.

When similar shifts in management focus have occurred in other organizations, staff workers and administrators have found themselves working in
an organizational culture that was suddenly more open to new ideas and
demanded improvements to their performance, including the acceptance of
new ideas and new ways of functioning (Senge 1990). This improvement in
productivity is a big part of the rationale behind the determination of governments to purchase, install, and train all staff members in how to use the new
information technology and enterprise management information systems that
have become the chief technological tools of knowledge management. Organizations that do not forge organizational cultures that foster and value organization-wide identification and sharing of knowledge, and that do not employ
the appropriate technology for establishing systems for knowledge management, will not develop the well-informed staff needed to succeed in the twenty-
first century (Alberts and Hayes 2003).

How Agencies Transform

An important question for government managers and administrators, then, is
how to develop a method for turning their old, bureaucratic organizations
into learning organizations that are open to change and ready to accept, and
preferably embrace, new ways of doing things. The methods organizations
seek must be right for their people, their time, and the environment in which
they serve.

The process includes adopting innovative ways to collect, distribute, and
store information. But more importantly, it requires helping all of the
organization's people learn to use the organization's knowledge to invent,

innovate, and improve. They must be brought to recognize that only when information is shared, combined, reframed, and put to use does it becomes knowledge—and knowledge is the critical ingredient for designing and implementing new processes and new and improved public services. Finding an appropriate answer to this question is made difficult for some government agencies because, as a rule, they do not have a history of searching out and adopting innovation and creativity.

Managers in the public sector are today employing whatever methods they can in order to turn their once-bureaucratic organizations into learning organizations that are open' to change and ready to accept new ways of doing things. This wave can be called "innovation in progress." When they achieve their goals, staff workers and other administrators will be open to new ideas and not be satisfied until they have improved their performance on their own.

Public services typically require close interaction with clients/customers/citizens. Therefore, innovation in service organizations is often not only about *what* is being offered, but also about *how* and *by whom* it is being offered. The following description of knowledge management and its role in innovation helps to make this connection clear:

> Knowledge management caters to the critical issues of organizational adaptation, survival, and competence in the face of increasingly discontinuous environmental change. Essentially, it embodies organizational processes that seek a synergistic combination of data and information-processing capacity of information technologies, and the creative and innovative capacity of human beings. (Malhotra 2000)

Organizational learning influences innovation in two key ways. First, when the people in the organization learn new information that they can then turn into useful knowledge, it makes the organization a better innovator. And second, learning and innovating bring about many, often small and incremental, changes in performance, outlook, and morale in the organization. Ideally, organizational learning becomes a never-ending social process that influences, shapes, and improves the behaviors of the organization's personnel. This social process is a mix of knowledge, behavior, habits, experiences, standards, and values—all of which are also the ingredients that form an organization's culture (Sundbo 2001).

Innovation in Technology

Government administrators are generally eager to adopt new technology when it promises to improve public service and reduce department operating costs.

Clearly, the published evidence indicates that the processes of innovation and creativity are alive and well in all levels of government, albeit perhaps not to the degree that they are in the private sector. For example, at the federal level the enterprise architecture program is aiding in the replacement of older, specific-purpose, legacy information systems—some of which date back to the 1970s or even earlier.

Agencies are implementing new comprehensive enterprise management systems, including new computers and software, and coordinating and improving the management of it all by making it subject to the needs of the people who will use the technology. To control these developments, they have adopted the leadership position of knowledge manager, or chief knowledge officer (CKO). By developing a single agency-wide database accessible to all municipal personnel in all departments (but excluding personnel records), the systems approach promises to reduce operating costs and improve staff productivity. In 2005, however, the jury was still out on the return on the investment. Possibly because of their later start, many government innovations have not always achieved the objectives set out for them.

Public services typically require close interaction with clients/customers/citizens. Innovation in information and communication technologies are driving change in governments everywhere (Kiel 1994). To achieve change in public organizations, government leaders must embrace innovation in all its manifestations. Information-Age needs further dictate that governments adopt innovative, jurisdiction-wide information-sharing capabilities.

Problems with Technology and Innovation

Counter to much common perception, governments do innovate; they have done so for a long time, and in many cases they have done it well. In describing twenty-five successful innovative state and local government programs, Wheeler (1993) reported:

> Despite public opinion, which holds a contrary view, government is capable of tremendous innovation and effective management. State and local government programs are in place, which are effectively addressing some of the most thorny issues of our time.

This does not mean that governments have not often stumbled in their attempts to innovate. One study of 365 public- and private-sector information and communications technology managers found that one-third of all IT projects were canceled before completion (Brown 2001). Only 16 percent of the projects were completed on time and on budget, and more than half of the projects exceeded their original cost estimates by almost 200 percent; one-third of the projects took from twice to three times as long to finish as estimated. In another study reported by Brown, the researchers claimed that 20 percent of all IT projects are cancelled before they are completed, and 80 percent of those that are completed finish behind schedule, over budget, and with lower performance than was projected. Reporting on experiences at the federal level, Brown quoted the U.S. General Accounting Office, which has for years pointed out the high failure rate of IT initiatives. Other studies point to similar failures at the state and local levels.

Not all the blame for these difficulties can be placed entirely on problems with the technology aspect of knowledge management systems. Successful management of innovation and change in government requires that equal consideration be given financial, administrative, cultural, social, and personal dimensions related to the use of technology in the organization. Failing to consider any of these factors increases the risk of not receiving all the potential benefits that such systems offer (Gagnon 2001). The behavior and mind-set of managers is often cited as one of the most important factors.

A Case of the Muddled Innovation

An often-heard criticism of public management is that government administrators do not embrace innovation and technology with the same ardor as managers in the private sector do. In response, apologists aver that business management and public management are different. Moreover, traditional bureaucratic management practices have been equated with program stagnation and leaderships' unwillingness to accept the risks associated with new actions and innovative ways of addressing old problems. Government workers and administrators, both elected and appointed, are often reviled for incompetence whenever they try something new that doesn't work as well as planned. Increasingly, public managers are being held accountable for program performance failures (Bhatta 2001).

What is forgotten when the press adopts the role of vigilante is that problems with implementing new programs and practices will almost always surface. Not all innovations succeed; failures invariably occur in both the public and the private sectors. But in government, when innovative programs, processes, and projects fail, results can be catastrophic (Altshuler and Zegans 1997; Bennett 1997; Entman 1997; Robson 2003).

In 2002 in the City of Tacoma, Washington, what only a year or so earlier had been seen as an innovative city council, mayor, and team of city administrators were subjected to charges of failure and malfeasance. The city thought they were buying new technology in the form of a new city department-wide enterprise management system (EMS). The public's perception was that all that the city succeeded in doing was to create more problems and waste more of the taxpayers' money. The officials' efforts to bring the city into the twenty-first century with the latest in knowledge and information technology ran into a series of unexpected problems and glitches. The criticism that surfaced in the later stages of the program installation and implementation resulted in calls for a retreat to the older, safer-but-inefficient way of running the city's business.

When government innovations stumble or fail, elected and appointed leaders are subjected to public abuse that includes public charges of incompetence. Administrators and managers quickly become the target of criticism and sanctions that can include loss of employment, recall, or failure to win reelection. Senior administrative employees can lose their jobs. And the public can lose out on the full benefits the innovation was designed to provide.

After such high hopes and seemingly adequate planning, why did installation of the citywide system run into difficulties? The argument selected by press reporting of the program seemed to be based in a failure of leadership at all levels, from the mayor to the city council, director of utilities, and program "czar" appointed specifically to manage the installation. Success in carrying through with change in an organization requires strong leadership by someone who is capable of asserting that leadership against resistance that can be expected within the organization.

For innovation to be successful, these four factors must be in place: growth, change, strong leadership, and a culture of success (Probst and Raisch 2005). In the public sector, one or more of these "essential factors" are often missing. For example, since the late 1990s, governments have been constricting rather than growing; budget reductions and/or spending caps are far more common than growth in resources. Agencies are told to "do more with less."

Typically, change is not desired in bureaucratic organizations; it has not been a common objective of public leaders. Strong, charismatic personalities, men and women capable of exerting strong leadership and who understand the complex relationships between the rules that govern systems behavior and the processes involved in managing complex systems, are not often attracted to careers in public service. It has been a long time since anyone has been willing to describe public service as a "culture of success." Citizens no longer trust government at any level, or the people who labor in government to serve the public.

KM Innovation in Public Safety

Police departments are incorporating many of the same information and communications technology tools and knowledge management systems used in business and industry, and which are increasingly common in large public-sector organizations (Brown 2001). In the last eight years of the Clinton administration, the Department of Justice distributed more than $6 billion in information technology grants, spread across nearly 11,300 local law enforcement agencies. In 1998, Congress enacted additional legislation authorizing spending $250 million in each of the following five years to promote integration of justice system information technology.

Studies have suggested that police officers spend something like 92 percent of their time collecting, coding, combining, and distributing information. As they perform their tasks, they rely on timely, readily available information. Such is information is a critical component in developing an officer's storehouse of tacit knowledge. Another name for such knowledge is "street smarts."

In 1997, the Charlotte-Mecklenburg Police Department (CMPD) of the City of Charlotte, North Carolina, received roughly $11 million in federal funds and added another $8 million in local funds to develop a comprehensive enterprise management system: the Knowledge-Based Community Oriented Problem Solving System (K-COPS). Implementing the City of Charlotte system was to take place in three distinct phases: First, an in-depth analysis of the potential users' needs was conducted; second, as much of the system architecture as possible—laptops, servers, networks, etc.—and several software applications (e-mail, word processors, etc.) was installed. The third step was similar to the plan in the City of Tacoma, in that it involved upgrading and combining wherever possible the CMPD's most-used databases. As in most public-safety organizations, crime statistics and other data—criminal records, arrest history, mug shots, fingerprints, etc.—were located in separate, unconnected databases. Phase three would involve replacing the legacy "information silos" approach with a single, easily searchable database.

Results of the first-phase needs analysis were highly critical of the department's information-sharing practices. Most respondents reported that crime-related information simply was not available to officers on patrol. Officers were also critical of the sufficiency of the information that was available. They were particularly dissatisfied with the way that information was shared among department units. Only 10 percent reported that case and suspect status information was available to them.

To address these and other problems, the master plan authorized by the city established an information infrastructure and implied knowledge management system based on the following four requirements:

1. The IT architecture adopted had to be geared toward improving the community policing efforts, specifically addressing the needs of the officer on the street.

2. All parts of the system had to deliver as much information as possible to the officers in the field; the police vehicle was to be considered the officer's office.

3. Officers were no longer to be simply "note takers." Rather, they were to "own" the cases in their neighborhoods, and were to receive all the information available about the case, thus vastly improving their knowledge base.

4. Finally, the program was to empower members of the community, helping them to become participants in community problem-solving efforts.

Initial Results

Although the early results of the program did indicate a number of positive results, Brown also noted that achieving these results was not easy (2001, 363–64):

> Transitioning from a minimalist approach to technology (a single mainframe, 200 dumb terminals, and 6 support staff) to a 19-server, 2000-client operation requiring 26 support staff members demanded a tremendous amount of resources in time, energy, and capital. Whereas the annual IT operating budget for the CMPD more than tripled from less than $1.8 million to more than $6 million, support requirements increased by a factor of 10 (from 200 dumb terminals to 2,000 client server devices).

Reading about the problems associated with implementing the program is a déjà vu experience. For example, many of the project's component tasks experienced cost overruns and schedule delays. The full extent of the efforts that would be required was underestimated. Cost overruns occurred primarily from changes in user requirements, which in turn led to project expansion. Equipment malfunctions and incompatibilities, lack of technical expertise, and high personnel turnover further exacerbated the problems.

On the positive side, most neighborhood officers report the project has improved their performance by making it possible for them to receive and put to immediate use knowledge they need to be more productive in their jobs—productivity and efficiency gains by a factor of three were reported by some officers. However, no improvements were reported on case feedback or perceptions of problems in the neighborhoods.

It is important to note that all the facts relating to the story of the experiences of the City of Charlotte police department's knowledge-based information system installation were not yet in; phase 3—improvements to the department's databases—had yet to be completed. Brown (2001, 365) offered this caveat in her conclusion to the case:

Coordination, communication and leadership commitment requirements placed heavy burdens on the organization. The extent to which public agencies are prepared for both the tangible and intangible costs that result from technology innovations is an important finding worth noting.

Government Innovation in Korea

Mr. Yang-sik Choi, assistant minister at the Korean Headquarters of Government Innovation, Ministry of Government Administration and Home Affairs (MOGAHA), prepared the following discussion on government innovation for a larger government report, *General Information on Innovation in Korea* (Choi 2004). The minister described a number of innovative government programs currently under way in Korea, including knowledge management and e-government. Significant portions of the minister's report are included here as a model of what government innovation can accomplish. The report has been modified somewhat, but is essentially as it was released.

Introduction

After the inauguration of the Roh Moo-hyun administration in February of 2003, the issue of government innovation became one of the top priorities of the new government, alongside eliminating corruption. The administration, named *participatory government,* stressed the paramount importance of government innovation in the process of improving the practice, perception, and implementation of governance: improvements that would contribute to stronger national competitiveness toward meeting the global standard. In the first eighteen months of the administration, an *Innovation Road-Map for the Five Main Sectors of Society* was developed. In 2005, the government designated *change management* as the key objective of government innovation.

Although it is still early to make a final evaluation of the outcomes in government reform, changes are becoming increasingly evident in the attitudes of public servants and the government itself. This presentation is aimed at reviewing the key visions and objectives that underlie government innovation in Korea, and synthesizing the outcomes and challenges that lie ahead. In addition, it will put forth the major features of this government's innovation in the context of global trends.

Key Visions and Objectives of Government Innovation

The concept of reform adopted by the preceding Korean national administration drew from concepts supported in the "new public management." These stressed efficiency, market orientation, and privatization. The main concepts of the reforms were:

- First, to establish a small government by reducing the size of the government at the central and local government levels;
- Second, to adopt a competition principle to the civil service;
- Third, to introduce a results-oriented fiscal system;
- And finally, to commercialize (privatize) some areas of the public sector.

Those government reform initiatives stimulated the reconstruction of the public sector and made considerable contributions toward tackling the financial crisis in Korea. However, excessive emphasis on efficiency, the top-down characteristics, and lack of participation have been widely criticized over the past few years. Moreover, the strategies for smaller government have noticeably weakened the government's capacity to perform.

Visions and Objectives of Government Innovation

Taking into account the past experiences of government reform, the government initiative has substantially changed the visions and strategies of government innovation. They can be differentiated from previous attempts in terms of:

- Setting up multiple innovation targets;
- Innovating government through participation and autonomy;
- Aiming to develop a competent and accountable government;
- And pursuing e-government founded on both hardware and software innovation.

First, innovation targets of the current government have been clearly established. The primary goal is to build a competent and interactive government. And under the primary goal, there are five subsidiary objectives toward government innovation. These are to build:

- An efficient government,
- A government that serves the people,
- A participatory government,
- A transparent government, and
- A decentralized government.

Second, the government promotes innovation based on participation and autonomy. The National Administration System has been readjusted to accommodate citizens' participation in identifying innovation tasks, implementing policies, and evaluating the subsequent outcomes. Furthermore, public servants were, are, and always will be considered as the very agents of innovation, and therefore, the success of government innovation lies in the active participation of public servants.

Third, the initiative focuses on establishing a competent and accountable government. Rather than adopting previous strategies toward smaller government, it is in the interest of this administration and the people that governments first become efficient and able.

Fourth, the government leads its innovation based on e-government, as advanced information and communication technology can immensely change the process of providing public services, the way of work, and organizational structures. In this regard, an e-Government Bureau has been created under the Headquarters of Government Innovation in conjunction with the government reform initiatives.

Finally, participatory government emphasizes software reform. Although it does not neglect to further hardware reform, the focal point of these reforms is to manage policy quality and link e-government with innovation.

Building Infrastructure for Fostering Innovation

Since building an innovative infrastructure is a critical factor for fostering government innovation, the new administration established the Presidential Committee on Government Innovation and Decentralization to provide macroscopic direction and strategy for government innovation. In addition, the government set up the Headquarters for Administrative Innovation within the Ministry of Government Administration and Home Affairs to devise innovation methods and help ministries implement such reforms. And, to coordinate with their counterparts and to stimulate innovation implementation, the position of *innovation officer* was created in each ministry.

The government has also formulated the legal foundation for government innovation with the enactment of two related laws: the Special Law for decentralization, balanced nationwide development, and a new administrative capital, and the revised Government Organization Law.

Establishment of an Innovation Road Map

The Innovation Road Map for the Five Main Sectors of Society has been completed. In this road map, 153 reform agenda were proposed according to the five main sectors of administration, personnel management, decentralization, e-government, and fiscal system.

Upon the completion of the road map, the direction and timeline of government innovation were set sufficiently enough to draw a broad picture of government innovation of the participatory government.

Building Consensus of Government Innovation and Sharing Strategy

Building a consensus emphasis toward government innovation and sharing innovative values are both crucial necessities. In line with this, the government has held a series of workshops for ministers and vice ministers and assigned Saturday as a *learning day* to realize these critical needs. At these workshops, participants analyze and discuss the innovative success of the private sector, and previous administrative policy failures.

The government has selected seventeen "common tasks" for reinventing government; work on each task is currently under way. The selected tasks include innovation on HRM, management of policy quality, conflict management, and deregulation. Each common task is being led by a host ministry assisted by some related ministries. In this process, the leading ministry shares successful cases and systems with other ministries. Among the seventeen common tasks, several were assigned to the Ministry of Government Administration and Home Affairs (MOGAHA). These include policy quality, knowledge management, business process redesign, and e-government.

Knowledge Management

Knowledge management (KM) aims to maximize the capacity of the government organization by accumulating and sharing practical knowledge. KM can be utilized as the effective means of government innovation by systematizing personal and organizational know-how, inventing high-quality knowledge, and maximizing the productivity of the administration.

In Korea, the government's knowledge management system (KMS) was introduced in the year 2000 and in 2004 was operating in sixty-eight organizations including central and district governments. Among them, twenty-six organizations were digitally sharing information internally and externally.

Business Process Redesign (BPR) and Improving Working Patterns

Redesigning business processes and improving working patterns are also a part of the transformation tasks at hand. By eradicating unnecessary work, and innovating ways of work, they aim to increase administrative productivity and change administrative culture.

Fostering E-Government

The e-government project aims to establish a ubiquitous government where public services are available regardless of place and time. In order to improve public services, the electronic public service system has been adopted and 420 items are available online. Also, citizens can receive digital certification for 8 items at their own personal computers. Future plans for e-government policy include establishing the e-participation portal system, which makes room for policy suggestions and feedback, and providing administrative services through mobile phones and PDAs.

A Global Trend in Government Innovation

The global trend in government innovation is today grounded on the viewpoint of "governance," which is characterized by the participation of various sectors and networks. In Korea, citizen participation in the policy-making process, partnerships between government and civil society, and continuous reform and management of innovation processes have become the major foci of government innovation.

Expanding Citizen Participation

The government initiative has adopted various innovative attempts to improve public service and expand citizen participation. Citizen participation has been extended in the areas of service production, consumption, and evaluation. In the policy planning process, procedures such as public hearings have been introduced to encourage citizen participation. In addition, the public portal service is being promoted for the same cause.

Building an Innovation Network

The participatory government initiative is in the process of building an innovation network within the government as well as in cooperation with civil society. This will enable various members in civil society to participate in the government's decision-making process. A committee comprising professionals, public servants, and citizens is being implemented as a measure to establish such networks. Also, to build a global network to enhance the global cooperation system, Korea plans to establish the OECD's Regional Center for Public Governance.

Three Stages of Reform

In order to succeed in this quest for reform, engraving reform in the minds of public servants is a must. At the next stage, reform must permeate into policy. And finally, reforms should be able to touch and move the hearts of the beneficiaries: the people. The most distinct feature of the participatory government's reform lies not within transforming individual policies, but in revolutionizing the way of thinking, ascertaining the problems of current government policies, and solving such problems by interacting with those who are affected by these policies.

Another feature of the participatory government's reform is the seeking of reform initiatives based on autonomy and participation. For this, the innovation officers in each ministry are appointed as change agents and formal/informal organizations have been activated.

Conclusion

Innovation is creating and applying new or distinctive ways of producing, distributing, and/or delivering products, services, or ideas from producers or suppliers to users. It also includes the design and implementation of new and distinctive organizational structures and processes, creating new services, or creatively experimenting with new combinations or products or services. Innovation can take place at any place in the value chain.

A primary goal of knowledge management in the public sector is to promote innovation and invention in government agencies. This includes applying new technologies, new and improved ways of delivering government services, and new or untried management processes and systems in organizations.

Previously, managing innovation in organizations focused on changing and improving processes. Until the global government reform movement took place in the 1990s, government managers and administrators had little opportunity or incentive to innovate. Today, however, government agencies, departments, and units must either innovate or explain "why not" to an active and knowledgeable electorate and legislative oversight bodies. A culture that rewards innovation in the way governments work and public-sector managers think has become common throughout the world, at all levels of government, from federal departments to the smallest local special service district. Managers in the public sector employ whatever methods they can in order to turn their once-bureaucratic organizations into learning organizations that are open to change and ready to accept new ways of doing things.

Public services require close interaction with clients/customers/citizens. Therefore, innovation in service organizations is often not only about *what* is being offered, but also about *how* and *by whom* it is being offered. Knowledge management helps make innovation possible by ensuring that information and knowledge are available when needed.

9

Knowledge Management in the Public Sector

The ability to draw on critical knowledge efficiently and reliably is what managing knowledge is all about. It is getting the right information, at the right time, in the right context, to support an identified need, strategy or action.
(DCMA 2004)

Although there are still government agencies in which it is not found in full-blown operation, the management function known as *knowledge management* has been widely embraced by a wide variety of organizations in the federal government. In those agencies where KM is found, it is often considered an important if not absolutely necessary management tool; implementing KM will enable the agencies to meet their service and performance requirements in spite of the many challenges government faces in this new century. Moreover, proponents of KM believe that by enhancing the collection, codification, storage, transmission, and sharing of knowledge, government agencies are able to succeed in their missions despite declining budgets, demands for more and improved services, and a skilled, knowledgeable workforce that is disappearing into retirement.

KM is far less visible in either state or local government, however. At the local level, many of the tasks of KM are managed under the auspices of a chief information officer, or similar IT-oriented managers. Because of the still-sparse adoptions of KM in state and local governments, the bulk of the discussion in this chapter must refer to KM as it is found in federal agencies, departments, and functions, with the few state and/or local applications added as they are found.

One of the reasons why government agencies at all levels may have been slow at adopting KM for their operations has been because they have had to fight entrenched agency cultures in which the norm was to keep information to yourself, not share it (Harris 2001). Proponents of KM believe that they have the power to change this culture. They point out that when knowledge resides in the group instead of an individual, the entire organization is made stronger. They point to the successes of organizational learning as examples of the power of shared knowledge. The culture of the organization must move from hoarding information to sharing information. In this way, organizations benefit from a new openness and continued support of upper-level management. Eric Lesser, a KM consultant at IBM, warned that the problems of opposing cultures are not the only barriers to successful KM programs in government. The most difficult task may be finding the time to give people the opportunity to talk with one another and share information. To deal with this problem, organizations often have to require their employees to participate in KM programs. When they fail to do so, the KM program also fails.

Chapter Objectives

The content of this chapter is designed to serve as an introduction to the series of public-sector KM case studies that follow in part 4. The objectives for this chapter include the following:

- To help readers gain a deeper understanding of the roles knowledge management is coming to hold in a wide variety of government agencies.
- To reinforce readers' recognition that, although it plays a big part as one of the fundamental legs of KM, information technology is only one of the primary drivers in a successful KM application.
- To help readers understand both the similarities and the differences in the roles of the chief information officer and the chief knowledge officer.
- To help readers, by reading about several case histories of agency experiences with and without KM programs, to understand where KM practices and procedures contributed to the ability of agency managers to achieve their missions.
- To help readers, again by reading case histories of successful KM applications, to see where and how KM can—or should—be applied in their own organizations.

KM in the Federal Government

Government adoption of KM began late in the decade of the 1990s, some ten years after a small number of businesses and industries first introduced the concept into their operations. The General Services Administration (GSA) was one of the first federal agencies to see how KM could improve their ability to carry out their operations. The FAA and the Goddard Space Center of the National Aeronautics and Space Administration (NASA) were not far behind (Ross and Schulte 2005). By the end of the decade and the beginning of a new century, enough federal agencies had expressed an interest in learning more about KM for the Office of Management and Budget (OMB) to take notice.

Initially, KM was more or less synonymous with Information Technology (IT). Private-sector IT vendors were engaged then—and now—in intense competition to sell their hardware and software to any and every agency even remotely interested. The OMB reacted quickly to bring a measure of rationality and planning into IT purchases. Another problem that concerned the OMB was that agencies were purchasing systems that could not communicate with one another, a practice resulting in independent systems with data contained in silos of information

A spokesperson for the Defense Contract Management Agency (DCMA) described how greater application of KM systems would contribute to the solution to these information hoarding difficulties:

> The Federal government is a vast storehouse of knowledge, and its employees are experts in thousands of subjects, from AIDS research to weather prediction. The real challenge is building an environment for a freer exchange of this collective intelligence among federal agencies; an exchange among Federal, state and local governments; and a more accessible exchange between the knowledge stores of the Federal government and citizens. The ability to leverage these extensive knowledge stores and increase the intellectual capacity of agencies to quickly find solutions improve decision-making and effectively respond to other government organizations and citizen is crucial to achieving a major improvement in the Federal government's performance and value to the citizen. (DCMA 2004)

Information technology is universally recognized as one of the four or five key components of a system for managing and leveraging an organization's knowledge. Before 1996, however, IT purchases and applications were considered to be the concern of each individual agency, with each unit's purchases controlled only through the budget and appropriations processes. Congress and the executive branch realized that something needed to be done to bring some measure of control to the ever-growing amounts being spent on IT. To do so, the position of chief information officer (CIO) was established in 1996 by executive order. Agencies appointed their own CIOs, who then began to monitor and manage their agencies' IT planning, purchases, applications, and architectures. The Office of Management and Budget then set up the Federal Chief Information Officers Council (CIO Council). The council is a network where CIOs can share problems, successes, and experiences. With the establishment of the CIO Council all federal CIOs also became members of a *community of interest* devoted to improving the use of IT in government.

The chair of the CIO Council is the deputy director for management in the OMB; members of the working group elect the vice chair from among the group membership. In 2005, the council had three working committees, with ad hoc groups formed as needed. The three committees are all responsible for some aspect of knowledge management. They are: (1) the *Best Practices Committee,* which focuses on identifying and encouraging the use of best practices to improve the development and delivery of IT solutions across federal agencies; (2) the *Federal Architecture & Infrastructure Committee,* charged with establishing a government-wide foundation for greater adoption of e-government by supporting the development of a common enterprise architecture and infrastructure platform, and by providing models and standards for federal systems; and (3) the *Workforce and Human Capital for Information Technology Committee,* which focuses on two programs: improving the federal government's ability to attract and retain a top-notch IT workforce, and expanding IT education and training opportunities for all federal workers.

By December of 2000, sufficient interest had been generated in KM across federal agencies for a few far-sighted leaders and CIOs in civilian and military organizations to form a special interest group on KM topics. The CIO Council officially formed the Knowledge Management Working Group (KMWG) on January 5, 2000, to be the interagency body that would bring together the best of what federal agencies were doing with KM. Although the working group is particularly concerned with KM in the federal government, it has begun discussions on collaboration and knowledge sharing with state and local governments.

The KMWG includes federal professionals, ICT consultants, vendors, and representatives from academia. The working group includes representatives from more than thirty federal agencies. The primary mission of the federal KM group is to ensure that all government agencies collect and share what the government workers *know.* Governance for the KMWG falls under the leadership of the Best Practices Committee of the CIO Council, which has formally charged the KMWG with responsibility for:

- Identifying best KM practices that can be found in government, business, and industry;
- Encouraging the dissemination of information related to KM; and

- Ensuring the development of competency profiles for public-sector chief knowledge officers.

The KMWG accomplishes these assigned tasks through a variety of special interest groups (SIGs). The number of SIGs operating at any one time varies with assigned tasks, needs, and available resources. Shortly after its formation, the working group identified four far-reaching benefits they believed would result from the growing emphasis on KM in government (Remez and Desenberg 2000). First, *information, knowledge, and expertise will be readily available by subject and interest area.* KM has the ability to break down barriers to learning caused by the practice of "stovepiping" people, their knowledge, and their skills into artificial groups and bureaucracies. It does this by bringing technology—i.e., the Internet, intranets, listservs, and other electronic communications tools—and people together to eliminate physical and organizational boundaries. This enables communities of practice to form and flourish. Communities of practice are informal groups of people located in geographically dispersed areas and groups, but who have a common interest in a work domain, project or product, and/or practice.

Second, *government services will be integrated and accessible.* Knowledge management brings together expertise and action, letting citizens transact business with all levels of government. For example, today it is possible for citizens to access such government services as renewing their pet or driver's license or their passports, and they can pay their utility bills online. Other agencies are working on making it possible for citizens to vote online. The old Web sites that used to be simply data repositories are rapidly becoming knowledge portals that provide real solutions.

Third, *one-stop shopping will come to government.* Knowledge management has the power to bring together different agencies and levels of government, not based on organizational structure, but according to purpose and function. In one Washington State example, an independent knowledge specialist has developed a Web service that makes it possible for citizens carrying out an activity that crosses a number of rural jurisdictions to complete the permitting process online. Applicants go to a single Web site to apply and pay for one permit that is valid in all jurisdictions, and receive the permit in just a few days—the goal is to eventually bring the response time down to just hours. The site brings together the combined knowledge housed in people working in six continuous small communities. Before, the citizens would have had to visit each site to apply for a permit valid in only that one community, meet different requirements in each community, and wait different periods of time for the community official to respond. Overall, the process might have taken weeks if not months.

Fourth, *tacit knowledge will become more accessible.* Many people still experience some unease when they find themselves trying to communicate with nonhuman automatic response systems, or a customer service individual who might be located several continents away. Instead, they prefer to either travel to a government office or wait on hold to speak with a live person in order to reap the benefits they receive from the knowledge of experienced professionals. Certainly, mountains of raw data have long been available for anyone who knows how to maneuver their way through the maze of the World Wide Web. However, the tacit knowledge and experience that a skilled person brings to a citizen's problem has, until just the last few years, been available only in a face-to-face meeting. Knowledge management applications have the power to harness this tacit knowledge and put it to use on a much wider scale. One way this is happening is by the wedding of Internet communications and television. Agencies are using televised vignettes—in stories used as examples of solutions to problems—to capture the tacit knowledge held by professionals on their staffs. Citizens can access these televised stories directly on their home computers. In some instances it is also possible to request and receive a connection to a live representative for real-time communication.

Presidential Support for KM

Federal agency interest in knowledge management was given a large boost early in the administration of G.W. Bush, who included KM in his President's Management Agenda (PMA), along with management improvements, enterprise architecture policies for IT, strategic planning, and e-government initiatives. The president's KM mandate was clarified in a 2002 OMB report:

> The Administration will adopt information technology systems to capture some of the knowledge and skills of retiring employees. KM systems are just one part of an effective strategy that will generate, capture, and disseminate knowledge and information that is relevant to the organization's mission. (OMB 2002, 13)

Today, most agencies in the federal government have appointed chief information officers to oversee their IT operations. In some agencies, the CIO is also responsible for managing the knowledge management system. However, today the KM director is more likely to be a separate, senior-level manager functioning with the title of chief knowledge officer (CKO) or something similar. The government agency CKO has broader responsibilities than the organization's IT. The CKO must plan, implant, and manage a comprehensive program that fosters knowledge collection, sharing, and usage. Under a

KM operating philosophy, IT is one of several equally important tools that help make a knowledge management system possible.

Early Federal Adopters of KM

The General Services Administration was one of the first federal agencies to take on KM as a major strategic thrust. The GSA is responsible for acquiring the buildings, products, services, technology, and other workplace essentials for federal agencies. The agency's knowledge management unit is housed in the Office of Applied Science–Knowledge Management Division. The division describes its responsibilities as follows:

> The Knowledge Management Division is responsible for leveraging the sharing of knowledge, information, and data across the [GSA] organization. It is responsible for identifying, capturing, and disseminating information. The Division will also evaluate he effectiveness of information and determine its relevance and validity to support [the organization's] business. (GSA 2006, 1)

The Federal Aviation Administration (FAA) is responsible for maintaining the safety of the nation's aviation system, including managing the air traffic control network and monitoring aircraft safety. The FAA has a long history of applying knowledge management concepts to its operations. The Knowledge Sharing (KS) office was an early group set up to promote knowledge management across the organization. A follow-on organization was the Office of Knowledge Management. Among the long list of KM programs in the FAA were the Environmental Occupational Safety and Health Event Management System, an FAA Logistics Center, the National Aerospace Information Architecture Committee, the Aviation Safety Knowledge Management Environment, the Technology Transfer Program, and the Traffic Flow and Enterprise Management Collaborative Communications System, among others. FAA'S Traffic Flow and Enterprise Management (TFEM) organization was one of the founding members of the agency's Knowledge Services Network (KSN), a group established to foster collaboration and research and develop the FAA's knowledge management effort (FAA 2003). The TFEM developed and implemented the Collaborative Communications System as a knowledge management tool.

NASA's Strategic Plan for KM

The KM professionals at NASA produced an early version of a strategic plan for knowledge management in April 2002. In the foreword to that plan the authors outlined a chief reason why getting a handle on the scientific and technical knowledge as NASA was so critical.

For most of its history, the majority of NASA's physical and human resources were directed at developing and managing a few long-duration programs such as the Apollo, Viking, and Space Shuttle programs. During those years, NASA had the luxury of its people willingly sharing knowledge throughout their tenure on the programs. Engineers and scientists spent years, sometimes decades, working on a project. During those years junior employees learned from senior members of the project team. Eventually, the juniors became seniors and they, too, mentored new junior team members.

For more than forty years, NASA'S knowledge base and abilities have continued to grow. Today, however, NASA has been forced to adopt a new operating philosophy, one in which it must apply the principles of faster-better-cheaper as appropriate. NASA can no longer sustain the earlier era of apprenticeship and the nurturing of the flow of experiential and tacit knowledge from senior to junior employees. Today, engineers and scientists may work from one to three years on a project and then move on to something new. Individually they gain a lot of knowledge, but what they learn stays with them; the knowledge is not captured or passed on across the organization for future missions. Knowledge management principles offer a solution for moving ahead, accepting today's constraints, and adapting to a world where technology and innovative processes must partially replace the mentoring and measured approaches formerly common throughout NASA. According to Jeanne Holm, chair of NASA's knowledge management team in 2002, "NASA's knowledge, its intellectual capital, is the Agency's primary, sustainable source of competitive advantage. Physical assets age, today's workforce is mobile, and technology is quickly bypassed. Our knowledge as an agency, however, can endure. This knowledge is a fluid mix of experience and know-how that allows NASA employees to strive for and achieve the improbable day after day" (NASA 2002, 1).

The strategic plan highlighted three key areas in which the agency needed to manage its knowledge and that the agency needed to address more effectively. The first was capturing more of the critical knowledge needed to safely conduct missions. The second was making it possible for virtual teams to collaborate more effectively in their work. And the third was managing more effectively the information already captured in the agency. The principles in this strategic plan have guided the agency's KM operations to where it is now one of the most proficient and effective at using KM in accomplishing its overall mission.

KM in the Navy

The Department of the Navy (DON) was one of the first branches of the military to successfully adopt the KM philosophy. Jim Knox, chief information officer for the DON, defined the navy's take on KM in a paper presented at a 2005 government KM conference:

> Knowledge Management systematically brings together people and processes, enabled by technology, to facilitate the exchange of operationally relevant information and expertise to increase organizational performance. (Knox 2005).

The navy's version of KM—the DON KM Framework—is formed from five key interconnecting spokes: content, processes, culture, learning, and technology. Each spoke is further shaped by a number of key factors developed from several knowledge management tools, techniques, or practices. The culture spoke, for example, includes commitment, sharing, building relationships, and communicating. The learning spoke is framed around building content, storytelling, creating, growing, experimenting, and establishing feedback loops. The content spoke includes value, relevancy, currency, credibility, and expertise, while the process spoke incorporates making knowledge explicit by capturing, categorizing, mapping, analyzing, and disseminating. The technology spoke is built on enabling, facilitating, empowering, and promoting innovation.

The navy employs KM in a range of applications, beginning with the DON Virtual Knowledge Repository. This tool is used as a clearinghouse for best practices data. Other DON operational applications include the Naval Network Warfare Command, the Tactical Training Group–Pacific, and the DON Business Innovation Team, among others. Recognized as a leader in KM government applications, the DON has distributed more than 20,000 copies of its Knowledge-Centric Organization (KCO) toolkit to different federal government agencies and units. The toolkit, recorded on a CD, provides information on how to create a KCO that connects people to the right information at the right time for decision making and action.

Varying Degrees of KM Adoption

Knowledge management and knowledge management systems applications have far to go before they become an integral management function everyplace they can contribute to agency performance. The principles and practices of KM have been embraced by such federal offices as all branches of the military, NASA, the Department of Transportation, and many similar offices where the collection and sharing of workers' knowledge is a critical component of operations. Surprisingly, however, in other organizations management's embracing of KM has been far less warm or demonstrative. The examples that follow illustrate situations where an installation of a comprehensive knowledge management system could improve agency performance. The first illustration is the office of the Architect of the Capitol; the second is the Department of the Treasury; and the third is the Department of Homeland Security and several mission-related operations.

The Case of the Capitol Architect

The office of the Architect of the Capitol (AOC) is responsible for the maintenance, renovation, and new construction of all buildings and grounds within the Capitol Hill complex. The U.S. General Accounting Office (GAO) is required by the Legislative Branch Appropriations Act to conduct a thorough review of all legislative branch operations, including the AOC. The purpose of these reviews is to identify where the organizations can improve their strategic planning, organizational alignment (structure), strategic human capital, and information technology—and knowledge—resources so that they might better achieve their mission.

The GAO's 2003 report on the results of their study of the AOC included the conclusion that *managing knowledge* is one of the key steps the agency must take in its legislatively mandated management transformation. The GAO report recommended that the architect's office implement three major management changes (emphasis added):

- Strengthen and consistently implement its human capital polices and procedures, including addressing ways in which management could better gather and analyze data on employee relations issues.
- Continue to improve its approach to financial management by developing strategies to institutionalize financial management practices that support budgeting, financial, and program management.
- *Adopt an agency-wide approach to information technology management by establishing appropriate leadership and developing the policies, procedures, and tools needed to effectively and efficiently manage information technology resources across the agency.*

The last recommendation is emphasized in order to point out that these are key steps in designing and implanting a knowledge management system. Specifically addressing the information technology management issue, the GAO added that they believed the AOC could benefit greatly from knowledge sharing, and by encouraging and rewarding employees who share and implement best practices across the various jurisdictions, teams, and projects. For example, employees included in the study's focus groups overwhelmingly reported that communications from supervisors to employees was insufficient.

In 2003, the AOC still did not have an agency-wide approach to managing its information technology (IT) functions; it had not implemented the requirement to prepare a technology architecture plan (i.e., a blueprint for current and future IT needs); nor had it named a senior-level executive to be responsible and accountable for IT management and spending. Rather, control of IT purchases and operations remained in each AOC organizational component.

GAO auditors concluded that without proper agency-wide management of IT, the Architect of the Capitol will be unable to effectively manage all the critical building and operating systems knowledge that resides in the minds of its personnel. When such problems as the anticipated retirement and departure of large numbers of senior-level professionals occur, the AOC may find itself forced to continue to "reinvent the wheel" for each solution, thereby unnecessarily increasing both the cost and the time to complete a project. Decades of critical knowledge will be irretrievably lost.

The Case of the Treasury Department

An illustration of what happens in a government agency when there is insufficient or unfocused management of data, information, and knowledge was reported in a GAO report on activities in one unit of the U.S. Treasury Department shortly after the September 11, 2001, terrorist attacks. The study was not tied to that catastrophic event, but clearly illustrates the notion of better control and sharing of information and knowledge.

The U.S. Department of the Treasury has many diverse responsibilities, organized in twelve separate bureaus. The department summarizes its many duties and responsibilities into three overarching tasks: promoting the nation's economic well-being, managing the government's finances, and ensuring the integrity of financial information both inside and outside of the federal government. In the August 2004 annual report of its operational results, the department succinctly summarized these responsibilities by identifying itself as the "chief manager of the nation's finances."

The department is also charged with enforcement of the laws and regulations that relate to such responsibilities and functions as the Alcohol and Tobacco Tax and Trade Bureau, the Financial Crimes Enforcement Network, the Inspector General, the Internal Revenue Service, and the U.S. Mint, among others. To carry out these enforcement duties, the individual bureaus typically coordinate and collaborate with other federal, state, and local law enforcement agencies. In March of 2002, the General Accounting Office (GAO) issued a report of its review of the department's Office of Enforcement (now the Office of Terrorism and Financial Intelligence, which combines the department's intelligence and enforcement functions). The enforcement office was established to provide oversight, policy guidance, and support to the department's enforcement bureaus. The GAO report spelled out why it is so important for government agencies to manage the knowledge that exists within their domain.

The GAO reported that they could not find any single comprehensive source in Treasury that provided guidance to either the enforcement staff or the bureaus in those instances when the bureau must interact with enforcement personnel, nor could they find any established documentation for twelve of the twenty-nine situations where such interaction is required. When documentation did exist, the GAO considered it to be (1) generally too broad in nature for its purpose, and (2) a failure at providing explicit information on half of the bureau/enforcement interactions. About half of the bureau officials interviewed said that they were not aware of any written requirements for their interactions with enforcement, nor did they know when to interact. The knowledge factors that influenced the requirements for interactions included professional responsibility, experience, judgment, and even common sense.

The GAO report emphasized that the agency's internal control needed to be clearly documented and that documentation should be readily available for examination by managers and field workers as needed—clearly a role for a knowledge management system. The GAO went on to add that, without a well-defined and -documented set of policies and procedures covering operational and communications activities, the enforcement office of the Department of the Treasury runs the risk of not being able to perform its functions and meet its goals efficiently. KM can help the department to surmount this threat.

The department has moved to rectify the shortcomings identified in 2002; progress on a number of change initiatives was spelled out in its 2004 President's Management Agenda report (DOT 2004). Those changes clearly reflect knowledge management thinking without the KM label. For example, Treasury's human resource offices, business units, and information technology offices now work together to identify current and planned technology, required skills, and current and anticipated skill gaps. This information is used to frame the department's long-term plans for closing the skill gaps and maintaining appropriate skill levels.

A program to enhance workforce capabilities has resulted in the implementation of a comprehensive, multidimensional, and integrated technology knowledge-sharing strategy. At the same time, greater integration and control over investments in technology and processes are being implemented to ensure that knowledge, skill, and training needs are included in all technology proposals and implementation plans.

Changes at Treasury that specifically address the lack of coordination and procedures with enforcement include an electronic information exchange system to allow law enforcement agencies—federal, state, and local—to quickly attain information from U.S financial institutions about suspects, businesses, and accounts in major money laundering and counterterrorism investigations.

The Case of Homeland Security

Homeland security is a classic example of an area in which significant efforts at managing critical knowledge are warranted. One of the reasons often cited for the failure of national and local law enforcement and intelligence agencies to identify and deter the terrorist attacks of 9/11 was the long tradition of protecting—hoarding—information of this type. This practice is referred to as collecting and holding agency-gathered knowledge relating to potential threats to the nation in secure "stovepipes" or "silos." In an Op-Ed article in the *Mercury News* of San Jose, California, the dangers of the practice of information and knowledge hoarding were described in a hypothetical case in which a field agent at the Chicago, Illinois, FBI office and a CIA operative in Kabul, Afghanistan, both become aware of separate leads regarding a possible biowarfare attack on Chicago. Under the traditional system, it is unlikely that the two reports would have been put together or that either agent would be made aware of the other agent's information (Baird and Barksdale 2004).

The authors of the "think piece" article were officials of the Markle Foundation, a nontraditional private foundation that sponsors research in counterterrorism, among other fields. The foundation has a long history of working to improve the nation's healthcare and medical education systems, promote interactive communications programs for children, and promote policy initiatives for adoption of IT in government. Its work on issues relating to the nation's security network was a logical outgrowth of its work in promoting IT applications. In this role, Markle brought together leaders and innovators from technology industries, various government agencies, public interest organizations, and business to promote technical and policy changes relating to new and better uses of IT in government.

After September 11, 2001, the foundation formed a study task force comprising leading national security experts from the Carter, Reagan, G.H. Bush, Clinton, and G.W. Bush administrations, and other experts on technology and civil liberties (Dempsey 2005). Their charge was to identify ways to strengthen the nation's security against the threat of terrorism. The progress reports, produced in alliance with the Brookings Institution and the Center for Strategic and International Studies, were issued in 2002 and 2003. The foundation described its interest in knowledge management in healthcare and national security thus:

> These are two of the most critical issues of our time, where the benefit to be gained from the ability to put the right information into the right hands at the right time is enormous. In each of these areas, the effective use of [shared knowledge] can literally save lives. These are areas where IT promises great breakthroughs, and where without better use of IT our nation's goals cannot be met. At the same time, healthcare and national security also highlight the major challenge in seeking better ways of using information: the risk such use poses to our established privacy and civil liberties. (Markle Foundation 2003, 2)

In its final report, *Creating a Trusted Information Network for Homeland Security,* issued in December 2003, the Security Task Force stressed the importance of creating a decentralized network of information sharing and analysis around presidential guidelines to address the challenge of homeland security. The report also identified the following seven key characteristics that are needed to enable homeland security units to take full advantage of the nation's strengths in information technology:

1. Handling of information should be decentralized and take place under users, following a network model rather than a mainframe hub-and-spoke model.
2. The network should be guided by policy that simultaneously empowers and constrains government officials by making it clear what is permissible and what is prohibited.
3. The government's security strategy should focus on prevention.
4. To deal with the difficulty of distinguishing between domestic and foreign threats, the government should avoid creating blind spots, or gaps between agencies, that arise from such distinctions. New rules must replace the old "line at the border" rules that distinguished domestic and foreign information-collecting responsibility.
5. The network must recognize that many key participants are not in the federal government, but instead may be in state or local government or the private sector.
6. The network must be able to use information gathered in clandestine intelligence activities, information from normal law enforcement investigations, and also information held by private companies. This should occur only after guidelines for its collection and use are formed.

7. Policies and actions for combating terrorism need to have the support—and trust—of the American people. Privacy and other civil liberties must be protected.

The report then identified a list of steps for implementing the policies, adding that the federal government needed to give greater priority to sharing and analyzing information. The report concluded that it is no longer possible to justify the practice of restricting access to information that characterized the intelligence policies of the Cold War. Rather, the agencies involved need to adopt a program similar to what the study termed the *Systemwide Homeland Analysis and Resource Exchange* (SHARE).

The report also spelled out a set of goals, policies, and practices that are part and parcel of a typical *knowledge management system.* Reaffirming the principles of the first report, the 2003 document included greater detail on how and why government must create networks for information collection, sharing, analysis, and use across federal, state, and local agencies and the private sector. The network as conceived by the task force includes more than just technological architecture; it must also focus on the people, processes, and information that must go hand in hand with the technology, including the rules necessary to govern how all the elements interact.

The task force did note that the federal government has made some progress in developing the envisioned network; both the executive branch and Congress now have an understanding of the need for more information sharing and for networks that break down agency "stovepipes." Steps have been taken at all levels of government to expand the sharing of terrorist-threat data among all agencies, while at the same time improving analysis of terrorism-related information.

One example of this greater coordination and cooperation is the Antiterrorism Information Exchange (ATIX) network developed by the Justice Department and the FBI to provide all law enforcement agencies and public safety, infrastructure, and homeland security groups access to some homeland security information. At the federal level, creation of the Terrorist Threat Integration Center (TTIC), a joint operation of the CIA, the FBI, the DHS, the departments of State and Defense, and other members of the intelligence community, was announced in January of 2003. However, the 2003 report also charged the Department of Homeland Security and the TTIC of laxity in developing the needed knowledge management system. Moreover, the DHS was apparently lax in its duties by not taking the necessary steps to build the communications and sharing network required to deal with a terrorist threat. Nor did the agency begin producing regular, actionable intelligence products for other agencies on time, as needed. The DHS had not produced a vision of how it would link federal, state, and local agencies in a communications and sharing network, or what the agency's role would be with respect to the threat integration center and other federal agencies. The report concluded that the DHS instead appeared to be focused on building a new information technology infrastructure to support and unify its twenty-two components. Finally, the study determined that neither the TTIC nor the DHS had accomplished much in the way of putting in place the necessary staff or framework for analyzing information and sharing it among the relevant federal, state, and local agencies.

By 2005, however, the Department of Homeland Security had made a number of important strides in resolving these critical shortcomings. One such advancement was the formation of a network for sharing information, connecting, and improving homeland security, Lessons Learned Information Sharing (LLIS.gov). LLIS is a national online network of lessons learned and best practices for emergency response providers and homeland security officials. The restricted and secure network serves approximately 12,500 members as the official clearinghouse for all homeland security–related information (Travis 2005).

One of the growing problems associated with the installation of a comprehensive terrorist information network is the large and growing number of government, nonprofit, and private-sector companies involved in one or more aspects of the field. For example, the LLIS program is sponsored by two agencies: the DHS Office of State and Local Government Coordination and Preparedness (SLGCP)—formerly the Office of Domestic Preparedness—and the National Memorial Institute for the Prevention of Terrorism (MIPT). Reflecting the special vertical sharing requirement for antiterrorist information, SLGCP is responsible for assisting states and local jurisdictions to prevent, plan for, and respond to acts of terrorism, while the MIPT sponsors research to discover equipment, training, and procedures that might assist first responders in preventing terrorism and responding to it.

The LLIS knowledge management system has become the official repository of lessons learned and best practices for the Department of Homeland Security. To encourage usage, access is both free and secure (only cleared law enforcement and antiterrorism professionals have access to the network). The network provides users the following KM benefits:

- Analytical Tools: Government analysts are provided with custom query building and recording tools.
- Collaboration: By connecting emergency response personnel across the country—users have access to a searchable member directory, secure e-mail message boards, and user surveys—a culture of collaboration and sharing is being formed.

- Document Library: The library supports the collection and storage of structured and unstructured data and multimedia content and organizes and categorizes content using a custom-designed taxonomy that permits users to find information following more than one path.
- Document Management: Manages a system for approving and posting documents, workflow management, and back-end document management, including archiving information and knowledge so that it is not lost.
- Feedback: The feedback tool encourages users to comment on system content and technical issues, as well as providing users an opportunity to add new content to the system.
- Integration: The system integrates system content and user communities with independent emergency response applications using Web services.
- Search: LLIS uses a third-party search engine to support full-text searching, category matching, and relevancy ranking.
- Security: LLIS assigns security and access rights to groups and individuals.

Law enforcement agency collaboration and information sharing about terrorists and terrorism is not only a problem in the United States. Box 9.1 describes examples of how the intelligence community in Europe is reacting to this need.

The United States is not the only nation affected by the actions of Muslim extremists and terrorist group activities. Bombings in Bali and Madrid, murders, and plots to set off dirty bombs in the UK are only a few of the terrorist activities taking place around the world. One of the problems in identifying and stopping terrorism in Europe is the porous nature of the borders within and without the European Union. Once inside any of the twenty-five nations composing the EU, it is possible for terrorist suspects to move easily to any other country.

Terrorist organizations have moved many of their planning and fundraising activities to Muslim population enclaves that exist from Norway to Spain and beyond. The intelligence and law enforcement communities of these European countries are finding it extremely difficult to maintain current information databases on terrorists because the needed information-sharing infrastructure is only now emerging.

KM at the FBI

The use of KM tools and processes is not new in government, although not always with the name for the practice. Agency innovators have long used KM to improve collaborative actions, capture and share best practices—a program that gained a strong following during the 1990s empha-

Box 9.1

Building an Information-Sharing Culture in Europe

Networks of Islamic jihadists are reported to exist all across the European Union. They are descendants of guest workers recruited in the years following World War II. Although those guest workers helped to create the postwar economic miracle in Europe, most remain social outcasts. They are, unable or unwilling to become full-fledged citizens of their adopted countries. Many of their children have joined terrorist groups, joining illegal aliens, asylum seekers, and students who came to Europe seeking refuge. Militant minorities in these groups carried out many of the terrorist activities across Europe. They were implicated in the September 11, 2001, attacks on the New York World Trade Center and the Pentagon, bombings in Spain, murders, and more than thirty other terrorist plots.

Many politicians and intelligence bodies in Europe consider terrorism to be a crime problem, not a war. Terrorism activities are considered isolated attacks and not part of a larger, coordinated plot against the West. Some progress in collaboration and coordination is occurring, however. For example, in France, Germany, the Netherlands, Spain, and the United Kingdom police and intelligence officers regularly meet to share information wiretaps and video or satellite photos. Yet, counterterrorism agencies in Europe are still reluctant to share sensitive information or cooperate on prosecutions. Fragmentation and rivalry among the EU's security organizations continue to hamper counterterrorism efforts.

Source: Leiken 2005.

sis on Total Quality Management (TQM)—and provide e-learning (often as distance learning).

The FBI has employed state-of-the-art knowledge management technology for several years, and is now coordinating its antiterrorism investigation and enforcement activities with Homeland Security. The FBI's systems allow the agency to gather, organize, share, and analyze both structured and unstructured data (Schwartz 2003). FBI agents are able to use KM tools to make connections they might never have been able to make earlier. Agents can now access information from other open FBI cases that might be relevant to their own cases. In addition, the bureau has forged agreements and is working out standards for cooperating with the CIA, the DHS, and other intelligence-gathering agencies—a benefit that expands the possibilities for fighting terrorism.

One of the key concerns of the FBI and other agencies involved in counterterrorism activities is how to change the traditional culture of keeping tight control of all intelligence information. Secrecy has been a hallmark of the intelligence network since it was formed. Often critical pieces of information discovered in an investigation were not reported to other agents because a first analyst determined the data to be immaterial. As a result, later analysts were not able to include the bits of information in their take on the situation, thus missing knowledge that might have raised alerts. The FBI has moved to change that culture. Early in 2003, a bureau directive was circulated mandating that all information be shared unless an agent can justify why it should not be. In the past, all FBI case files were restricted to the agent on the case, making it impossible for other agents to know what they contained. Agents working on similar cases could not share information.

The next step in moving to a knowledge-sharing culture was moving information into the FBI's counterterrorism database, the Secure Collaborative Operational Prototype Environment for Counterterrorism (SCOPE). A variety of search engines and other knowledge management tools are used to access and share information in the database. Agents are now able to have all information relating to a case they are working on tagged and sent directly to them without additional searching.

Despite the accomplishments of the bureau and other agencies involved in the war on terrorism, significant challenges remain to be resolved. The biggest challenge still seems to be determining how to share data effectively so that safe, secure, efficient, and effective knowledge management is ensured. The FBI, the CIA, and the DHS must find ways to share knowledge internally, horizontally, and vertically—internally so that all their personnel have access to the information they need when they need it, horizontally with other intelligence agencies at the federal level and internationally, and vertically with state and local law enforcement groups and private-sector security organizations. That is where the systems, procedures, and tools of knowledge management are already helping the FBI and its sister agencies.

Conclusion

The federal government, with only few exceptions, appears to have adopted the knowledge management philosophy that emphasizes sharing of knowledge, and has implemented many of the processes, procedures, and tools developed for this still-evolving management initiative. State and local governments are still waiting to see whether KM will really provide enough of the performance improvements promised to warrant making the sometimes-substantial investment required.

The federal government's Chief Information Officer Council formed the first knowledge management working group early in 2000. As of 2004, the KMWG had grown to include membership from more than thirty different government organizations.

Among the federal agencies that have been leaders in adopting KM are the General Services Administration, the FAA, NASA, the Department of the Navy, and many others. The chapter also touched upon some of the difficulties agencies such as the Architect of the Capitol, the FBI, and the Department of Homeland Security have encountered in meeting their KM mandates. Later chapters will include in-depth KM application case histories of the experiences of some federal agencies.

10

The Public-Sector Chief Knowledge Officer

*The CKO is an administrator, a planner, and a marketer of the
[organization's] knowledge assets.*
(Wang, Hjelmervik, and Bremdal 2001, 28)

*The chief knowledge officer shall act as the systems owner for all data
and information warehouses, and shall provide assistance to all
knowledge workers in the sophisticated use of knowledge and
information tools.*
(Gaston 1997, 117)

*A still-controversial practice called knowledge management is winning
converts throughout federal agencies. Leading the movement is a
group of jump-up-out-of-your-seat evangelists known as chief
knowledge officers. Already, 13 agencies have added these CKOs or
some other knowledge management official to their hierarchies,
usually reporting to the chief information officer.*
(Harris 2001)

A number of uncertainties continue to plague the practice of knowledge
management (KM) in both the private and the public sectors. These uncertainties may be exercising a braking effect on more widespread adoption
of KM departments and functions. Among the more salient ambiguities is
lack of consensus on exactly what KM *is,* and *where* in an organization the
function should be located. Despite these still-unsolved difficulties, a consensus is emerging on the responsibilities and critical skills of the individual or individuals selected to guide its functioning in organizations. This
chapter examines the responsibility and governance question, and then reviews some of the agreed-upon skills and responsibilities of the public-sector KM manager.

Chapter Objectives

This chapter has been framed on a set of objectives designed to help readers become familiar with the history and development of the chief knowledge officer position in government, and to:

- Understand how and why KM has gained acceptance among government managers, administrators, and elected officials.
- Appreciate some of the operational characteristics that shape the activities of the CKO.
- Understand the duties and characteristics of a public-sector CKO.
- Recognize some of the challenges public-sector knowledge managers face.
- Learn that a professional certification program exists and what it entails.

Growing Acceptance for KM

Government managers, administrators, and knowledge users are rapidly discovering what KM can do to improve government products and processes. This information is being spread rapidly. In 2005, at least three and probably more KM conferences were held in Washington, D.C., and in other cities in North America. Many of these maintained free attendance for government workers. In addition, KM conferences are also being held in cities across Europe. One such conference, Knowledge Content-UK, included speakers from such organizations as the Bank of England, the Home Office, the British Council (a public organization that promotes the UK and UK products abroad), and others, together with representatives from a variety of industries. Although KM is now a widely understood concept in most high-level government agencies, it is still not widely adopted in state or local government organizations.

One of the reasons for this spotty application of KM is that not everyone agrees on what KM is or should be. Although it may be hard to believe, a universally accepted role for KM is still being forged. Mark McElroy, a founder and president of *Knowledge Management Consortium International,* sees this as an expected sign of the relative youth of the discipline, explaining it thus:

> One of the clear indicators of knowledge management's youth as a discipline is the extent to which its position in corporate [and government and nonprofit organization] structures can vary widely from one firm [organi-

zation] to another. Indeed, one of the more vexing problems for would-be knowledge managers is determining where to position themselves in the corporate [organizational] hierarchy. (McElroy 2003, 82)

Government administrators are increasingly cognizant of KM programs, but still have not come to an agreement on a definition of the function, let alone who in their organizations should lead the implementation and performance evaluation of the function. Illustrative of this lack of agreement on the content and scope of KM, what it can and should do, and who ought to be responsible for its implementation is the following question posed in the preface of a 2005 text on what the author believes is becoming a recognized discipline in organizational management:

> Why [should] anyone dare if we still don't have a globally accepted definition of KM; let alone universally accepted frameworks, principles, and best practices? Many executives and managers don't even know that KM exists, or that it is the solution to many issues concerning improving organizational efficiency, effectiveness, and innovation. (Stankosky 2005, ix)

Managing the KM Function

Although many public- and private-sector organization leaders have accepted the need and rationale for knowledge management activities, not everyone agrees where management of the function should fall in the organization. Addressing this issue, Professor Nick Bontis observed:

> We have a long way to go before we can be seen to be effectively managing our [organizational] knowledge, but the concept of knowledge management is here to stay. So too is the position of chief knowledge manager. (Bontis 2002, 25)

Emergence of the CKO Position

The position title of *chief knowledge officer* (CKO) appears to have surfaced as the preferred (although still not universally accepted) title for the person or persons who are charged with leadership of the function. However, many other titles are still extant. In government and nonprofit organizations, KM function leaders are still known by a wide variety of titles. To name a few: such diverse positions as chief information officer, chief learning officer, special advisor on learning and knowledge management, director of information services, knowledge management director, knowledge management technologies program manager, knowledge management and technology transfer director, and many others. One observer even reported seeing business cards of persons working in the KM field with the whimsical titles of "Idea Percolator" and "Imagination Evangelist" (Bontis 2002).

The CKO title may have been a logical extension or emulation of the already accepted organizational positions of chief executive officer (CEO), chief operating officer (COO), chief financial officer (CFO), and chief marketing officer (CMO). However, it is more likely an evolution of the chief information officer (CIO) position title that is common in information technology functions. An indication of the close connection that remains between knowledge managers and chief information officers can be seen in Box 10.1, a partial job description announcement for a CKO position at the U.S. General Services Administration (GSA).

Two additional KM position openings were announced by GSA in 2003: one for a *knowledge manager* and one for a *Web-based knowledge manager.* The role of the knowledge manager was to plan, develop, and "articulate Knowledge Management Policy, Programs and concepts to the GSA culture." The task of the Web-based knowledge manager was to conceptualize and execute "web-based Knowledge Management systems that are nationwide, GSA-wide, [and] business-specific in nature. [He or she] reviews market trends and technology changes and recommends specific functionality and appropriate technology investments to GSA top management, [and] provides Web-content through interconnections and relationships with research, academic, and business organizations" (Andre 2003).

Knowledge and the "Open Enterprise"

Mark McElroy (2003), a leader in the evolving KM discipline, cited an e-mail communication of Joseph M. Firestone regarding the KM leadership question in a discussion on what is needed to facilitate an "open enterprise." Firestone, another pioneer in development of the discipline, was quoted as describing a collective approach to the leadership question by proposing a joint chief knowledge officer/ombudsman position, with the ombudsman reporting directly to the board of directors and not to the management hierarchy (McElroy and Firestone 2003). McElroy found that, even in those organizations where management of knowledge is led by a person with the title of chief knowledge officer, actual oversight of the function still varies widely, ranging from the IT office to research and development (R&D), finance, or human resources. He took issue with each these alternatives, opting instead for a greater degree of autonomy in the organization (McElroy 2003, 88).

Box 10.1

**Excerpts from a Job Description for a
Chief Knowledge Officer at GSA**

Nature and Controls

The position of Chief Knowledge Officer is located in the immediate office of the Administrator of the General Services Administration and reports directly to the Administrator. A key leadership position, the CKO is one of four "Chiefs:" knowledge, information technology, human resources, and finance. The incumbent has a broad mandate to maximize GSA's intellectual capital, and manage knowledge to the benefit of its mission and employees.

Duties and Responsibilities

The incumbent is responsible for ensuring that GSA employees have the right information at the right time in the right place. Knowledge lives in people, while data and information reside in computers. The CKO provides the leadership required to successfully transform GSA into a learning organization that is flexible, agile, and open to change.

Working cooperatively with GSA's CFO, CPO, and CIO, the CKO builds collaborative work environments, infrastructure, resources, and skills to provide the necessary enterprise architecture for knowledge management within GSA.

The CKO: (1) serves as a chief advisor to the Administrator . . . on all matters pertaining to knowledge management, including identification of goals, strategy, tools, measurements, targets and project management; (2) develops program management structure to support GSA's major business lines and regional offices in selective pilot and demonstration projects related to knowledge management; (3) encourages, coaches, steers and directs, where necessary, these GSA initiatives to deliver positive and measurable results to the organization; (4) serves as a primary spokesperson within and out of the agency for GSA's knowledge management program; (5) represents GSA at conferences, forums, consortia and academic seminars, as well as to the print media; (6) identifies highly knowledgeable and skilled employees and ensures that they maximize these skills in their jobs and careers, providing guidance and encouragement.

Source: Andre 2003.

Box 10.2

Excerpts from a CKO Job Description for the Federal Energy Regulatory Commission (FERC)

Chief Knowledge Officer (Information Technology)

Major Duties

The chief knowledge officer (CKO) will oversee a new function, the Office of Knowledge Management and Integration, under the chief information officer. The CKO, breaking new ground in embracing the new, evolving knowledge management concept, is responsible for managing and overseeing the FERC knowledge management and technology resources in a manner consistent with the FERC missions and program objectives. The CKO ensures the management of knowledge and information assets enterprise-wide to improve decision-making processes.

Knowledge management includes all actions to ensure collection, storage, distribution, integration, and application of knowledge within an organization. In order for the FERC to evolve into a knowledge-based organization, the CKO must effectively manage its intellectual capital (knowledge) and information and records assets.

The CKO must ensure timely and accurate information to the staff and the public. This requires designing and implementing the FERC knowledge management architecture to support multiple roles and missions.

(continued)

An example of the IT connection is the position title found in the Federal Energy Regulatory Commission's announcement of a new CKO position (Box 10.2).

McElroy (2003, 82) described what he saw as a "clear distinction" between the roles of a chief information officer (CIO) and a chief knowledge officer (CKO). This distinction is not universally recognized, however. In agencies where KM is under the direction of a CIO, the organization tends to see KM as an application of information technology (IT). The CIO literature appears to be supporting his position, as McElroy noted: "This approach accounts for the fact that many IT trade publications, such as *CIO* magazine, have embraced KM as *one of their*

Box 10.2 *(continued)*

The CKO is responsible for ensuring effective knowledge collection and transfer of corporate knowledge and information assets to achieve gains in human performance and competitiveness. The CKO must promote electronic filing and electronic issuance, and make information readily available at the source versus submission of forms, and the establishment of standards for industry. This includes the responsibility for overseeing the overall planning, direction, and timely execution of the knowledge management program. In fulfilling this responsibility, the CKO role must include the acquisition of appropriate information and technology resources to enhance the ability of the workforce to gather knowledge-based information to perform missions more efficiently and effectively.

Qualifications

• Ability to manage knowledge, corporate strategies, and technology for leveraging intellectual capital and know-how to achieve gains in human performance and competitiveness.
• Ability to formulate and implement knowledge management policy initiatives, and to direct an organization in the accomplishment of short- and long-term objectives.

Source: FERC 2005.

own, and now routinely treat it as though KM is nothing more than the latest rage in IT."

Another example of the connection between IT and knowledge management in government can be found in the listing of the responsibilities of a public-sector CIO in the U.S. Air Force's 2005 appointment of a new CIO. The new CIO was to hold the newly established title of "office of the secretary of the Air Force, chief warfighting integration and chief information officer." According to the appointment announcement, the office would bring all IT policy formulation, execution, and resources, and workforce governance activities, under a single organization. The new organization consolidates the offices of communications operations, chief information officer, and deputy chief of staff for warfighting integration (Tiboni 2005).

Practices Shaping the CKO Role

Laurence Prusak, one of the pioneers of modern knowledge management, identified three organizational practices that have brought most of the content and energy to knowledge management (Prusak 1997). These are information management, the quality movement, and the human resources and human capital movement.

Information Management

This movement evolved during the decades of the 1970s and 1980s as a synthesis of the broader fields of information technology and information science. Information management refers to the activities and management theories that focused on how information in organizations is managed, independent of the technologies involved in collecting, storing, and processing the information. In a word, it was more concerned with the *social* side of communication. Information is studied to determine how it is valued in an organization, the operational processes involved in dealing with information, control and governance of the function, and the rewards and incentives associated with its management.

This aspect of the greater responsibilities of the CKO requires a focus on the values that knowledge users place on information—that is, their satisfaction with the availability and receipt of information—rather than on improving the efficiency of the technology that stores and delivers the information to users. Information management and knowledge management are concerned with the *quality* of the information, and how much it benefits its users.

The Total Quality Management (TQM) Movement

Developed from initiatives to improve manufactured products—promoted to its zenith in post–World War II Japanese industry—the TQM movement in government focused on improving the delivery of products and services to internal "customers" as well as external clients. The movement evolved from what some perceived as a one-time effort to instead become a constant process of continuous product (or process) improvement (CPI).

Knowledge management owes a large debt to the CPI process, although with a much broader scope. Instead of focusing on the product or service delivered, KM and the CKO are involved in applying lessons learned and best practices to improving everything the agency does. The knowledge officer is involved with helping to facilitate a valuing of information and knowledge not for itself, but for what it can do when shared and combined. A quality perspective results in improving products and services; knowledge management results in innovation in products, processes, procedures, and services. Moreover, knowledge management has the power to assist the agency toward becoming a learning organization.

The Human Capital Concept

Human capital refers to the management processes of empowering workers and valuing their knowledge, experiences, and abilities to create and innovate. The knowledge management philosophy looks upon workers as assets rather than expenses. Organizations gain benefits far greater than the costs involved in making investments in their people; these investments are usually in the form of training and development programs. On this basis, one of the most important responsibilities of the CKO is collecting the stories of employees' past successes and failures and making that collected knowledge available to other government agency workers. The community of practice developed by U.S. Army company commanders is an excellent example of the value of this KM activity.

The next section outlines some of the chief functions of public-sector chief knowledge officers—regardless of their actual title—and includes several case examples of evolving government CKO positions. The cases represent KM developments in the U.S military, one of the branches of the federal government to more fully integrate knowledge management programs and policies into their operating systems.

Functions of the Public-Sector CKO

If some voids in the framing of the KM function still remain, it is no wonder that establishing the focus of leadership and responsibility for the person charged with carrying out the function is still somewhat fuzzy. However, steps are being taken to rectify this state of affairs. Beginning in 2000, a group of public-sector KM practitioners and vendors (providers of hardware, software, and related services) came together to chart some preliminary steps in the path toward consensus on what it is that knowledge managers do and how to hold them accountable for their actions. Calling themselves the Federal Government KM Working Group, they met in a series of brainstorming sessions to define and frame KM applications in government organizations. The sessions were held at the Information Resources Management College of the National Defense University.

A key product of those early sessions was an outline of the fundamental roles, skills, knowledge and intellectual capacities, and performance responsibilities of the typical public-sector knowledge officer. To be successful in the role of knowledge manager, a public-sector CKO has to exercise competency in the following management processes: leadership and management, communications, strategic thinking, IT tools and technologies, personal behaviors, and personal knowledge and cognitive capabilities (intelligence).

Illustrative of the tasks typically assigned to the public-sector CIO are those described in 2005 for the newly appointed information officer for the U.S. Air Force, Lieutenant General William T. Hobbins (Tiboni 2005). General Hobbins was the first director of a newly reorganized office that combined the offices of communications operations, chief information officer, and deputy chief of staff for warfighting integration. In his new position General Hobbins became responsible for all of the Air Force's IT policy determination, execution of IT policy, and resource and workforce governance.

The Federal Working Group also emphasized that a government chief information officer (CIO) is not the same thing as a public-sector chief knowledge officer (CKO). The government CIO is typically focused on management of the organization's physical computer and network assets. The CKO, on the other hand, is more likely to be concerned with a complex set of activities that reflect *human behaviors* in organizations. These include, but are not limited to, such actions as work processes, reward systems, knowledge collecting and sharing, information dissemination, and similar social actions. Accordingly, the work of the public-sector CKO was seen as involving the following primary activities:

- Participating in forging and implementing a knowledge management strategy.
- Developing leadership skills in managers and workers.
- Determining best practices and/or processes within and without the organization.
- Fostering a knowledge-sharing culture among individuals, groups and teams, and the organization as a whole.
- Identifying and promoting establishment of *communities of interest* and *communities of practice* within and without the organization.
- Recommending and administering rewards and other incentives for knowledge sharing, innovation and creativity, and learning within the organization.
- Specifying ICT tools and related technologies to leverage the existing intellectual base in the organization.
- Identifying and rationalizing taxonomies (classification schemes) of organization information.
- Managing the organization's education, information, and communication technology resources.

The KM Working Group summarized its recommended skills, knowledge, and abilities of a public-sector knowledge officer by stating that the function of the chief knowledge officer is first to create and maintain an environment and atmosphere within which all workers deliver value to the organization. (Adding value occurs with the collection and application of existing and unexploited explicit and tacit knowledge resources.) Second, CKOs must be engaged in identifying, charting, and discovering connections and networks in organizational and information processes, classification schemes, and tools to access and use existing data, information, and explicit and tacit knowledge in a manner that promotes sharing across time, space, and boundaries (FKMWG 2000).

Stephen J. Gaston (1997, 128), a former PricewaterhouseCoopers management consultant, identified these eight activities and responsibilities for a chief knowledge officer:

- Maintains a repository defining the location and meaning of the organization's data, information, and knowledge.
- Provides advice to others on the available data, information, and knowledge.
- Defines and communicates availability and instructions on the organization's information and knowledge tools.
- Assists others in the uses of advanced information and knowledge tools.
- Assesses how data may be obtained, stored, and accessed in the most effective and efficient way.
- Keeps abreast of information and communications technology as they relate to information and knowledge tools.
- Works with the chief information officer to define and maintain the organization's enterprise architecture as it relates to sharing of data, information, and knowledge, and the nature and availability of knowledge tools.
- Acts as a "systems owner" for all data and information warehouses.

Characteristics of a Public-sector CKO

A research team led by Michael J. Earl and Ian Scott (1999) conducted a series of in-depth interviews with chief knowledge managers in North America and Europe to determine which common characteristics, if any, are held by CKOs. Earl and Scott found that the KM managers had at least two chief characteristics in common: First, they were all highly knowledgeable in information and communications technology. Second, they also exhibited strong organizational environment skills and awareness. Their technical knowledge included understanding what information and communications technologies (ICTs) were needed in their organizations to capture, store, manage, organize and interpret, and, in particular, share knowledge within and without the organization. Anecdotally, they also found that most of the CKOs in the study were firmly entrenched in the ICT operations of their organizations. The organizational skills may be grouped into the more recognizable category of "people skills." The following statement by one of the respondents adds further clarification to the concept:

> Unless I can persuade people [in the organization] that knowledge management is not just for the benefit of other people, I haven't got much hope of persuading them to buy into it. They have to believe there's something in it for them and that I care about that as much as they do. Otherwise it just comes across as the latest form of cynical manipulation. (Earl and Scott 1999, 4)

A common thread found to exist across the sample of CKOs was a mix of activities that could be grouped together under the category of "conceptual design." This included designing knowledge directories (who in the organization knows what and where to find them), knowledge-intensive business and management practices, and events where knowledge exchanges can occur. In addition, CKOs were involved in the design of physical spaces to facilitate knowledge sharing (such as "in-house coffee shops" and the like). Finally, CKOs also designed methods, policies, and processes for knowledge protection.

According to Stankosky (2005), a general consensus exists on what should be considered the fundamental tenets of KM. He added that, despite the confusion that remains in many areas of the concept, widespread agreement has emerged on most of the basic principles of KM. He identified the following four fundamental principles as forming the core of all knowledge management applications and, therefore, necessary characteristics for holders of the CKO position: *leadership,* which must frame organizational culture, vision, strategic planning, and communication; *organization,* which involves the forming of such operational aspects as which functions, processes, procedures, and formal and informal structures are best for the organization; *technology,* which, of course, means the information and communication technologies (ICTs) that make knowledge sharing possible in organizations, including such tools as e-mail, data warehousing, search engines, content management programs, and similar technological functions, hardware, and programs; and *learning,* which includes such behavioral aspects of operations as innovation, creativity, invention, teams, shared information and results, exchange forums, and other activities. Stankosky added that subsequent developments in the discipline, including a growing list of published professional and academic literature, suggest that these four pillars of the discipline have been accepted as the basis upon which all KM programs must be established.

Activities of Knowledge Managers

In a study of a mixed bag of forty-one industrial, service, and service-sector KM-function managers from the United States, Canada, Europe, and Asia, McKeen and Staples (2001) identified nine key KM activities carried out by the respondents:

- Creating and managing an intranet
- Creating knowledge repositories
- Establishing and managing a data warehouse
- Creating internal networks of knowledge workers in communities of interest (CoIs) and/or communities of practice (CoPs)
- Implementing groupware to support collaborations
- Mapping sources of knowledge and expertise in the organization
- Launching new knowledge-based products or services
- Establishing new knowledge roles
- Implementing decision-support tools

Of these nine key activities, the most commonly cited activity was creating and managing an intranet (more than 90 percent), followed by creating knowledge repositories and data warehousing (80 percent each), and creating internal networks (nearly 70 percent).

The 1999 Earl and Scott findings were generally replicated by Bontis in a 2002 study of more than twenty-five international CKOs. Bontis determined that the two most common characteristics of the international sample were: (1) an understanding of the technologies that contribute to the capture, storage, and sharing of knowledge, and (2) skills and knowledge in human resource management that gave them an ability to understand social network behavior in their organizations.

Key Challenges Facing the CKO

A number of authors have identified a variety of issues and concerns that CKOs reported as among the chief challenges they faced (Wiig 1994; Duffy 1998; Ruggles 1998; McKeen and Staples 2001).

Wiig identified the "central challenge" as determining how to effectively create, build, and leverage knowledge of both the individual employee and the entire organization. A second challenge was how to establish a way to include the best possible knowledge in creating and managing products and services in ways that provide the greatest possible value to customers, clients, and other stakeholders.

Duffy (1998) reported the results of an earlier study of fifty-two CKOs in which the following challenges were discussed:

- Setting knowledge management strategic priorities
- Establishing a knowledge database of best practices
- Gaining the commitment of senior executives to support a learning environment
- Teaching seekers of information/knowledge how to ask better and smarter questions of their knowledge resources
- Putting in place a process for managing intellectual assets
- Obtaining customer satisfaction information in near real time
- Globalizing knowledge management

Ruggles found that CKOs considered these three activities to be their greatest challenges: (1) changing people's behavior (to value and share knowledge); (2) measuring the value and performance of the organizations' knowledge assets; and (3) determining which knowledge needs to be managed.

McKeen and Staples found that little had changed over the three years since the completion of the Ruggles study. Using a five-point scale ranging from *Not a Problem* (1) to *A Severe Problem* (5), McKeen and Staples found changing people's behavior to still be the CKOs' greatest challenge. This was followed by measuring the value and performance of knowledge assets; justifying the use of scarce resources; mapping existing organization knowledge; attracting and retaining talented people; and determining what knowledge should be managed.

Government-Approved KM Certification

In December of 2000, the Federal KM Working Group (FKMWG) invited industry and academic institutions to join them in developing a list of the most important skills and knowledge needed for a government-approved KM certification program (Faget 2004). The group identified fourteen learning objectives important for KM certification. These objectives covered necessary competencies, ways to facilitate the flow of information, and tools needed for implementation of KM programs in the government sector. Although they were developed specifically for the federal government, they can be seen to apply equally to both state and local government as well. The fourteen objectives, published as a "candidate list" of learning objectives for a KM certification program, are as follows (Fagot 2004):

1. Knowledge of the value added by knowledge management to the [organizational purpose], including the return on investment, performance measures, and the ability to develop a business case.

2. Knowledge of the strategies and processes to transfer explicit and tacit knowledge across time, space, and organizational boundaries, including retrieval of critical archived information enabling ideas to build upon ideas.

3. Knowledge of state-of-the-art and evolving technology solutions that promote KM, including portals and collaborative and distributed learning objectives.

4. Knowledge of and the ability to facilitate knowledge creation, sharing, and reuse including developing partnerships and alliances, designing creative knowledge spaces, and using incentives structures.

5. Knowledge of learning styles and behaviors, striving for continuous improvement, and being actively engaged in exploring new ideas and concepts.

6. Working knowledge of state-of-the-art research and implementation strategies for knowledge management, information management, document and records management, and data management. This includes project management of knowledge initiatives and retrieval of critical archived information.

7. Understanding of the global and economic importance of developing knowledge-based organizations to meet the challenges of the knowledge area.

8. Ability to use systems thinking in implementing solutions.

9. The ability to design, develop, and sustain communities of interest and practice.

10. The ability to create, develop, and sustain the flow of knowledge. This includes understanding the skills needed to leverage virtual teamwork and social networks.

11. The ability to perform cultural and ethnographic analyses, develop knowledge taxonomies, facilitate knowledge audits, and perform knowledge mapping and needs assessments.

12. The ability to capture, evaluate, and use best-known practices, including the use of storytelling to transfer these best practices.

13. The ability to manage change and complex knowledge projects.
14. The ability to identify customers and stakeholders and tie organizational goals to the needs and requirements of those customers and stakeholders.

Examples of Public-Sector CKO Positions

CKOs in government and in business and industry clearly have similar responsibilities and skills. However, the political dimension of government results in a difference in focus for the public-sector CKO, who is not influenced by bottom-line constraints. The following examples of federal CKO activities illustrate these differences.

The U.S. Defense Department CKO

In 2003, the Department of Defense (DoD) published a detailed, seven-page description for a support position for the newly established office of the director of knowledge management: a *computer specialist (knowledge management)*. The person hired for the new position was required to have the qualifications described in Box 10.3. The U.S. Defense Information Systems Agency (DISA) locates its knowledge management close to the IT function. A 2003 job description for an information technology specialist placed the position in the office of the chief transformation executive (CTE), Knowledge Management Office. The role of the specialist is to "develop and manage an integrated approach for capturing, sharing, and reusing enterprise information and intellectual assets, including the development of KM policies" (Andre 2003).

It is interesting to note that this announcement signals an as yet little-spoken-about power of knowledge management: the ability of both terrorists and our own military to use information technology and knowledge management to wage cyber warfare—and the military's efforts to protect against such terrorist activity. A primary role of the specialist was to provide information and knowledge program management and senior staff–level support for the Command, Control, Communications and Intelligence (C3I) of the Secretary of Defense.

The objective identified for the new office was to "improve the organizational environment for valuing, generating, sharing and applying knowledge." A typical C3I activity is management of the Information Warfare (IW) program. The DoD has issued the following unclassified definition of IW:

> [IW includes all] actions taken to achieve information superiority by affecting adversary information, and information systems, while defending

---

Box 10.3

Required Qualifications for a DoD KM Specialist

• Broad and expert knowledge of planning, conducting, and directing Knowledge Management efforts. In-depth knowledge of DoD policies, processes, and procedures related to KM and related disciplines and technologies.

• Expert skills in working closely with high ranking officials (Assistant Secretaries, flag officers, Pentagon officials, Joint Chiefs, OMB, White House officials, etc.) in order to gain support for and evolve the KM program through shared resources, techniques, and partnerships.

• Expert knowledge of federal and DoD contracting to manage large KM, and related technological projects for KM.

• In-depth and current understanding of planned KM trends, standards, approaches, and tools.

• Expert skills in project management to be applied to large, critical, and complex DoD systems.

• In-depth and expert understanding of the trends and characteristics of the industrial base that supports KM and information systems.

• Expert writing skills to justify and acquire resources to accomplish projects. Expert marketing and strategic planning skills to accomplish Departmental technology transfer. Skills in writing business/ process documentation, developing models and graphics, and making oral presentations to senior DoD officials, conferences, and task forces. Expertise in facilitation or high-level group analytic sessions to include skills in resolving conflicts and achieving consensus.

Source: U.S. DOD 2003.

---

one's own information, information-based process, and information systems. (Fredericks 2002)

The CKO in the U.S. Navy

The U.S. Navy has identified knowledge management as a distinct career path for civilian staff, with eleven different job positions. The navy prefaced a description of the position titles with this broad definition:

> The Knowledge Management Career Area involves creating a knowledge-centric organization. This is accomplished by providing the right informa-

tion to the right decision maker at the right time, thus creating the right conditions for knowledge to be created. Employees in this new and evolving career area possess a commitment to put information to work for the Department of the Navy enterprise. (Knox 2005)

Job titles and brief descriptions for the eleven positions included in the announcement are included here because of their general applicability across all public-sector agencies considering adopting a KM initiative. The positions, as defined by the KM.gov paper, are as follows:

Chief Knowledge Officer (CKO): Manages the knowledge-sharing process at the command level; leads efforts to move the organization to knowledge centricity; requires a dedication to KM principles, the ability to discuss the benefits of knowledge sharing, and the vision to ensure that KM initiatives are adopted by the organization . . . fosters cultural change, defines roles, skill sets and opportunities for knowledge workers, and facilitates training and education of knowledge workers.

Knowledge Manager (KM): Working with the CKO to implement KM initiatives; manages KM efforts. Looking across KM processes to capture tacit and explicit knowledge and often involves balancing technology, information, processes, and individual and organizational learning within a culture of shared values.

Knowledge System Engineer (KSE): This involves turning KM ideas into workable solutions by engineering appropriate knowledge-sharing Internet/intranet sites, rules-based systems, portals, databases, etc. Requires intimate knowledge of the systems, architectures, technologies, standards, and protocols for KM.

Knowledge Process Manager (KPM): This position involves focusing on the organizational processes of KM and content integration; manages the efforts of the knowledge transfer engineer, knowledge research engineer, and knowledge life-cycle engineer. Develops process models for optimal organizational effectiveness.

Knowledge Transfer Engineer (KTE): Involves capturing and codifying tacit knowledge, making it available for reuse. Connects people to enable the transfer of tacit knowledge to explicit knowledge.

Knowledge Research Engineer (KRE): Involves making explicit knowledge from available resources and integrating content in KM systems into easily accessible knowledge for decision makers.

Knowledge Life-Cycle Engineer (KLE): Ensures information for knowledge systems is current, appropriate, and changed as needed; handles information creation and disposal for the organization.

Knowledge Community Leader (KCL): Facilitates the operation of communities of practice across organizations to foster innovation, improved performance, and collaboration.

Intellectual Capital Manager (ICM): Develops the workforce and ensures the human capital aspects of KM are fully integrated. The ICM uses KM to increase the performance and the learning of the organization and identifies gaps in KM competencies.

Performance Measurement Engineer (PME): Focuses on measuring and assessing the knowledge-centric organization model implementation and architecture. The PME performs analysis, develops predictive models, shows the potential impact of change, and provides implications for validation of the knowledge-centric organization model.

Knowledge Assurance Manager (KAM): Ensures the assimilation of information and knowledge is protected from unauthorized access and/or disclosure.

Conclusion

Many public- and private-sector organization leaders have accepted the need and rationale for knowledge management activities. However, not all agree where management of the function should fall in the organization. The position title of *chief knowledge officer* (CKO) is the person charged with leadership of the function, although many other titles still exist, including chief information officer, chief learning officer, special advisor on learning and knowledge management, director of information services, knowledge management director, knowledge management technologies program manager, knowledge management and technology transfer director, and others.

Three of the management practices that have contributed the most toward the development of the knowledge management discipline and to the shaping of the CKO position are the information management concept, the product/service quality movement, and the growing awareness of the value to an organization represented in its human capital.

The government chief information officer (CIO) has different responsibilities than the public-sector chief knowledge officer (CKO). The CIO focuses on management of the organization's physical computer and network assets, while the CKO is more likely to be concerned with a complex set of activities that reflect *human behaviors* in organizations, including but are not limited to, such actions as work processes, reward systems, knowledge collecting and sharing, information dissemination, and similar social actions.

Part 4

Stories of Public-Sector KM in Action

11

Knowledge Management at NASA

Edward Hoffman, Jon Boyle, and Anthony J. Maturo

NASA has always made program and project management a central tenet of its approach to completing complex, multifaceted, and highly technical missions. Borrowing concepts of program/project management from the military in the late 1950s, NASA recognized that having an effective project management workforce was critical to the undertakings of the agency (NASA 1994). From the agency's beginning, project managers were tapped to direct the day-to-day work on NASA's missions and were responsible for overall mission success. Although most of NASA's first project managers were scientists, NASA began placing engineers in these positions on many of the earliest missions (Naugle 1991).

The early years of NASA witnessed the rapid evolution of a variety of systems and techniques for directing the combined efforts of thousands of individuals cooperating in close-knit programs in which government, universities, and private industry played mutually reinforcing roles. Many of the major learning experiences gained from NASA's earliest missions, such as the Apollo management system, were subsequently applied to the next generation of projects (NASA 1994). At the same time, with the success of the Apollo program and its unmanned mission precursors, it became recognized outside the agency that one of the valuable byproducts of the U. S. space program was the body of knowledge concerning management of large, complex development project activities (Kloman 1972).

Although the commitment to project management was clear from the agency's beginning, program administrators discovered early on the difficulty in determining how managers could best be selected, trained, and rotated (Kloman 1972). Compounding this problem was an inability to identify qualifications that distinguished the ideal candidate for project management assignments from other types of managers. In 1970, NASA commissioned the National Academy of Public Administration (NAPA) to study ways to improve and refine the agency's project management techniques. After extensive research and interviews, however, the study found no scientific basis for drawing conclusions on the kinds of personal characteristics, skills, or management styles that best lend themselves to the responsibilities of being a program or project manager (Chapman, Pontious, and Lewis 1971).

In practice, NASA's project managers have always been differentiated from those in other management positions in the agency. First, these individuals have typically been engineers or technicians with no formal background or training in management. Second, their roles have primarily been involved with guiding cost, scheduling, and technical aspects of an engineering project with a definite beginning and end. Finally, these individuals have not been directly involved, as an engineering manager would be, in directing the day-to-day technical decisions about design, development, and testing of engineering systems, nor have they been responsible for a functional area that provides an ongoing product or service, such as marketing, accounting, or manufacturing (Duarte et al. 1995).

Preparation of project managers has been a conscious undertaking throughout NASA's history. For much of its early history, NASA had a tradition of using individual managers as the "conduit" for the transfer of project management learning experience. Writing about the history of project management on the Surveyor and Lunar Orbiter missions, Kloman (1972) pointed out that:

> Although each manager setting out on a new task may view his assignment as a completely new departure, he is actually part of a continuum. Just as he brings to his task his own past knowledge and experience, so his colleagues bring theirs. The successful project manager is one who is able to provide the kind of leadership that effectively taps this experience, focusing a common effort upon common goals through a progression of commonly accepted intermediary steps.

NASA successfully continued to rely on this tradition of preparing project managers for many years by transferring "lessons learned" from manager to manager, and using on-the-job experiences supplemented with targeted training for specific skills. However, mission failures beginning in 1988 doomed this effective but inefficient transfer of knowledge. In addition, national attitudes were working against NASA as a result of a series of failures that followed the Apollo program.

Outside of NASA, the idea of more and bigger government was an unpopular alternative for most people since the country's collective loss of innocence resulting from events such as the Vietnam War and Watergate. Some came to the conclusion that government cannot provide all of the answers, and additionally it cannot be trusted. This was developing as a worldwide phenomenon. The worldwide public-sector expansion occurring after the end of World War II was accompanied by many international reform movements as a result of poor service delivery and other economic difficulties.

In the United States, Congress and the executive branches were taking steps to fundamentally change government work. Departments and agencies shifted to a focus on results, and were operating like businesses. Budget pressures, political realities, technological advances, and shifting priorities forced government organizations to change as rapidly as private-sector organizations in order to meet their mandates and responsibilities to the country. Out of this environment of change and technological advances grew the conceptual framework of knowledge management (KM).

The National Aeronautics and Space Administration (NASA) has attempted to instill effective KM practices through the NASA Academy of Program and Project Leadership (APPL) and its various incarnations since the late 1980s. The following narrative provides an appreciation of one part of NASA's KM effort and the continuing impact of this particular brand of KM on the organization, stimulating consideration of how organizations evolve in the use of knowledge to foster innovation, creativity, and performance in a federal government environment.

The First Generation of NASA Knowledge Management

In 1988, the *Challenger* tragedy was a watershed event for NASA. Enormous energy and thought went into understanding what went wrong and how to repair the NASA legacy of project excellence. There were numerous Tiger Teams (special interdisciplinary teams of experts convened to sove a specific problem), commissions, and boards originated with the single task of improving NASA project management. Out of this climate of introspection and commitment was conceived the notion of the Program and Project Management Improvement (PPMI) program, the precursor of NASA APPL. The initiative was sponsored by then deputy administrator J.R. Thompson, who assigned a training budget to this effort.

One full-time civil service employee, Dr. Ed Hoffman, was assigned to change the way NASA project managers were developed. On top of that, Hoffman was an anomaly at NASA, possessing a PhD in organizational development in an organization that valued engineering and technical excellence above all else. But Hoffman was smart enough to see that NASA was a project-based organization, and that anything that had to do with creating and sharing knowledge across projects would provide a huge benefit to the organization.

The mission of the original PPMI effort was articulated as promoting project management excellence and competency in advance of NASA's need through training and development services. Any early observer of PPMI would see a traditional training and development office. Managing knowledge and using it to increase performance was still years away, and would not have survived without a strong career-development infrastructure first being in place. Therefore, the early years of PPMI were focused on establishing a robust and relevant curriculum of courses, defining and providing a baseline of knowledge and competence that would better prepare a future generation of NASA project professionals.

Hoffman planted the seeds of KM early on with the adoption of a strategy that training would represent only a fraction of the performance equation, no more than 10 percent of the preparation necessary for producing a successful generation of project professionals. The remainder of the performance equation was represented by real professional experience in NASA projects and a reliance on the knowledge of a previous generation of project talent who would serve as mentors, coaches, and expert guides. Unbeknownst to NASA overall at the time, but intentionally created by Hoffman, the foundation for understanding and better managing explicit and tacit knowledge had been created.

PPMI's goal was to provide sound fundamental skills. These fundamentals would then be developed and further sculpted through years of incrementally more challenging assignments at NASA field center locations. Overall engineering capability would be nurtured through progressive learning on increasingly challenging work with an abundance of experienced mentors ready and willing to offer any necessary guidance, tips, and encouragement. This was reflected through policy documents such as the first program plan for the PPMI:

> The primary mission of the PPMI effort is to develop NASA personnel through a number of parallel activities: developing and delivering formal classroom and on the job training, capturing and disseminating past Agency experiences, studies focused on current and future technical management requirements and skills and the documentation and communication of current and new program and project management methods.[1]

For Hoffman, such a mission was well conceived for the organizational setting at the time. NASA in 1990 was still a traditional leader in managing large, expensive, long-duration programs and projects. The history of Apollo,

Shuttle, Viking, and the Hubble Space Telescope offered technologically challenging programs that allowed a natural progression of learning in a more deliberate and hierarchical context. It was also personality dependent, with project managers building their reputations on smaller projects as they moved up the chain and were increasingly recognized by their peers. It was at this higher level of experienced practitioners that Hoffman recognized the need to leverage and transfer knowledge effectively and efficiently through some type of sharing mechanism.

In terms of anything beyond training, the initial PPMI career development efforts were necessarily limited in scope to traditional training approaches, reflecting the status of adult learning theory and technology at the time. PPMI provided a sound foundation for progressive preparation of project management capability, while individuals could expect the time to learn and fine-tune expertise in a work setting loaded with experienced professionals. In an environment of a few very large programs, with an abundance of project expertise cultivated through the challenges of Apollo and Shuttle, such a strategy was both logical and desirable. However, there was little sense in wasting effort in sharing of knowledge across the organization since NASA centers often viewed themselves as in competition with each other for dwindling resources. KM activities were thus limited in scope to noninstitutional individual successes within programs and projects.

The Second Generation of NASA Knowledge Management

A new era of revitalization started in 1992 with the appointment of Dan Goldin as the new NASA administrator. Immediately upon taking leadership of NASA, Goldin initiated a dramatic remodeling of NASA program and project management adjusted to the political and budget realities of the time, emanating from the broader context of government reform efforts attempting to increase the efficiency and effectiveness of government organizations in their delivery of products and services to the public.

The era of managing projects in a faster, better, and cheaper (FBC) framework was established, doing more with less, greatly increasing the volume of project work, and doing it in a way that emphasized safety, innovation, low cost, speed, and quality. Such a demanding vision with seemingly inherent conflicts dramatically altered the nature of both project management and the way talent needed to be developed within the agency. The unspoken corollary to this type of management approach was that the raw material of knowledge, critical to innovation and better decision making, needed to move faster, better, and cheaper across the agency as well.

Goldin appointed a Program Excellence Team (PET) to strengthen and streamline the policies and processes governing the management of our major system development projects and to issue a single comprehensive policy document to combine its program and acquisition management procedures. In essence, this team discovered ways to shorten and improve project management. The team was working in an environment where the *average time* from authorization to actual launch was about eight years, and the typical program cost and schedule overruns averaged a growth of over 60 percent from commitment estimates.

The PET cited eight major factors that drove NASA program cost and technical risk:

- Inadequate Phase B (formulation) requirements definition
- Unrealistic dependence on unproven technology
- Annual funding instability
- Complex organizational structures, including multiple/unclear interfaces
- Cost estimates that are often misused
- Scope additions due to "requirements creep"
- Schedule slips
- Acquisition strategy that does not promote cost containment

These factors were further aggravated by the fact that they did not represent anything that was not already understood. The organization possessed this knowledge, but did not realize it or did not possess the political willpower to solve the issues. In fact, over thirty previous NASA studies and working groups during the previous twenty years had consistently identified these factors as a drag on effective, efficient project management. This led to the establishment of the NASA Program Management Council (PMC) and Program Management Council Working Group (PMCWG), initiating the first critical task of forming a project management policy and guidelines document that would promote "faster, better, and cheaper" (FBC) projects. This was a problem tailor-made for KM to address, a strategic issue that could be focused on by providing existing organizational knowledge to decision makers at the right time and the right place.

Up to this time, the PPMI had been fundamentally a curriculum-driven entity, carrying on through the charter originally established subsequent to the *Challenger* mishap. The purpose was to identify workforce topics (e.g., project management, cost estimating, requirements definition, and systems engineering) and to design, develop, and implement training programs that would correct deficiencies in these identified areas. This led to a human resource development culture that emphasized curriculum, but without metrics toward performance and outcome success.

With the arrival of Goldin, it became increasingly clear to Hoffman that PPMI required significant modification. It was no longer reasonable to generate courses without a clear link to mission success and requirements. Therefore, he initiated a major effort to identify the core competencies required for success at different stages of a career, with the idea that senior-level employees required the capability to share knowledge as they progressed in the organization. Competency-driven project management development was inaugurated.

This approach centered on a formal career development strategy (eventually called the NASA Project Management Development Process, or PMDP) that was intended to link critical project competencies to NASA-sanctioned learning and education. This systematic analysis made it possible to match curriculum content to organizational customer requirements. It also created the first possibility to tie mission success to the transfer of learning which, in turn, made it possible to tie human resource requirements directly to mission success. It introduced the building blocks of KM to the agency, using the concepts of competencies, capability, knowledge sharing, expertise, innovation, creative and critical thinking, and information technology (IT) tools to enable organizational implementation of KM fundamentals. In this way, knowledge management was infused in NASA through identified standards of behavior described by competencies and performance capabilities. As Holtzman (1999) points out, "by establishing proven and accepted standards today, project management professionals can be better prepared for the challenges of the future."

As a result of this fundamental shift in thinking, Hoffman initiated several changes. There was an increased emphasis on career development, curriculum certification, benchmarking, and research, and a greater emphasis on job aids and tools. These represented a natural extension of the learning environment and also represented significant advances in adult learning theory, educational technology, and IT. While NASA was undergoing dramatic change, there would be a continuous demand to upgrade PPMI services and products. Once personnel started to consider the competencies necessary to increase project management capability, this would lead to requests for new courses, certification of learning and competency, online computer support, and intact-project team performance support. During these years, the groundwork would be laid for a significantly broader and different developmental organization than originally envisioned. In addition, assessment and certification began to be discussed more frequently as budget pressures grew. Crawford (1999) makes the case that assessment links learning outcomes with learning objectives in a meaningful way.

With this new set of issues and challenges, Hoffman quickly realized that he needed more help, fast. He recruited Dr. Jon Boyle, an expert in human development from the private sector, and Mr. Anthony Maturo, a highly talented NASA training and development and budget expert at NASA Langley, to help to achieve the new organizational strategy. Boyle possessed deep experience in KM across the public and private sectors, and taught KM at the Virginia Tech graduate program in human development. Maturo also had extensive education and training experience, and knew the NASA culture and budget structure intimately.

The transition from a NASA "initiative" to a formal training "academy" was promoted by Administrator Goldin as part of an effort to cultivate program and project managers who could adapt to the new project environment with a significantly different mind-set and methodology. In 1999, the PPMI became formally known as the NASA Academy of Program and Project Leadership (APPL). The purpose of APPL was to provide total team and individual professional development support through training, developmental activities, and tools for the organizational benefit of developing and maintaining "world-class" practitioners of project management in advance of NASA's requirements. The mission of APPL shifted to providing outstanding and continually improving developmental activities and support for individuals and teams that accomplish NASA's programs and projects through career development activities and tools, performance enhancement projects, knowledge-sharing communities of practice, and cutting-edge research and development. KM had now become institutionalized in the mission of the organization as well as being defined as a critical competency and performance capability.

The importance of APPL increased substantially, since the number of projects increased as the workforce was decreasing. NASA reduced its overall civil service workforce by 26 percent between FY 1993 and FY 2000, and reduced the headquarters staff by 50 percent during the same period. Organizational restructuring and reductions resulted in a 52 percent reduction in supervisory positions and a 15 percent reduction in SES. On an agency-wide basis, the supervisor-to-employee ratio went from 1:6 to 1:10. These changes reduced the number of on-site mentors and experienced project managers, placing new demands for innovative and accelerated strategies to enhance learning and development.

APPL flourished under the era of FBC, contributing to significant gains in agency performance even as the agency's resources dwindled. APPL leveraged retiring NASA PMs and assigned them as mentors and coaches to active programs and projects, capturing lessons and success formulas and transferring these lessons across the agency. Partnerships that stimulated innovation were established with professional organizations such as the Project

Management Institute (PMI), and new leadership initiatives were implemented with universities and colleges such as the Massachusetts Institute of Technology (MIT). NASA APPL also moved to the forefront in implementing change for the agency, as evidenced by APPL's being selected to manage the rewrite of the organization's project management policy and procedures documents, NPG 7120.5b. As a result of the progress and accomplishments of NASA APPL, Hoffman, Maturo, and Boyle were highlighted in the November 1999 issue of *Fast Company* magazine as innovators in the human development field.

The Third Generation of NASA KM

During Dan Goldin's tenure, APPL provided multifaceted support to the leaders and teams that made up NASA project management. In normal times, such a strategy and commitment should endure. However, the current NASA environment proved again to be far too dynamic for Hoffman, Maturo, and Boyle to remain static in terms of APPL and still to meet the requirements of the workforce.

Perhaps if the changes taking place in project management were the only changes occurring in NASA, the transition would be smoother for both the organization and the individual practitioners. In reality, Hoffman realized that NASA was proceeding through accelerated change in virtually every facet of the organization, and was reflecting other changes in the greater business environment that were occurring worldwide. The APPL management team was grappling with a new extended list of challenges:

- Implementing the President's Management Agenda (PMA)
- Implementing the President's Vision for Space Exploration
- Adjusting to new NASA administrators
- Transferring APPL from Human Resources to the Office of the Chief Engineer
- Aligning to the federal Human Capital Plan (HCP)
- Adjusting to the increasing importance of a knowledge management strategy
- Adjusting to a revamped project management policy and procedures (NPG 7120.5c)
- Reacting to pressure to operate in a businesslike mode
- Emphasizing competition to increase productivity
- Shifting from FBC to a results-oriented approach
- Coming to terms with shrinking budgets
- Coming to terms with shrinking human resources

- Adjusting to fewer experienced personnel
- Implementing the Government Performance and Results Act (GPRA)
- Adjusting to higher customer and stakeholder expectations
- Shifting to performance-based contracting and budgeting
- Implementing full cost management
- Adjusting to new technologies
- Adjusting to a dramatic increase in the number of projects
- Reacting to a need for better strategic planning and management
- Shifting program management to the centers and then back to HQs
- Revamping commercialization and technology-transfer processes and procedures
- Creating more international partnerships
- Adjusting to a higher employee-to-supervisor ratio
- Increasing reliance on electronic government and information technology
- Reacting to career volatility
- Adjusting to an overall increase in speed, uncertainty, and scarcity of time
- Adjusting to greater project complexity
- Addressing a demand for speed and low cost
- Addressing a demand for accelerated leadership development
- Addressing increased concern about the competency and capability of the project workforce
- Integrating systems engineering and project management

At the level of a project manager, the rapid pace of change impacting social, technical, strategic, and administrative systems seems to be a volcano of activity. Much of the fallout from this activity is placed squarely on the shoulders of the project management workforce. In a short span of time, the responsibility of project managers shifted from a pure focus on mission (technical, business, safety, and customer satisfaction) success to responsibility for business management, commercialization, new technology identification and development, customer satisfaction, strategy, and much more. Hoffman, Maturo, and Boyle realized that this is an intractable issue to address without putting an integrated KM infrastructure into place, since even the current environment represents a total change from only ten years earlier.

In terms of the President's Management Agenda, the strategic management of human capital is the number one issue. This is because as much as 50 percent of the current federal workforce is eligible for retirement over the next five years. As in most agencies, the recent and continued retirement of experienced personnel puts NASA at risk, due to the loss of valuable knowledge and expertise that is critical for continued mission success. NASA, along with twenty-three of the twenty-six executive agencies, received red-light status on the Office of Man-

SpaceX has avg age of 29

why — focus on experience

agement and Budget (OMB) Human Capital Scorecard at the beginning of 2002. Additionally, at a time when experience and talent is at a premium, there is an increasingly young and inexperienced workforce in place.

At a time when innovation and creative approaches are needed, many of the most experienced project managers lack the preparation that comes with education and training. They cannot depend on having a ready pipeline of college students equipped with technical and engineering degrees on hand. Having succeeded in an environment of slow change and stability, some of these managers may be ill equipped to flourish in a workplace that demands a wide array of competencies and flexibility, because they have not received the educational preparation gained by project personnel.

In the early 1990s, the vast majority of NASA's project managers were "homegrown." In 1993, for example, three out of four of NASA's senior project managers had started as entry-level engineers in an engineering organization, and all had worked for NASA by the middle stage of their careers (Duarte et al. 1995). The majority of these project managers had been with the agency for fifteen to twenty-five years, and these were the "mentors" who were being asked to pass on their knowledge and wisdom from lessons learned to prepare the next generation of project managers.

By 1998, NASA had more scientists and engineers over the age of seventy than below the age of twenty-five (NASA 2001). The number of scientists and engineers under age thirty-five leaving NASA was three times greater than the intake of the same age group over the prior several years. During the post-*Challenger* period, FY 1988 through FY 1991, the hiring of scientists and engineers averaged about 1,000 per year. However, the number of scientists and engineers hired over the whole period from FY 1992 through FY 1997 totaled only 1,150.

By the mid-1990s, the group of senior project managers represented an "age lump" of personnel, all about the same age, who had joined NASA in the 1970s and 1980s. As often happens with an age lump phenomenon NASA has experienced a crisis of continuity as these individuals retire, exacerbated by early retirements and buyouts that have characterized the downsizing of NASA since 1993. A recent report on the FBC policy by the NASA Office of Inspector General (NASA 2001) noted that:

> By 1998, the effects of NASA's downsizing efforts began to take their toll. The downsizing affected program delivery because managers could not recruit new staff to correct skill imbalances and to bring new ideas to the workforce. In addition, the Agency-wide buyouts encouraged the loss of highly experienced managers and created a void in management and technical expertise. (16)

In the wake of criticisms launched as a result of high-profile failures in the Mars Program, coupled with reports of wiring issues on the Shuttle, NASA administrator Dan Goldin testified to the Senate Subcommittee on Science, Technology, and Space in March 2000 that NASA had experienced "less than desired effectiveness" of project management and systems engineering practices with respect to the failed missions. In that testimony, he reported that:

> a major cultural change was underway. Programs were staffed with next-generation managers without always making sure that they had been adequately trained and mentored. What was needed was access to resources from lessons learned from past experience and the use of new tools and techniques.

The Inspector General's FBC policy report further noted that, faced with budget cuts and downsizing since the mid-1990s, NASA had been focused on overall staff reduction and had not given sufficient consideration to the alignment of human resources with its strategic goals. The workforce had been reduced, resulting in a loss of experienced personnel in all skill categories. As a result, NASA had not determined the appropriate number of staff and competencies needed to effectively carry out strategic goals and objectives for its programs and was now at risk of losing core competencies. It was noted that 25 percent of that time's most experienced managers would reach retirement age in 2005. The Inspector General's report concluded that:

> As part of workforce planning, management should consider how best to retain valuable employees, plan for their eventual succession, and ensure continuity of critical competencies and capabilities.

The Fourth Generation of NASA KM

In 2003, the *Columbia* tragedy represented another watershed event for NASA. Again, enormous energy and thought went into understanding what went wrong and how to repair the NASA legacy of project excellence. The Columbia Accident Investigation Board (CAIB) was chartered, led by Admiral Harold W. Gehman, and found that NASA management and culture were as much to blame as the technical cause of falling foam shattering reinforced carbon-fiber wing panels (CAIB 2003). Out of this climate of introspection and commitment, NASA APPL was ordered to transition into the Office of the Chief Engineer (OCE) due to its importance to project practitioners and its track record of success. Hoffman, Maturo, and Boyle were now in a place where increased responsibility and scrutiny would be the norm, but where increased credibility was available due to the position of the OCE within NASA. Again, human capital experts were placed into senior-level positions within an organization that valued engineering and technology above all else.

The new organization became the Integrated Learning and Development Program (ILDP), an appropriately engineer-titled organization, and includes not only project manager development but system engineering and engineering discipline development as well. The new transition continues the transition states that drive the organization:

- From classroom training to total system performance support
- From training success to mission success
- From event-driven to outcome-driven activities
- From how to think to how to behave
- From classroom to virtual learning
- From stable systems to managing change and uncertainty
- From training the individual to learning as a team
- From one best way to competition
- From knowledge hoarding to knowledge sharing

Hoffman is currently guiding APPL (now ILDP) through a process of adaptation and growth in order to meet the demands of the President's Vision for Space Exploration. There is a need for a closer relationship to mission success by offering competitive services and products that support the practitioners in the work they do, resulting in a transition from Human Capital to the Office of the Chief Engineer during 2004. However, Hoffman continues to emphasize a few core issues that help clarify ILDP's role in NASA's project environment.

First, at a most fundamental level, the core values of NASA are achieved through science, engineering, and the management of projects. These core competencies are essential in that the existence of NASA is based on the capability of these disciplines. Everything else derives value from contributing to these critical core competencies. Second, there is a significant opportunity to develop a sharpened coordinated focus on the domains of program and project management and engineering to support these critical NASA core competencies, and to achieve better organizational integration and coordinated activity through KM tools and processes. Third, the window of opportunity to achieve this improved focus on project and engineering excellence is rapidly closing. NASA historically seems to be easily distracted by generic institutional changes that redirect energy, focus, and attention from the critical core competencies. For NASA, an uncoordinated abundance of strengths and resources in human capital across independent centers can serve to camouflage real problems and embedded systemic weaknesses agency-wide.

Hoffman, Maturo, and Boyle are now moving the new organization toward serving as an agency-level KM office that provides recognition, prioritization, and mobilization of developmental efforts in an integrated fashion under an integrated and cohesive framework. The overall framework consists of four separate but integrated engines of developmental innovation:

- The career development business area provides products and services around professional development competencies and training and development opportunities for increasing levels of expertise and capability in NASA.
- The performance enhancement business area brings world-class experts and learning design directly to NASA's programs and projects, bringing knowledge, wisdom, learning, and support to the practitioner and project team when they need it, where they need it, and how they need it, increasing practitioner learning while simultaneously increasing the probability of project success.
- The knowledge sharing business area builds and supports NASA communities of practice for the express purpose of promoting leadership development through mentoring and teaching, capturing and communicating knowledge and wisdom from the best practitioners, and enhancing open communication and dialogue, employing the tools of *Master's Forums, Transfer Wisdom Workshops* and the award-winning *ASK Magazine,* compiling best practices from practitioners through the ancient art of storytelling, edited by one of the most respected names in KM, Larry Prusak.
- Research in project management and systems engineering through the Center for Program and Project Management Research (CPMR), a cosponsored activity between the Universities Space Research Association and NASA, focusing on applied research on NASA issues, importing new ideas and innovation into the organization, and stimulating the other business areas.

The focus and initiatives of KM are contained in the knowledge sharing (KS) business area. Let's take a closer look at these key elements.

Key Elements of the NASA Knowledge-Sharing Approach

Over their many years of experience, senior program and project managers naturally accumulate a reservoir of critical knowledge. The purpose of ILDP's various knowledge-sharing activities is to capture, code, certify, house, and disseminate this knowledge and leverage the experience of these practitioners. In this way, through agency leaders and experts, ILDP cultivates the current NASA skill sets and supports developing project and program leaders who will take the place of retiring NASA personnel. Ultimately, KS develops a knowledge-sharing community of program and project managers within the agency that shares lessons learned, transfers best practices, archives critical project data, and develops leadership skills.

The key elements of the ILDP KM strategy include the following conceptual guidelines for the design, development, and implementation of KS products and services:

- Successful and experienced project practitioners are the central source of knowledge creation and sharing.
- New strategies will go through a period of piloting (testing) and the determination of success will be based on practicing project professionals.
- Knowledge sharing will be successful only if participants are primarily NASA's most successful experienced and emerging project leaders.
- The primary role of senior practitioners is sharing knowledge, and ILDP's responsibility is to provide effective and efficient forums for leadership development and networking.
- Meaningful impact only happens at the local level, where strategies should be tailored to maximize the benefit to project managers, project team members, and project organizations.
- Knowledge sharing can be successful only if it is based on the development of a personal relationship and a process of genuine dialogue among participants.
- Reflection, dialogue, storytelling, and sharing of experiences are the best mechanisms to facilitate forums and construct online resources.
- Contributors to knowledge sharing and mentoring are highly valued and will be appropriately appreciated, recognized, and rewarded by the agency.

The expected benefits that result from implementation of the KS strategies are:

- Transform tacit knowledge into explicit knowledge to support current NASA skill sets and mission success.
- Disseminate knowledge within NASA to support the President's Vision for Space Exploration.
- Disseminate knowledge outside of NASA to support citizen-centered government as directed by the President's Management Agenda.

- Change NASA culture to enhance networking and collaboration and create a greater desire for knowledge.
- Accelerate leadership development to meet the human capital and succession planning needs of the agency.
- Support and improve the image of NASA here and around the world.
- Inspire and energize people to emulate successful practitioners and thus improve performance and results.
- Develop practitioners to become more reflective, to support and improve program and project outcomes.
- Technology must be driven by the needs of participants, not the other way around.
- Make knowledge sharing an integral part of people's work; it must be kept simple and natural, and it must be part of performance reviews.
- Expect that different divisions and departments may want to do things differently, but that a case can be made for identifying what data and processes can be standardized and centralized, to avoid costly repetitive efforts and more effectively share information across facilities.

Transfer Wisdom Workshops

Project management Transfer Wisdom Workshops (TWWs) are held at individual centers. They are one-day workshops based on small-group discussions of mini case studies from the experiences of top NASA project managers, and serve to populate a story database. The ILDP team facilitates the discussions as practitioners analyze the applicability of the stories to the challenges of their own center to support new and upcoming program and project managers. Follow-up to the workshops includes the distribution of a community document containing the pictures and contact information of the attendees to enable future knowledge sharing. The feedback from the workshop is compiled into a report and shared with the center contacts in order to capture lessons learned and provide a better product for the next workshop.

ASK Magazine is distributed quarterly both as an online magazine on the APPL Web site and as a hard-copy NASA publication. It is an award-winning vehicle intended to create a knowledge base for present and future NASA project managers. *ASK* provides a medium for implicit knowledge translated to explicit knowledge through the ancient art of storytelling. Its articles include project management stories, lessons learned, interviews, book reviews, and a column on best practices, which serve as resources for higher levels of achievement and results. The stories in *ASK Magazine* also form the basis for the learning in the TWWs.

The Leaders as Teachers and Mentors initiative supports the development of human capital by leveraging the knowledge and experience of an identified set of current and retired agency leaders and experts to serve as teachers and mentors to the current and future generations of NASA practitioners. It offers senior and retired NASA practitioners the opportunity to share their knowledge, skills, and expertise as they give back to the agency through guest lecturing, teaching, consulting, and mentoring. The program framework includes established processes, recognition/reward systems, a candidate expertise database, and a file of opportunities for teaching, mentoring, and skills development of these leaders as well as the practitioners they serve. Project managers that are currently participating in other APPL knowledge sharing programs are recruited to participate in the Leaders as Teachers and Mentors initiative and are recognized by the agency for their contributions. They also serve as a source for referrals for other teachers and mentors.

Conclusion

Hoffman, Maturo, and Boyle are still working at the new ILDP effort and implementing KM. The years have literally rocketed by (appropriate to working at NASA). Since the first PPMI effort in 1988, KM efforts, gradually implemented, have borne fruit in allowing practitioners to turn implicit knowledge to explicit and to possess mechanisms to share this knowledge and wisdom across the organization and indeed around the world. Most of the effort now is spent on integrating KM practices and procedures across all developmental activities in ILDP. The stories generated through KS serve as a catalyst for many program and project improvements, and the sources of these stories continue to expand internationally from project managers across industry, academia, and the government.

In talking with Hoffman, it can be seen that he still has the passion for the work, and that the emphasis on serving practitioners in a practical way is the key to success for NASA. Reflecting on the history of KM at NASA he remarked:

> I never expected the success that we had over the past years. Who would have thought that cutting-edge human development and organizational development concepts would find a home in such a technically oriented organization as NASA? But as reports such as the CAIB continue to point out, it's all about the culture. KM tools and techniques allow us to share knowledge in a way that helps to prevent accidents like the *Columbia* from happening in the first place.[2]

Notes

1. As quoted on the NASA website, "History of the NASA Academy of Program/ Project and Engineering Leadership (APPEL)." Available at http://appel.nasa.gov/node/ 12.accessed September 2006.

2. Personal discussions with the author, May 1–15, 2006.

References

Chapman, R.L., R.H. Pontious, and B.B. Lewis. 1971. *Project and Program Management in NASA: The System and the Men.* Washington, DC: National Academy of Public Administration.
Columbia Accident Investigation Board (CAIB). 2003. "The CAIB Report," Vol. 1. Washington, DC: U.S. Government Printing Office.
Crawford, L. 1999. "Assessing and Developing Project Management Competence." Paper presented at the Thirtieth Annual PMI Seminars and Symposium, Philadelphia, PA (October 1999).
Duarte, D., A. Lewis, E. Hoffman, and D. Crossman. 1995. "A Career Development Model for Project Management Workforces." *Journal of Career Development* 22, no. 2: 149–64.
Holtzman, J. 1999. "Getting Up to Standard." *PM Network* (December), 44–46.
Kloman, E.H. 1972. *Unmanned Space Project Management: Surveyor and Lunar Orbiter.* Washington, DC: NASA SP-4901.
NASA. 1994. *Project Apollo: A Retrospective Analysis.* Monographs in Aerospace History no. 3. Washington, DC: National Aeronautics and Space Administration.
———. 2001. *Faster, Better, Cheaper: Policy, Strategic Planning, and Human Resource Alignment.* Washington, DC: NASA Office of Inspector General.
Naugle, J.E. 1991. *First Among Equals: The Selection of NASA Space Science Experiments.* The NASA History Series. Washington, DC: National Aeronautics and Space Administration.

12

KM at the Army's Communications-Electronics Command

Susan L. Nappi, Knowledge Manager,
U.S. Army Communications-Electronics
Life Cycle Management Command

Early in April 2002, my career as a U.S. Army management analyst took a sudden turn down a path I had never envisioned. I was sitting at my desk at Fort Monmouth, New Jersey, doing the quarterly review and analysis for the command—the U.S. Army Communications-Electronics Life Cycle Management Command (C-E LCMC). Next thing I knew, my director at the time, Rich Kelly, was standing by my desk telling me that our two-star general, Major General William Russ, wanted to do knowledge management. Not only was it a game of "tag I'm it," but we were going "live" on May 13! I had a little over a month and I hadn't a clue what knowledge management was. In my twenty-plus-year career with the army I've faced several assignments that required me to pave new ground. I've learned that these assignments are the most difficult but also the most rewarding—it was clear from the get-go that this was going to be another one of those "opportunities."

As soon as Rich walked away from my desk, I immediately tapped into my local library's online journals and periodicals (God bless the Internet!) and searched for every recent knowledge management article. From those articles I gleaned who were the major theorists/players and the books I needed to read. I read Nancy Dixon, Larry Prusak, and Etienne Wenger, among others.

I don't want you to think that I had no help at all—I did have three aces in the hole: an existing Web portal, local knowledge management expertise to tap into, and the assignment of an intern to assist me.

I didn't need to develop a new Web portal—the decision had already been made by Raoul Cordeaux (one of our information technology folks) to leverage a product that a co-located army entity at Fort Monmouth, led by Emerson

Keslar, had already developed. As a result, my true focus was to be knowledge management, not information technology. I had the luxury of developing a program for an audience of 8,000 users that focused on ensuring they had the right information and knowledge at the right time to do their mission—providing key command and control, communications, computers, intelligence, surveillance, and reconnaissance systems for the warfighter (a member of the armed forces who engages in combat). Information technology was just the enabler—just as the textbooks said it should be.

Second, there were existing knowledge managers in two of the business centers within C-E LCMC. Ken MacFarlane from acquisition, and Grace Keslar and Rosemary Matura from research and development, had been doing knowledge management for well over a year using Emerson's portal. I immediately tapped into MacFarlane, Keslar, and Matura's expertise. They freely shared insights on what had worked for them and what didn't and why. What they had learned was immensely helpful (my first "peer assist"). However, we now had a two-star general behind the effort and the situation wasn't exactly the same—we were moving from sharing information and knowledge at a business-center level to sharing it at a command or enterprise level. The needs for information and knowledge within each business center had similarities but they also had vast differences. My plan had to accommodate their differences, but also had to define, plan for, and accommodate what information and knowledge needed to be shared across the enterprise.

Last, I was assigned one of my organization's best interns, Claudia DeCarlo. She was sharp and as enthusiastic about the project as I was. The stage was set.

Developing the New Knowledge Center

After reading everything I could, and talking to Emerson, MacFarlane, Keslar, and Matura, it was readily apparent that there was much more to the job than ensuring that documents were posted to the Web portal, known as our knowledge center. I learned that I needed to capture tacit knowledge and make it available to others. Tacit knowledge is the result of years of experience and education. This knowledge isn't easily codified—this knowledge resides within the heads of subject matter experts (SMEs), those senior leaders who seem to have the right guidance/answers to the hard questions. I didn't have a clue how I was going to capture tacit knowledge and make it available for reuse. I wrote my plan (which included capturing tacit knowledge) and briefed it to General Russ. He fully endorsed the effort and was instrumental in getting the command to use the Web portal. But I wondered, just how was I going to pull off capturing tacit knowledge?

DeCarlo and I spent the next few months getting the right content on the knowledge center and training users. We worked extremely hard and many long hours. Since very few were familiar with the Web portal, we wound up loading much of the original content ourselves. I needed more help and realized that I needed points of contact within each C-E LCMC business center who could oversee the content within their organization. The concept of organization leads for knowledge management was born! Over time, these individuals became key to the implementation of the command knowledge management program—but back to my story on capturing tacit knowledge.

While DeCarlo and I were still buried in content in August of 2002, I received a phone call. A group from the Office of the Secretary of Defense's Change Management Center was coming for a visit. The purpose of the visit wasn't clear to me. All I was told was that they wanted an hour-long briefing from me on the command's knowledge management program. Mary Margaret Evans, a member of the senior executive staff, headed the party, which included a vice president of Science Applications International Corporation (SAIC), a government consulting science and engineering organization.

On the day of their visit, Evans and a host of others huddled in my conference room, stared at a blurry monitor (now long since replaced), and listened to my spiel on how C-E LCMC was implementing knowledge management. They seemed very impressed and even "pleased" with the breadth and depth of our program and the maturity of our Web portal. When I got to the chart that stated the command's goal to capture tacit knowledge they looked at each other and asked me what I had done to date. I was embarrassed, as everything else on which I had briefed them had a significant amount of substance behind it and I could easily point to examples of what we had accomplished. Honesty is the only way to go: I told them that I had no idea how to accomplish it; I only knew that it had to be done. My embarrassment quickly faded—it was clear that was the answer they had come to Fort Monmouth to hear.

Back at the Beginning

Flashback to earlier that same month: Evans had met Cordeaux (I introduced him earlier in my story as one of our information technology folks, but he probably prefers to be known as our chief information officer) at a recent army information technology conference. Evans learned from Cordeaux that we were doing some "neat" stuff with knowledge management. Evans had a burning issue that needed to be addressed—the aging of the acquisition workforce in the Department of Defense. She was concerned that within five years there could be a mass exodus of experienced acquisition professionals, professionals who would be eligible for retirement.

Evans estimated that over 40 percent of these individuals would be eligible for retirement in five years. These acquisition professionals possess tacit knowledge key to negotiating the complex process of procuring products and services in support of the warfighter. Evans saw this as an area ripe for applying a tacit knowledge capture model. She wanted to do a tacit knowledge capture pilot project and, based on its success, promulgate the concept throughout the Department of Defense. She had hired SAIC to run the pilot project, as they had had success in capturing tacit knowledge in the private sector. Based on her conversation with Cordeaux, Evans decided to visit Fort Monmouth and test the waters.

So unbeknownst to me, as I was sitting in my conference room, I was being delivered the solution to my dilemma of how to capture tacit knowledge on the proverbial silver platter. Based on my briefing and a larger meeting that day with C-E LCMC's senior leadership, Evans selected C-E LCMC as her pilot site. My adventure began!

The Pilot Project

The philosophy behind the pilot was not for SAIC to do the project, but to work with us onsite to teach us, coach us, and then leave us; their plan was to work themselves out of a job. When they left, we had the skills to continue to capture tacit knowledge, and SAIC had succeeded. The SAIC team was led by Rick Wallace and included Kevin Roth and Page Miller. Wallace, Roth, and Miller taught us their technique and the resulting product was a "knowledge asset"—the Web-based video clip repository for the tacit knowledge captured. After their departure, the exact model they taught us evolved, responding to our organizational culture and needs. The model we are using, however, is well rooted in the basic principles and resulting product we learned from SAIC.

Before I go into the specifics of the model we are using to capture tacit knowledge, let me be clear on this—the aging of the workforce is not the only reason or even the most important reason to capture tacit knowledge. There are a host of reasons to capture tacit knowledge, including the following:

1. *Globalization.* We no longer have the luxury of dealing face-to-face with others in our business processes. We are far flung around the globe—information technology tools have made this all possible. C-E LCMC has experienced globalization pains firsthand. In the early 1990s, C-E LCMC was primarily located in one large leased-office building near Fort Monmouth, New Jersey. To seek out knowledge, we rode an elevator up and down the six floors and walked the four color-coded building wings. In 1993, a Base Re-

alignment and Closure Action (BRAC) directed that C-E LCMC move from the leased building into a dozen government buildings on the main post, Fort Monmouth.

Other business decisions followed that added elements to C-E LCMC, permanently changing its complexion. The vast majority of C-E LCMC no longer resides at Fort Monmouth. Sharing became difficult once the command was no longer within one building; sharing became more difficult when we were no longer at one locale. With distance, we no longer saw the faces of the experts. Then e-mail arrived and we now no longer even heard the voices of the experts.

2. *Information Overload.* The information age has really meant information overload. There is too much information available—how can you weed through all the information residing on the Internet and within databases and glean knowledge? Try this exercise on the Internet using any of the search engines: Search for information on army transformation. In June of 2005. the Alta Vista search engine provided 133,405 results. How can you determine what information is relevant to what you may need and how can you tell if it is current? And who are the experts in transformation to whom you can reach out?

3. *Quickened Pace of Activity.* The availability of information technology tools has resulted in increased pressures to work faster and more efficiently. An action/task that used to take a month now needs to be completed within a day. How do you tap into the knowledge needed to get the job done? There is just too much information to sort through; the experts we need to connect with are not located in the next office; they may even be in another time zone—and we probably don't even know who the experts are!

4. *Anticipated Loss of Knowledge.* Purposefully, I've kept this as the last reason to capture tacit knowledge. The primary reasons to capture tacit knowledge are outlined above in reasons one to three. You shouldn't be waiting for your experts to announce retirement to get concerned about capturing tacit knowledge. Rather, you should have been doing it all along. Sitting down with an expert thirty days before their retirement is too late. You will never be able to capture more than a sliver of what they know. They may not even want to share it at that point—especially if they can "sell" their knowledge to a government contractor.

The Big Question

Here comes the million-dollar question. If you only capture a sliver of what your experts know, then why should you even undertake the effort to try to capture their tacit knowledge? I've found that the real benefit comes from how we present the results of our knowledge capture: the video clips. Watching a video clip, a novice is influenced by the expert's body language and speech patterns. From what they watch, the novices learn the range of knowledge the experts possess. It is rare that the exact knowledge a novice will need will be already captured. However, a novice can determine which expert has the experiences and resulting insights that will be of benefit. Watching the videos, novices begin to feel like they know the experts and feel comfortable in reaching out for advice for their unique situations. The best resulting scenario is for a mentoring relationship to develop between the novice and the expert and for knowledge transfer to continue over a span of time. To allow time for true knowledge transfer, the optimum time to capture an expert's knowledge is at least five years before their anticipated departure.

Watching a video really does make you feel like you know the SME. Renee Ullman, one of my team members, was helping me to put together a training session. As part of the preparation she had watched several video clips of Rick Riccelli, one of our acquisition SMEs. Weeks later, she was driving in her hometown (around thirty minutes away from Fort Monmouth) and was stopped at a light. She looked to her left and saw a familiar face; she immediately felt as if she knew him, and knew him well. She wanted to beep and wave a greeting. However, she was having a little trouble placing who exactly he was, when it hit her: He was Rick Riccelli. She really didn't know him at all other than through the video clips. A few months later she saw him at a work social event and introduced herself and told him this story. Ullman felt completely at ease in approaching him; his video made her that comfortable with him. We now teasingly call this the "Rick Riccelli effect."

Video: The Perfect Medium

Video is the perfect medium for knowledge capture. Consider this statistic: When people process information, only 7 percent is based on what was actually said, 38 percent is based on how it was said (for example what words were emphasized), and a whopping 55 percent is based on body language. You learn much more from watching and hearing a person than from reading the text transcription. When I demonstrate our knowledge asset I usually show a video clip of Victor Ferlise, one of the three deputies to our commanding general. He speaks very persuasively about the importance of C-E LCMC's mission. He states that if we don't do our mission, "somebody will die." After showing this stirring video clip, I show my audience the text for the clip. The same emotion simply can't be captured in the text; the difference between text and video is startling.

Continuing the Program

Since the departure of SAIC, our knowledge capture activities have continued. The C-E LCMC knowledge asset is the place to go on our Internet-based Knowledge Center to tap into tacit knowledge. Our knowledge asset comprises the following key elements:

- *Basic Employment Information/Knowledge.* In four years, C-E LCMC hired over 2,000 new employees, many of whom had never worked for the federal government. This area of the asset is an electronic employees' handbook that includes instructions for basic employment processes and procedures and links to key forms, samples, and Web sites. For example, new employees can find instructions on how to fill out and submit a request for leave, and even link to the form needed.
- *Workplace Expectations.* When your organization is as large and spread out across the globe as ours, with over 8,000 civilians, military personnel, and contractors worldwide, you need a means to communicate the organizational culture and values. In this part of the asset, senior leaders are captured on video in one- to three-minute clips talking about what an employee needs to know to succeed. The video clips are organized into eight major themes that emerged through the interview and distillation process (these processes will be discussed later).
- *Mission Knowledge.* Again, with our organization so large and dispersed, many employees have never seen or heard the commanding general speak. In this part of the asset, employees can learn about the mission of the command and their business center directly from the leaders themselves via video clips. All of this increases their organizational knowledge and value to C-E LCMC.
- *Key Processes.* This is the part of the asset in which we provide knowledge on key business processes via video clips from SMEs. Within each process, video clips are organized into themes that emerged through the interview and distillation process. We also included links to resources such as information or explicit knowledge (guidebooks) residing in the larger document repository on our knowledge center.
- *Expert Locators/Question and Answer Forums.* In this part of the asset we provide access to a database of management-approved SMEs. Click on their name and you have access to their phone number and e-mail address, and if they are online, you can instant message them. In situations in which you can't figure out under which subject matter area your situation falls, we provide the capability to pose a question and our support center determines who should answer the question. The center

uses the database of experts and also reaches out to the organizational leads for knowledge management to help route the question.

• *Links to Communities of Practice (CoPs).* Rather than develop C-E LCMC-level communities of practice, we link to army-wide and Department of Defense–wide CoPs. We discovered early in building our asset that CoPs larger than our organization provided the best opportunities for cross-fertilization of knowledge and ideas.

Steps in Capturing Knowledge

Capturing knowledge occurs through a distinctive sequence of procedural steps. C-E LCMC followed this five-step process in developing each key process in our knowledge asset:

Step 1. Identify a Key Process

When you select a process, you need to ensure there will be some expected gain in doing knowledge capture. The gain can be efficiencies/savings, improved effectiveness, better decisions, or more innovation. Capturing knowledge is resource intensive, so you need to focus on areas that will result in a quantifiable or perceived improvement. It is very hard to measure the outcome of knowledge capture. We have been tracking our standard business metrics—if they continue to improve, part of the reason may well be our knowledge capture efforts, but it could also be other reasons (changes in policy or procedures, etc.). We have also been relying upon anecdotal stories as indicators of success.

Be careful how you size your efforts—too big an effort will be undoable. For example, when we were working with SAIC we decided to capture knowledge about creating effective source selection evaluation criteria. When we contract for a product or service we don't go with the lowest bidder; we go for "best value." There are times when we want to pay a higher cost to get a better technical solution. Best value allows us to evaluate the bidders against evaluation criteria, differentiate among the bidders, and pick the contractor that will provide the best product within the amount we want to spend. The entire source selection process is too huge—focusing just on developing the criteria seemed to be about the right size. Being able to size your capture efforts will come through experience. We had the benefit of SAIC's expertise in helping us to size our initial effort.

This next thought seems obvious, but I need to state it anyway—before you start an effort make sure there is tacit knowledge to capture. The key process should have both a "science" (the explicit knowledge and information) and an "art" (the tacit knowledge). Don't waste your limited resources on something that has already been codified.

Finally, don't even try to capture tacit knowledge unless you have the sponsorship of the senior process owner. No one is going to support your efforts if the senior leader isn't supporting it. SMEs are busy people—there was many a time when we relied upon the senior process owner to "prod" a participant to "play" with us.

Step 2. Identify Knowledge Harvesters and the SMEs

Based on the process chosen, the next step is to identify who will capture the knowledge. These individuals are the "knowledge harvesters." Use junior employees (interns for example) as knowledge harvesters since they are the employees who will be inheriting the process. For the source selection evaluation criteria, we used acquisition interns. If they get their questions answered, then we know we are on the right track.

Knowledge management practitioners make excellent knowledge harvesters. We trained the KM practitioners in the knowledge capture process (to include the interview and distillation process) so that they can lead and train the other knowledge harvesters in the process and techniques. The KM practitioners become knowledgeable about the subject matter by reading and organizing the existing resources that will be linked to the knowledge asset. My KM practitioners were members of the team supporting the entire command's knowledge management efforts: In addition to DeCarlo and Ullman I was supported by Mary Buchwald, Cyndia Halsey, Susan Jackson, Anthony Paskvan, and Kathleen Reilly. Additional support came from my organizational leads for knowledge management. One of these leads, Ilene Mulhern, was affectionately called our "grammar queen," and we relied upon her to ensure the grammar was correct in everything we produced.

We also used acknowledged experts to harvest knowledge because they know the process and as a result can help us to frame interview questions to elicit higher levels of knowledge. Acknowledged experts also add validity to the effort. If they become involved, SMEs are more likely to participate. For source selection evaluation criteria, Tom Carroll from the legal office, an acknowledged leader (not just at C-E LCMC, but in the army), became heavily involved in our efforts. This was especially helpful since it was our first effort and we had no track record to show how well we could accomplish the capture of tacit knowledge. Knowing that Carroll was involved in the effort was a key element that helped to convince the SMEs to participate.

You also need to identify who possesses the tacit knowledge—the SMEs to be interviewed. Be sure to validate them with management. The one time we didn't validate and relied upon a peer referral we wound up wasting valuable time interviewing a disgruntled employee.

Step 3. Interview the SMEs

First, prepare for the interview by developing the questions. Run them by the experts. You're looking for the secrets of their success and what has been learned from mistakes. Don't ask closed questions like "Was it a success?" Rather, ask "What made it a success?"

After the questions are developed and approved by the experts, the interviewer needs to set up the date and time for the interview. Believe it or not, this was one of the most difficult elements to accomplish. We had to work to coordinate four schedules: the SME's, the interviewer's, the videographer's, and the room availability. It's important that you have a "quiet" room where you are unlikely to be disturbed during the filming.

After a date and time has been selected, an interviewer must conduct a preinterview with the person. People only share with those they know. If the interviewer meets the SME for the first time at the interview, there's a good chance that the SME won't share failures and the resulting knowledge gained from those failures. Even if the interviewer does know the SME, an appointment should be made to meet with the SME and explain face-to-face the purpose of the project, the interview, and what the SME should expect. Also, before the interview, e-mail the SME and give that expert a general outline of what will be asked, but don't give them the verbatim questions to avoid scripting. The SME requires time to reflect on their past experiences so that they will be ready to effectively answer your questions.

In addition to the primary interviewer, always have a secondary interviewer. The purpose of the secondary interviewer is to pose follow-on questions that the primary interviewer may have missed. For example, if the SME states "Oral proposals didn't work," and the primary interviewer doesn't ask why, the secondary interviewer can ask that question after the primary interviewer is finished asking all of their questions. The secondary interviewer waits until the end to not interrupt the flow between the interviewer and the SME.

The interview is not a Steven Spielberg production, nor is it a home movie. Don't overwhelm the interviewee with too much equipment. We use a digital camera on a stand, one light, a microphone clipped to the SME, and one mike on a table stand shared by the interviewers. Sit the SME in a chair without wheels (so they don't move in and out of the frame), face them to the interviewer, and have the camera at a forty-five-degree angle. You want to tape a personal discussion between the SME and the interviewer, not a "deer caught in headlights."

Most important, before and after the interview, be sure to tell the SME that nothing will be used on the asset without the SME's approval. The SME most have complete confidence that you will not ruin their credibility or embarrass them. In some cases, we had to wait months to get final approval for posting videos to the knowledge asset. We had a situation in which a sponsor wanted to post an SME's video without approval because it was taking so long, but I stood fast. If I break my word, and something is remiss, it will be impossible to regain trust. In our interviews we talk about times in which the SME failed and what they learned from it; the SMEs need to be secure in knowing that we will treat their disclosures properly.

Step 4. Prepare Key Learnings Documents

Following the interview, the video is transcribed into a Word document with time codes. The time codes will allow the knowledge harvesters to identify the start and end times needed to make the video clips. The interview transcript is given to four knowledge harvesters (we found four to be the magic number) to read through, much as they would school homework. The homework includes the identification of key learnings. Key learnings are not the same thing as best practices. Best practices are applicable to every situation within a standard business process. They are a proven tactic that everyone should follow. Best practices are used for the "science" part of the knowledge asset development process. Key learnings refers to the "art" part of the process. You need to know the context from which that key learning emerged. When you read a key learning it contains an "insight." Key learnings are expressed as a one- to two-line summary sentence focusing on a specific action and the resulting benefit, for example, "In order to succeed, you need to be technically competent, hone your soft skills, develop your leadership competencies, and mix in a dose of creativity."

Upon completion of their homework, the four knowledge harvesters meet for a collaborative knowledge distillation. The purpose of the collaborative distillation is to reach a consensus on the key learnings and the supporting texts (which will become the video clips). We have found that it takes about four hours to distill a one-hour interview and that as lunchtime approaches, we can distill faster. Each of the knowledge harvesters comes to the collaborative distillation with a copy of the interview transcript marked up with their notes. One of the knowledge harvesters (the best typist) documents the consensus of the group by converting the interview transcript into the key learnings document while the rest of the group watches. A portable projector connected to a laptop aids this process; while the typist makes the changes, the rest of the group can view the Word document and guide the changes.

Upon completion of the collaborative distillation, it is not unusual for a few clean-up actions to remain for the typist. After those actions, the draft key learnings document is sent to the knowledge harvesters for a short review period to ensure that they got it "right." This is accomplished electronically via e-mail.

After the completion of this review, the key learnings document is provided to the SME for final approval. We ask the SME to make sure the key learnings summary sentence is accurate and they are comfortable with the supporting text. They can edit words in the text, but we made it clear that the audio/video will reflect the original words. Anything that the SME is not satisfied with, we do not use. Upon final approval by the SME, the key learnings document is provided to the videographers to create the video clips for the asset.

Step 5. Categorize by Major Themes

When several interviews have been completed, the key learnings are categorized by major themes (five to eight). The major themes are then presented in a graphic on the asset. When a viewer clicks on the graphic, he or she can drill down into the key learnings and supporting video clips.

Conclusion

This has been a short version of the knowledge capture process I've been involved with at the U.S. Army Communications-Electronics Life Cycle Management Command. We've codified the process in a guidebook that we make available to all of our knowledge harvesters. We've also interviewed ourselves (the knowledge management practitioners) and captured our key learnings about capturing tacit knowledge. The harvesters keep changing (based on the key process) so we are constantly in a training mode.

I feel you can capture tacit knowledge for reuse, as long as you fully understand that you will never capture it all, or even a majority of it. However, if you codify key learnings, organize them, and deliver the supporting text via video clips, something special happens. When you view multiple video clips, you walk away with an insight or knowledge that you didn't have before. Many times you can't point to one specific key learning that provided the insight—it was the summation of the pieces that resulted in the insight.

Most important about the asset is that you've allowed novices to identify and get to know the experts. The novices now know who to go to for help in solving their dilemmas. You've reintroduced the personal contact that has degraded within the organization due to the advent of globalization and e-mail.

The video clips and the delivery via the Internet also appeal to novices. Many of the novices are the younger members of the workforce who grew up watching videos and have spent much of their time on the computer searching for information and knowledge. What better way to capture their attention and interest than video clips on the knowledge asset? Reading long texts doesn't always cut it for these members of the workforce.

Since we began to capture tacit knowledge we've realized that it is not a one-shot deal. You have to keep going back and refreshing the asset. As we add more key processes, we have been relying upon leads we designate for each key process to assist us in identifying and updating the knowledge captured.

Beginning in 2001, we have had our ups and downs in the process; there are times we surge ahead and make great progress, while at other times we stall for weeks awaiting support from a sponsor or just trying to make time to conduct interviews and distillations. The other obstacle has been the constant turnover of the knowledge management practitioners I use to capture tacit knowledge. It turns out that knowledge management practitioners have skills and knowledge that are attractive to the rest of the organization. Through their participation in knowledge capture as well as in content management of the knowledge center, knowledge management practitioners gain a significant amount of organizational and networking knowledge that makes them "ripe for the picking." DeCarlo began the adventure with me, but later moved on for a promotion. My team has ebbed and flowed, consisting of between two and six individuals who support all aspects of knowledge management as well as the capture of tacit knowledge.

The adventure continues. The most recent news affecting our efforts is that Fort Monmouth was selected for closure in BRAC 2005. The majority of the workforce will be relocated to Aberdeen Proving Ground, Maryland, sometime around 2010. How BRAC will impact tacit knowledge capture is yet to be seen, but I expect our tacit knowledge capture activities to increase.

Afterthought

Here I am again, sitting at my desk at Fort Monmouth, New Jersey, making the final edits on my story. I can say honestly that this "adventure" was the best assignment I have had with the army. I've thoroughly enjoyed being able to provide employees with the information and knowledge they needed to accomplish their mission in support of America's warfighter.

13

KM at the Virginia Department of Transportation

Maureen L. Hammer, PhD, *Director, Virginia Department of Transportation KM Division*

With about 9,200 employees, the Virginia Department of Transportation (VDOT) is one of the three largest state agencies in the Commonwealth of Virginia. Virginia has the third-largest state-maintained highway system in the United States. The VDOT is responsible for the construction, maintenance, and operation of the roads, bridges, and tunnels in the state's 58,082-mile system. The agency has nine district offices, which oversee construction, maintenance, and operations within the designated geographical area. The districts are further divided into forty-two residencies and two district satellite offices and also staff an area maintenance headquarters in each county. The VDOT central office headquarters is located in Richmond and has thirty-five operational and administrative units. The knowledge management division is part of the central office but is located in Charlottesville, in the geographical center of the state.

In the mid-1990s, the agency lost experience and valuable institutional knowledge following a statewide workforce reduction that offered early retirement to long-term employees. To mitigate the loss, the agency hired former employees as contractors to continue the work. Today, about 28 percent of the current employees are eligible for retirement in the next five years and the former employees hired back as contractors are approaching second retirements. To prevent a recurrence of the knowledge loss, the agency instituted a knowledge management division in late 2003 to address critical knowledge identification, collection, organization, and dissemination.

When Philip Shucet joined VDOT as the new commissioner in 2002, he introduced the concept of two new incubator programs to address the intellectual assets of the agency, knowledge management and the learning center.

240

His expectation was that the KM program would address the identification and sharing of critical institutional knowledge, and the learning center would ensure that the organization would incorporate that knowledge and emerging core competencies into training and learning opportunities. The KM division was established in the spring of 2003 and a director was hired in November of that year. Due to a hiring freeze in state government, hiring for additional positions in the division was put on hold for six months. As the new director came from outside the agency, the chief of technology, research and innovation, Dr. Gary Allen, assigned a research scientist and long-term employee, Bill Bushman, to temporary duty with the new division to act as a guide to the agency for the new director. The research council, located in Charlottesville, provided administrative support. The KM division was given two directives: (1) establish a community of practice for the project managers of the major construction projects, and (2) take baby steps but make this happen quickly.

Goals of the KM Division

The goals of the division are to preserve and make accessible institutional knowledge and memory, to establish an environment that supports knowledge creation and sharing, and to help the organization know what it knows. The objectives are to identify knowledge experts and to support the redundancy of knowledge within the agency. These are accomplished through knowledge mapping and the establishment of communities of practice. The agency has included measurements for these activities in its strategic plan for 2006–2008. The division will map the knowledge network of one district and will double the number of communities to twenty.

Original Community

As directed by the commissioner and chief, the first community was to comprise the project managers of major construction projects, such as the Woodrow Wilson Bridge, the Springfield Interchange, Pinner's Point in Hampton Roads, I-81, and the Coalfields Expressway. The value of these projects taken together was approximately $8 billion. An initial meeting with these seventeen project managers was held in early December 2003, during which the commissioner stated that he truly believed that just bringing them all together in one room to talk with each other about what was happening in their projects, their issues, their concerns, and lessons learned would result in tremendous savings for the agency. He also stated that due to the project managers' heavy schedules and responsibilities, the community would need to be established electronically as they did not have time to meet in person on a regular basis. During the meeting, the project managers provided brief overviews of the construction projects to acquaint each other and the new knowledge management officer with the current status of the projects. The group agreed to meet again in early 2004 for a community kickoff, at which time the technology platform would be introduced.

As the agency did not have software for online communities at that time, the information technology division developed an interim solution for an online discussion board using Microsoft Office folders, which would allow the participants to send e-mail messages. The intent was to provide a forum with which project managers were familiar and that would allow them to participate while performing a familiar activity, corresponding through e-mail. Knowledge management also partnered with the project management office to establish a taxonomy to organize the discussion and to ensure that lessons learned were captured in a consistent way.

There were a few difficulties in establishing the discussion forum, however. In February 2004, the system went live and was introduced to the community during another face-to-face meeting. An initial topic was selected and the knowledge management office populated the forum with notes from that meeting. During the next two months, not a single community member used the system despite repeated requests, reminders, and encouragement. What the knowledge management director had not realized was that members of this group were new to their positions and had never had consistent interaction, nor were they necessarily familiar with each other. A successful community requires trust between members who are knowledgeable and have expertise in their field. Discussions should improve practices and increase knowledge, not criticize:

Trust plays an important role in the sharing and use of knowledge. If people believe they will benefit from sharing their knowledge, either directly or indirectly, they are more likely to share. Whether people use the knowledge of others depends on whether they know and trust the source of the knowledge (KM Working Group 2001, 2).

As Edwards and Kidd (2003, 133) have noted, "knowledge sharing, even without any kind of formal system, inevitably raises issues of trust." Ribiere and Sitar (2003) have suggested that dialogue and communication are the basis for all knowledge sharing because they facilitate the development of social relationships, and if people are to start talking freely without the fear of becoming vulnerable, trust is absolutely necessary. The willingness to share what is known requires the presence of trust.

Trust involves a belief that the source and recipient will be respectful of the knowledge exchanged and that the exchange will be beneficial to each. It also encompasses a belief that the source of knowledge is competent and reliable. According to Abrams et al. (2003, 65):

> In the context of knowledge creation and sharing in informal networks, research suggests two dimensions of trust that promote knowledge creation and sharing: benevolence ("You care about me and take an interest in my well-being and goals") and competence ("You have relevant expertise and can be depended upon to know what you are talking about").

In our early program, participants perceived the initial system as "clunky and unfriendly," and did not feel that they had time to learn how to use it. A meeting was called for June, at which time all the participants were to be brought together to discuss the lack of use of the system and to continue discussions on lessons learned to that point. The KM director admitted to the project managers that the attempt to establish an online community had been a complete failure. The ability and freedom to admit to this mistake established for the community that it was acceptable to say that something could have been approached differently. From this we learned a lesson that could be used in the future, which later helped establish trust and demonstrated what could be shared.

The decision was made for the full group to meet quarterly for similar discussions. The knowledge management office would conduct interviews of specific project managers prior to the meeting to collect lessons learned that the group would review prior to publishing them to the agency at large. The lessons learned by the knowledge management division included: (1) know the participants, (2) develop the community of practice to suit them, (3) participants need to know and trust each other to share knowledge, and (4) although communities can be supported by online interaction, they require periodic face-to-face meetings.

Office Expansion

The hiring freeze was lifted in 2004 and three new project managers were hired. The office now had four full-time and two part-time employees, along with administrative support staff. A list of possible knowledge management projects had been gathered and these projects were assigned to the new members of the team, who quickly began to implement new communities. There were also parallel activities in knowledge mapping: identifying experts, identifying knowledge held by experts, identifying knowledge gaps or potential gaps, and promoting and defining knowledge management within the agency. In addition, the division welcomed the addition of the VDOT library. The expertise and skills of the librarians would be utilized by knowledge management in organizing the knowledge collected to ensure that it would be retrievable.

Communities and KM Projects

By the end of 2004 there were four active communities, two emerging communities, a lessons learned collection project, and three active knowledge mapping projects. By the end of June 2005, ten communities, three lessons learned collection projects, and four knowledge mapping projects were functioning, along with a waiting list of proposed communities and mapping projects. The division had doubled its activities in six months.

Each community is unique in its purpose and outcomes. Membership in communities varies to include:

- Employees within the same division or functional area,
- Employees who have the same role in different geographic areas,
- Employees who have different roles but perform related functions,
- Current and former employees addressing an identified knowledge gap, and
- Employees of VDOT working with employees of other agencies or organizations.

The original community is still active and developing lessons learned that can be shared within the agency. It is currently organizing an interactive conference to promote and share ideas on project management within the agency, thus expanding the reach of the lessons learned and best practices. Three communities evolved out of the original community as a result of issues raised and lessons learned during community meetings and interviews of the project managers for construction projects. These communities are looking at ways to improve cross-functional knowledge sharing, promoting the practice of project management within the agency, and establishing best practices for quality assurance and quality control.

To improve cross-functional knowledge and the promotion of project management, the construction project managers teamed with representatives of the location and design and structure and bridge divisions. After two meetings and the formation of a subcommunity, the group realized that the goal was to establish regular feedback between the design and implementation of a construction project using a project management approach. This shared feedback leads to the development of lessons learned and best practices that can serve as resources for future projects in support of the agency goal of

delivering projects on time and on budget with quality. An additional outcome was the formation of a constructability issues panel discussion between three representative project managers and the location and design
division statewide. This panel discussion contributed to lessons learned and
the sharing of best practices. The panel shared what worked well as well as
challenges faced during construction that directly related to the design.

The second community that developed out of the original community
was established within the right of way and utilities division to address
the pending knowledge loss that would result from the retirements of
about 40 percent of its employees and 90 percent of its managers. Knowledge management has partnered with human resources to work with this
community to establish what skill sets will be needed in the future, how
to develop these skills, and how to hire for these positions. This endeavor
is a pilot for how the agency will address the same issues with other
divisions. The community also established quarterly project days to discuss current and upcoming projects and how to best use existing staff to
address needs, including assigning employees across multiple districts
when needed. When the community brought the ideas for addressing the
anticipated knowledge loss in front of the district administrators committee, the response was unanimously positive and supportive. Leadership
was pleased to have the community of practice proactively identify the
problem and recommend a solution.

The third community that was developed out of the original community
involved construction quality managers with the anticipated outcome of developing best practices and improving day-to-day operations. The agency is
facing a serious shortage of experienced inspectors, so the community established a quarterly statewide project day to share information and to break
down barriers in districts. The community presented an idea for a best practice that will enable inspectors to spend more time in the field and to produce
statewide consistent records, which has been enthusiastically endorsed by
the district construction engineers committee.

One of the construction project managers invited knowledge management
personnel to participate in a "lessons-learned" meeting on a public-private
partnership construction project. This participation led to the formation of a
group to look at all lessons learned in this new type of project and to close
the loop by developing a feedback process and identifying lessons learned
that could be a knowledge resource for future projects. The lessons developed from this project are serving as the basis for the development of a repository and taxonomy for the organization's intranet.

Another community was established to address an identified knowledge
gap in the rehabilitation, dismantling, and relocation of historic truss bridges.

This community includes retired employees who hold the missing knowledge and will result in published best practices that will be used throughout the country. This community was interested in supplementing in-person meetings and interviews with an online team room.

Two more communities were developed to determine best practices for a new function for the agency, intelligent transportation systems, and to share lessons learned across the state. One community was formed to look at what the core functions of the smart traffic centers were as part of a research project. A member of the group expressed his satisfaction with the process by saying that the community was the most useful and rewarding activity of his professional life as it allowed him to learn from others, to meet with his peers, and to be creative in problem solving. The other community was developed for the entire intelligent transportation system function and the focus there is to set up an online environment in which members can share lessons learned and best practices and can ask questions.

A community linking the agency with representatives of cities and towns within Virginia is in the developing stages, and a subcommunity has developed that provides the members with the opportunity to ask questions of the experts in managing their own construction projects during round table sessions. This has led to cities' beginning to use each other as resources.

Knowledge Mapping Projects

Knowledge mapping projects include identifying and capturing the knowledge held by experts who are eligible for retirement, identifying lessons learned and best practices from long-term employees to be used by new employees, and identifying and capturing knowledge held by a sole source. An example of a sole source knowledge mapping is the highway performance monitoring system, a process that affects federal allocations for state road construction but that is currently only known by three people, all of whom are eligible for retirement. Lessons learned are captured for new and established functions for the agency both within communities and external to communities. An example of this would be the asphalt forum, which is attempting to collect lessons learned and best practices over the past fifty years from both within and external to the agency.

The knowledge management office is developing an online team site for the forum. The division plays a major role with the intranet to ensure that it is a knowledge-sharing tool and to establish a taxonomy that will allow for quick retrieval of needed knowledge and information. Online communities have also been established and are facilitated by the division on the agency intranet and learning management system.

Research to Identify Networks

The Virginia DOT recently sponsored a study to identify the types of networks within the agency in which employees participate, to determine what knowledge is shared, and to determine what roles employees play within the networks. Results of this study were then used to design new knowledge management projects within the agency and to identify what agency actions were needed to support knowledge sharing. The goal was to identify and make available expert, internal knowledge and external knowledge on the intranet so that an employee can search on a topic and have a retrieval that encompasses all three knowledge types. This allows the user to select the type of knowledge most needed or with which they are most comfortable—regardless of whether it is a written document or access to an internal or external expert.

The inclusion of experts in the system was necessary because not all knowledge can be codified and because people do not know what they know until they are asked a specific question. Study results were grouped by years of service with the organization, as follows:

Employees with Thirty or More Years of Service

These employees indicate having active roles in networks with strong ties (frequent interaction) with colleagues in the same geographical location as themselves, with counterparts in other geographical locations, and with consultants. Strong networks share institutional knowledge and experience and inform employees of who knows what. These long-term employees also participate in networks with weak ties (infrequent interactions) as peripheral members with employees within the same functional area in which knowledge is shared. These employees are the experts who are consulted or who offer knowledge and advice upon request. Employees became aware of these networks through mentors and as a result of long tenure with the agency. There was management support for regular face-to-face interactions with contacts and for informal knowledge sharing. As contacts retire, the networks are dissolving and interaction is decreasing. Long-term employees have a strong desire to share institutional knowledge, expertise, and experience with newer employees, but do not perceive that management has allocated time or budget resources to support the activity in the last decade.

Employees with Twenty Years to Less than Thirty Years of Service

Long-service employees have active, central, and spanner (links between networks) roles in networks. Moreover, they have forged strong ties with colleagues in the geographical area, with jurisdictions, and with consultants. These strong networks share experience, provide referrals, and inform employees of who knows what. These employees also participate in networks with weak ties, as peripheral members with previous coworkers and with employees in the same functional area in which relevant knowledge is shared. Employees became aware of networks through family members who also worked for the agency, through on-the-job training, by invitation, through involvement in special projects, or because of reputation. There was management support for regular face-to-face interactions with contacts and for informal knowledge sharing during the early years with the agency but that diminished since the 1990s. Participation supports these employees in knowing the function, providing institutional knowledge, and informing them of who does what. As networks dissolve through retirements, position changes, and departures from the agency, employees lose contacts and knowledge is limited to the immediate functional area. Periodic, temporary networks are relied upon. Employees perceive that management support for participation has decreased dramatically.

Employees with Ten to Twenty Years of Service

These employees indicate having active and central roles within networks, with strong ties with friends, colleagues in the same geographical area, localities, consultants, and those on Internet forums. Strong networks share career information, functional knowledge, how-to knowledge, and interpretations of explicit knowledge and inform employees of who knows what. The employees also participate in networks with weak ties in central roles, with previous coworkers, with employees in the same functional area within the agency, and with counterparts in other geographic locations in which functional, technical, historical, and cross-functional knowledge is shared. There are employees within this tenure group who are isolated from networks, primarily by choice. Employees became aware of networks through family members who also worked for the agency, mentors, job requirements, tenure, predecessors, or participation in special projects. There was support for participation in networks if required by the job or encouraged by mentors, although support has decreased since the mid 1990s due to budget and staff cuts. Management is focused on getting the job done today. Participation supports these employees in streamlining work processes, sharing workloads, knowing the questions to ask, and demonstrated value of expertise. Dissolution of networks has resulted in lack of communication, loss of contacts, lost institutional knowledge, and employees' no longer knowing who to ask.

Employees with Less than Ten Years of Service

These employees indicate having active or central roles within networks, with strong ties with friends, immediate coworkers, and previous coworkers; across functions when required by the job; with consultants; and through Internet forums. Strong networks share career information, functional knowledge, technical knowledge, and institutional knowledge. These employees also participate in networks with weak ties, in peripheral or spanner roles with counterparts in other geographic locations, localities, vendors, and colleagues in professional associations. Knowledge shared within networks with weak ties includes functional, institutional, and professional knowledge; lessons learned; and informing the employee of who knows what. There are employees who are isolated but wish to be more involved. Isolation can be attributed to a fear of providing wrong information as well. Employees became aware of networks through family members who work for the organization, the engineer trainee program, previous experience with networks, long-term employees, managers, and by invitation. Employees perceive there is management support if required by the job or if it results in improved technical knowledge. Lack of support is attributed to the unavailability of budget allocations to support networking. Participation in networks eases work assignments. Dissolution of networks results in lost institutional knowledge, not knowing who to ask, and a low awareness of organizational issues.

This study revealed that strong tacit knowledge networks in this state agency are primarily restricted to local groups due to a lack of time, budget restrictions, reduction in staff, high workload, the weight of paperwork, rules and regulations, and lack of management support. The assumption is that employees would share more if more time and resources were allotted to support the transfer of knowledge. Networks that do go outside the local area, primarily weak networks, result in more efficient and effective work practices. However, because these are weak networks with infrequent interaction, the agency does not fully benefit from the collective knowledge of its employees.

Effects of Organizational Culture

The participants perceive that the organizational culture is one of a command-and-control approach, which interferes with knowledge sharing and transfer through networks. "Culture embodies all the unspoken norms, or rules, about how knowledge is to be distributed between the organization and the individuals in it" (DeLong and Fahey 2000, 118). Knowledge creation and sharing is also affected by this organizational culture. "An organizational culture that enforces a policy of command and control to create an order seldom provides opportunities to create knowledge" (Bhatt 2000, 1).

Status as a government agency also impedes network participation, as employees are often overloaded with paperwork, rules, and regulations. According to Chiem (2001), unlike workers in private enterprise, government workers must complete paperwork for even the simplest tasks—a requirement that can potentially hamper workers' productivity and create an institutional tendency to perform only the minimum job requirements. Chiem also suggested that presenting knowledge sharing as a way to make jobs easier can assist in making KM practices appealing to government employees.

In the DOT study, employees with less than twenty years of service do perceive knowledge sharing as making jobs easier. Employees do not know what to share or what is known until the opportunity to network with other employees arises and through discussion the knowledge is revealed. There is a perception that talking is not productive; this study reveals that it is. "The non-information sharing culture of many government agencies is perhaps one of the greatest barriers that many agency directors will face" (Auditore 2003, S4). The KM Working Group of the Federal Chief Information Officers Council (2001) identified several reasons employees do not share knowledge: (1) people may not know what they know, (2) they do not know how to share or with whom to share, or (3) sharing may be seen as too difficult or time consuming.

The DOT study found that lack of time, failure to recognize employees, and rules and regulations produced by legislation all impacted networks. Similar information was found in a study of the U.S. Social Security Administration by Rubenstein-Montano, Buchwalter, and Liebowitz (2001), in which they identified the following barriers to sharing knowledge:

1. Lack of resources;
2. Failure to recognize individual contributions;
3. Assignment to leadership positions not based on merit or experience;
4. Hierarchical organizational structure; and
5. An organization driven by legislation.

The strong networks found to exist in the Virginia Department of Transportation were most often local, with few networks reaching across geographical or functional locations. A rationale for this finding was suggested by Ruddy (2000), who found that a great deal of knowledge in an organization is undocumented and therefore isn't easily available to everyone. It may be shared among a few individuals or within local groups, but it rarely migrates outside those circles. This is especially true for practical know-how, but is also true for the more formal kinds of knowledge that people discover and create every day. This restriction to local sharing of knowledge prevents that knowledge from being accessible to the rest of the organization.

The Impact of Worker Loss and Isolation

In the DOT study results, retirements, failure to retain employees, and reorganizations were all cited as contributors to knowledge loss and the inability to know who to call, a finding that was also seen by Burk (2000, 18):

> New staff or staff facing new problems are unaware of these ad-hoc communities and are unable to tap into their expertise. Expertise learned from experience is lost with retirement. Staff turnover and restructuring break down the informal networks to the point where even long-term staff do not know who to call.

Employees with less then twenty years of service may feel isolated (Connelly and Kelloway 2003, 297). Fifteen of the seventeen participants interviewed in the DOT study indicated a desire for more participation in more networks, particularly those that go outside the local area. These finding contradict Chatzkel (2002), who suggested that the main barriers to knowledge sharing in government organizations were the "not invented here" syndrome and personal power issues. Chatzkel also concluded that government employees hoarded knowledge to support the security of their role in the institution—barriers that were not found in the DOT study.

Lack of Management Support

A number of researchers have suggested that management is often unaware—or aware but not providing support or focus—of the role of networks in sharing knowledge across an organization. The literature indicates that management effort and support are required for successful knowledge transfers. Organization leaders have direct control over which activities are rewarded, which behaviors are encouraged, and how work is measured and valued in an organization, factors that all influence workers' motivation and ability to develop new knowledge (Bryant 2003). It is the organization's responsibility to establish a culture or environment that supports the forming of these networks, both loose and tight, to encourage the sharing of knowledge.

Implications and Recommendations

Findings of the knowledge sharing and networking study conducted in Virginia have implications that may be applicable to other organizations, including:

1. Barriers to knowledge sharing are greater than management support as evidenced by time allotted and resources provided for networking;
2. The loss of knowledgeable employees since the mid-1990s through retirements and attrition resulted in dissolutions or weakening of networks through which tacit knowledge was shared;
3. The continuing loss of employees further impedes the sharing and preservation of institutional knowledge;
4. Government employees need the visible and articulated support of management to engage in knowledge sharing;
5. Knowledge sharing results in benefits to the organization through improved processes, shared workloads, and easing of work assignments;
6. Younger employees desire to have the institutional knowledge recorded and made available electronically whenever feasible or to make tacit knowledge explicit; and
7. Long-term employees have a desire to share the knowledge gained over the years.

Agency-Related Recommendations

Recommendations resulting from this study for the agency are:

1. Increase management awareness of the value and impact of networks on the work performed;
2. Provide time and budget resources to support employee participation in cross-functional and cross-geographical networks to increase knowledge shared;
3. Develop networks for knowledge sharing;
4. Identify knowledge experts; and
5. Transform tacit knowledge to explicit when feasible and make it accessible electronically.

Lessons Learned

The agency hired a knowledge management director from outside the organization. Although the director had the knowledge and experience to develop a KM program, the new director did not have knowledge of the organization. To address this gap, a long-term employee was tapped to act as a guide for the new director. In this role he explained the history of the organization, the functions, and how they interacted; defined acronyms and terminology that were unfamiliar; and introduced the director to agency employees. As this long-term employee was well known and respected within the agency, this provided the new division with instant credibility.

That temporary assignment evolved into a permanent one, primarily at the request of the employee, who recognized the need for and value of a knowledge management program. The now-permanent staff person was also able to translate this experience into language that was instantly understood by his colleagues. The lesson learned is that an organization needs an experienced knowledge management professional to develop the program and to explain and define knowledge management for the organization, but it also needs the expertise and familiarity of a long-term employee to ensure that the program addresses the unique needs of the organization.

No two communities are alike within this agency. However, all communities were developed to provide something specific that would benefit the organization, whether that is the sharing of lessons learned that leads to cost avoidance, the development of a plan to address pending knowledge loss, the recovery of lost knowledge, or the sharing of knowledge between functions. Communities have an executive sponsor to ensure that participation is supported and that the community will provide the organization with a return on its investment. The knowledge management division provides coordination and organization for the community, facilitation of discussions, and the collection, organization, and dissemination of the knowledge across the agency. The lessons learned are that communities have unique needs and purposes but all must demonstrate value to the organization and to be successful community members need to meet face-to-face periodically to establish the necessary trust to share knowledge.

The knowledge management program was the direct result of the commissioner's initiative and vision, which was shared by the chief of technology, research and initiative. Both actively promoted the program prior to its inception and after, resulting in a willingness of employees to listen and to grant knowledge management the opportunity to pilot several programs. At that point, it was up to the KM team to demonstrate and persuade employees of the value of the program. The lessons learned were that the support of the top executive team was vital, particularly in the early days of the program to ensure that employees were given the support to participate. It was then important to demonstrate value to build grassroots support within the agency. Today, the program has the benefit of both.

To identify the impact of the knowledge management initiatives, participants were surveyed. The following statements by involved VDOT personnel illustrate sharing of lessons learned and current information in the original community:

- I view the reports from other PMs as adding value, as they provide unique real-time information and solutions from the other districts and projects.
- Allows me to see how others deal with issues and alerts me to potential issues.
- Other reports have given me insight into the management of the Virginia Public-Private Transportation Act of 1995 (PPTA) and design/build projects. For me, they have also proven to be a good tool to allow me to think of ways to develop and (at least) try to streamline some of our antiquated practices.
- Review of others' issues provides insight into issues that could surface on my projects and provides me time to consider them prior to their becoming a crisis.
- The reports are a valuable communication tool in what is happening and just as importantly in what is not. The reports can only help in strengthening the administrative team. We have had limited experience with multiple major projects . . . the reports keep us focused.

Members of the right of way and utilities community (formed to address the pending knowledge loss that will result from the retirement of about 80 percent of its employees) were surveyed on what value they perceived the agency gained from the community. The following received the highest ratings from the members:

- Ongoing—improved communication/collaboration
- Ongoing—improved processes and/or integration of people, ideas, differing objectives, or needs
- Lessons learned (can be related to projects, processes, or planning)
- Best practices (can be related to projects, processes, planning, or staffing)
- Effective process model for use elsewhere in the agency

The survey also questioned members of the right of way and utilities community on what value they perceived that the knowledge management office brought to the community:

- Effective facilitation of meetings
- Effective communication support (documentary or verbal)

- Collection of important and useful information
- Analysis of information to provide a useful result
- Integration of a working group that respects differences among people, ideas, and objectives or needs
- Neutral perspective—not associated with any specific group
- Access to decision makers
- Understanding of how to increase/improve collaboration

Conclusion

The development of a knowledge management division at the Virginia Department of Transportation has provided demonstrated value to the agency. Understanding of its role and goals has increased and has resulted in increasing support from both management and employees. The initiative is still in its early stages but a plan is in place to address the pending knowledge loss due to the retirements of long-term employees and to make that knowledge available to current and future employees.

References

Abrams, L.C., R. Cross, E. Lesser, and D.Z. Levin. 2003. "Nurturing Interpersonal Trust in Knowledge-Sharing Networks." *Academy of Management Executive* 17: 64–76.

Auditore, P.J. 2003. "Governments Worldwide Poised to Exploit Knowledge Management." *KM World* suppl. (June): 4.

Augier, M., and M.T. Vendele. 1999. "Networks, Cognition and Management of Tacit Knowledge." *Journal of Knowledge Management* 3: 252–61.

Bhatt, G.D. 2000. "Information Dynamics, Learning and Knowledge Creation in Organizations" (electronic version). *The Learning Organization* 7: 89.

Brown, J.S., and P. Duguid. 2001. "Knowledge and Organization: A Social-Practice Perspective." *Organization Science* 12: 198–213.

Bryant, S.E. 2003. "The Role of Transformational and Transactional Leadership in Creating, Sharing and Exploiting Organizational Knowledge." *Journal of Leadership and Organizational Studies* 9, no. 4: 32–44.

Burk, M. 2000. "Communities of Practice." *Public Roads* (May/June): 18–21.

Chatzkel, J. 2002. "Conversation with Alex Bennet, Former Deputy CIO for Enterprise Integration at the US Department of Navy." *Journal of Knowledge Management* 6: 434–44.

Chiem, P.X. 2001. "Knowledge Management in the Public Sector." *Destination CRM.* Available at www.destinationcrm.com/dcrm_ni_article.asp?id=560&art=mag&deptid=8. Accessed October 4, 2001.

Connelly, C.E., and E.K. Kelloway. 2003. "Predictors of Employees' Perceptions of Knowledge Sharing Cultures." *Leadership & Organization al Development* 24: 294–301.

Cross, R., T.H. Davenport, and S. Cantrell. 2003. "The Social Side of Performance." *MIT Sloan Management Review* (Fall): 20–21.

DeLong, D.W., and L. Fahey. 2000. "Diagnosing Cultural Barriers to Knowledge Management." *The Academy of Management Executive* 14: 113–27.

Droege, S.B., and J.M. Hoobler. 2003. "Employee Turnover and Tacit Knowledge Diffusion: A Network Perspective." *Journal of Managerial Issues* 15: 50–64.

Edwards, J.S., and J.B. Kidd. 2003. "Knowledge Management *sans frontières.*" *Journal of the Operational Research Society* 54: 130–39.

Knowledge Management (KM) Working Group of the Federal Chief Information Officers Council. 2001. *Managing Knowledge at Work: An Overview of Knowledge Management.* Available at www.km.gov. Accessed October 10, 2001.

Reagans, R., and B. McEvily. 2003. "Network Structure and Knowledge Transfer: The Effects of Cohesion and Range." *Administrative Science Quarterly* 48: 240–67.

Ribiere, V.M., and A.S. Sitar. 2003. "Critical Role of Leadership in Nurturing a Knowledge-Supporting Culture." *Knowledge Management Research & Practice* 1: 39–48.

Rubenstein-Montano, B., J. Buchwalter, and J. Liebowitz. 2001. "Knowledge Management: A U.S. Social Security Administration Case Study" (electronic version). *Government Information Quarterly* 18, no. 3.

Ruddy, T. 2000. "Taking Knowledge from Heads and Putting it into Hands." *Knowledge and Process Management* 7: 37–40.

Swan, J., S. Newell, H. Scarbrough, and D. Hislop. 1999. "Knowledge Management and Innovation: Networks and Networking." *Journal of Knowledge Management* 3: 262–72.

14

Conclusion: Knowledge Management's Role in the Drive to Transform Government

By 2006, four separate administrative policy themes had come together to shape a far-reaching movement with the objective of bringing greater cohesion, responsiveness, accountability, and overall improved performance to governments in the United States and elsewhere. These four management concepts included (1) implementing a business-driven approach to government administration; (2) forging an organizational culture that honors knowledge acquisition and sharing; (3) acceptance of a commitment to control the acquisition and use of information and communication technology; and (4) bringing a greater transparency, accountability, and accessibility in all government activities. These concepts are incorporated into the broadly based approach to transforming the federal government that is spelled out in detail in the 2002 President's Management Agenda (PMA).

The discussion in this chapter was inspired by federal agency representatives' presentations at federal e-government conferences over a period of several years, and from readings in government reports and professional and academic monographs. A framework for the chapter was suggested by a U.S. General Accounting Office (GAO) report presented to Congress in October of 2003: *Electronic Government: Potential Exists for Enhancing Collaboration on Four Initiatives.* The four PMA initiatives and their respective federal agencies—selected from twenty-five cross-agency e-government initiatives— in the GAO's collaboration study included e-payroll (Office of Personnel Management), Geospatial One-Stop (Department of the Interior), Integrated Acquisition Environment (General Services Administration), and the Business Gateway (Small Business Administration).

This chapter looks at four closely related transformational initiatives also promoted in the PMA: knowledge management, enterprise architecture, e-

Figure 14.1   **A Model of the Forces Shaping Transformation in Government**

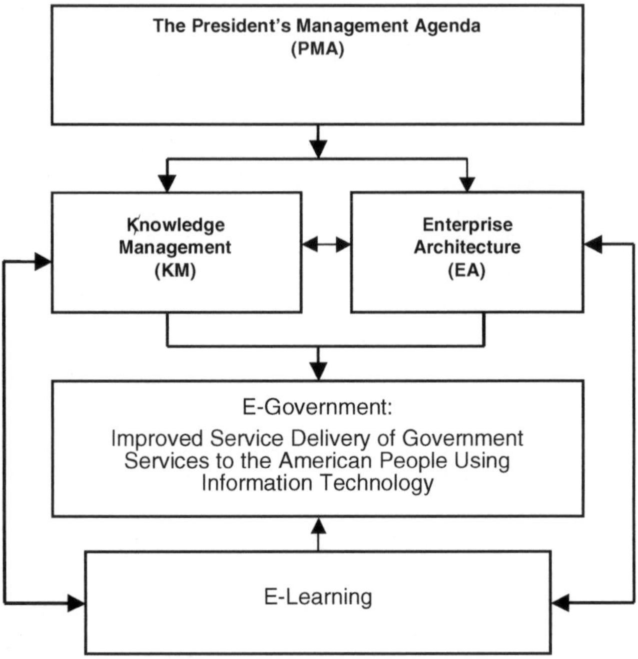

government, and e-learning. A model illustrating the interconnectedness of the four concepts is presented in Figure 14.1.

IT: The Unifying Element

Clearly, the unifying element in all of these transformation forces is the government's policies toward the use of information and communication technology (ICT). In fact, without the widespread application of ICT, e-government, e-learning, and knowledge management would not be possible. The federal government's dependence upon ICT was succinctly noted in the Whitehouse report on the third anniversary of the E-Government Act:

> The United States Government is one of the largest users and acquirers of data, information and supporting technology systems in the world, currently investing approximately $65 billion annually on Information Technology (IT). The Federal Government should be the world's leader in managing technology and information to achieve the greatest gains of productivity, service and results. (U.S. OMB 2005c)

PMA: The Transformation Policy Directive

The President's Management Agenda is the engine driving implementation of the initiatives and the programs they are spawning. As with all of the elements in the PMA, these initiatives are designed to help make government more transparent, efficient, accountable, and accessible. Because the PMA plays such an important role as the force for transformation, a brief review of its scope and content is presented prior to the individual elements. The objective of the chapter is to show how the four integrative management initiatives contribute as a whole to transforming the way our society is governed.

In the United States, the set of directives, policies, and procedures included in the PMA were designed to serve as a broad restructuring plan for reforming the way the U.S. government functions. Key objectives for the PMA include making the federal government (1) citizen-centered rather than bureaucracy-centered; (2) more results-oriented; and (3) market-based in its operations. This last objective referred to actively promoting—rather than stifling—innovation through competition (OMB 2002).

The PMA focuses on five government-wide and nine agency-specific goals, all of which are designed to improve management at the federal level. The five government-wide goals are: (1) strategic management of human capital; (2) competitive sourcing; (3) improved financial performance; (4) expanded electronic government; and (5) budget and performance integration.

These five goals are all interconnected and are continually being improved. One way this improvement is taking place is by requiring implementation of a federal *enterprise architecture* (EA) plan in every federal agency and department. Many of the programs included in the PMA have also been adopted at the state level—with varying levels of success. Knowledge management, the federal enterprise architecture initiative, e-government, and e-learning/e-training are examples of these transformation initiatives. State adoption of enterprise architecture initiatives is discussed in this chapter.

E-Government

The core outcome sought for this paradigm shift is the ongoing drive for the management and delivery of government services online—the process known as *digital government* or simply *e-government*. The General Accounting Office's definition of e-government is:

> The term "electronic government" (or e-government) refers to the use of information technology (IT), particularly Web-based Internet applications,

to enhance the access to and delivery of government information and service to citizens, to business partners, to employers, and among agencies at
all levels of government. (U.S. GAO 2003b)

Thus, e-government refers to a variety of government programs associated with the application of technology and information to accomplish the
greatest possible gains in productivity, service, and results. This plan to expand e-government is one of the key outcomes planned for in 2002 President's
Management Agenda, and therefore is a central product of the four initiatives discussed here. Overall, the underlying objectives of e-government continue to be achieving greater operational savings, better program results, and
better delivery of services (U.S. OMB 2005d).

The Bush administration's e-government program is off to a good start;
by 2006, improvements facilitated by the E-Government Act of 2002 were
being experienced both by citizens and throughout the government. In
the tax filing season, for example, 5.1 million citizens filed tax returns
online using the no-cost IRS Free File. In other activities, more than 17,000
grants applications had been received electronically; disaster management interoperability services were used in 111 disasters and 624 training exercises; and federal job seekers had filed more than 1,900,000
resumes online.

Comparing overall goals with actual agency results give a mixed picture
of how well implementation of the federal enterprise architecture is progress-
ing. While all 25 agencies assessed had a mature enterprise architecture plan
in place and more than expected had an acceptable business case (84 percent
compared to a goal of 75 percent), many of the agencies had not meet OMB
targets for 2005. The OMB's goal was 90 percent of all federal IT systems
certified and accredited. However, only 85 percent of the agencies met that
target. The goal of 90 percent of government agencies with certified IT systems was replicated for 2006.

Half of the identified gaps in the IT workforce were also targeted to be
filled in 2005, with the same target identified for 2006. In addition, at least
50 percent of the federal agencies were to be able to manage their IT portfolios in accordance with the OMB earned value management standard. However, only 28 percent of agencies had fully implemented earned value
management, with another 52 percent having implemented some parts of it.
Again, the goal for 2006 remained at 50 percent of agencies having fully
implemented the earned value management requirement.

To improve the development and use of common solutions across the federal government, the Office of Management and Budget (OMB) has developed e-government implementation plans with each agency to promote and

monitor their adoption and utilization of government wide solutions in order to avoid unnecessary redundant systems.

One of the most visible accomplishments to citizens was the development of a single-site entry point for accessing federal agencies; this was the PMA's *firstgov.gov* website. Through this website it became possible for citizens to change their address and file taxes online, as well as to access information from nearly all agencies branches of the federal government. The website received more than 6 million visitors per month in the first half of 2006.

Now that many agencies' enterprise architectures plans and analyses are beginning to mature, the federal government is exploring the opportunity to develop one federal enterprise architecture framework for use by all agencies. The problem, however, is that different agencies have used at least four major frameworks. While the difference between those frameworks is limited, a translator will be necessary to harmonize different frameworks' terminology, thus defeating one of the chief purposes of the exercise.

As the preceding chapters illustrate, the knowledge management initiative is one of the key products and management philosophies that federal administrators are employing to help bring about government transformation. Although it has already been discussed in some detail, the need for changing the culture of an organization before KM can function is discussed briefly below.

KM and the Needed Culture Change

A key integrating force is the knowledge management (KM) movement—itself one of the more recent of the procedures adopted from the public sector and the chief topic of this book. As we have seen in the earlier chapters, knowledge management involves a management philosophy and set of processes and procedures for collecting information about an organization's practices, processes, strategies, and programs. KM also integrates into an organization programs designed to collect, process, store, and disseminate needed internal and external information or organization stakeholders. KM includes developing and fostering a culture of knowledge sharing rather than hoarding. Finally, the KM activity in organizations includes administering data warehouses and supporting and developing knowledge workers through such methods as communities of practice, enterprise portals, story-telling, and other activities. KM has become particularly important in light of the extensive loss of knowledge expected to occur with the waves of retiring government workers expected over the next decade.

Figure 14.2 is a schematic representation of the basic structure of the

Figure 14.2 **KM in the Federal Enterprise Architecture Reference Model (FY07)**

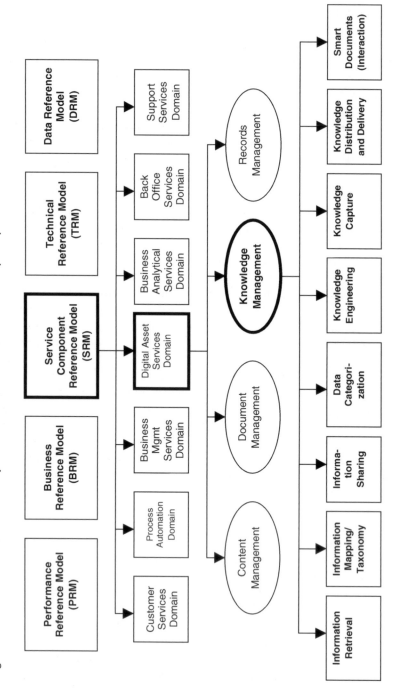

Federal Enterprise Architecture (FEA) initiative. It is included here because it shows where the government's knowledge management activities fall in this important management transformation program. FEA is constructed around five interrelated core elements: a Performance Reference Model (PRM), a Business Reference Model (BRM), a Services Component Reference Model (SRM), a Technical Reference Model (TRM), and a Data Reference Model (DRM).

Each of the five reference models incorporates a number of different "domains," or business activities under its umbrella. For example, the Services Component model covers the following domains: customer services, process automation, business management services, digital asset services, business analytical services, back office services, and support services. Each domain then frames a distinct set of "capabilities" or tasks that contribute to achieving the mission of that domain. For example, four capabilities are included in the Digital Asset Services Domain: content management, document management, knowledge management, and records management. The eight primary functions or responsibilities that are considered to be knowledge management capabilities are displayed in the bottom tier of Figure 14.2.

To summarize, the federal government's knowledge management functions and processes are one of the four capabilities in the Digital Asset Services Domain, which is one of the seven domains included in the Services Components Reference Model (SRM), which is one of the five reference models that make up the Federal Enterprise Architecture Program.

The objectives of the management agenda initiatives are simple and easy to understand. Moreover, many of the implementation elements have been carefully specified by the OMB and other agencies. Successful implementation of these initiatives has involved a significant change in the organizational cultures of public sector (and indeed private sector) organizations—in particular, changes in the mindsets, assumptions, and habits of legions of managers and employees. Careful architectural design and technical requirements planning alone are not enough (McNabb and Barnowe 2006).

The organizational culture model most conducive to successful knowledge management is the learning organization (Senge 1995). Learning organizations, with their focus on knowledge sharing and continuous learning, are the antithesis of large bureaucratic-mechanistic organizations, which are inherently oriented toward operational efficiency and control. In bureaucracies, information is concentrated at the top—the very stereotype of many public sector organizations, at least in the past. As Daft (2004) has noted, the changes in organization shape and design associated with learning organizations "require new values, new attitudes, and new ways of thinking and working together. A learning organization cannot exist without a culture that supports openness, equality, adaptability, and employee participation" (421).

Changes in organizational cultures are notoriously difficult, especially where existing cultures are entrenched (McNabb and Sepic 1995). For some public sector organizations, changes of this type and magnitude would be transformational, not simply incremental. Nonetheless, researchers in countries as diverse as Brazil (Guimaraes et al. 2001), Bulgaria (Pavlov and Katsamunska 2004), Canada (Lawrence 1998), El Salvador (*Conectándonos al Futuro*, 1999), and the USA (Apple 2000) are beginning to extol the benefits of the learning organization model for public-sector organizations (McNabb and Barnowe 2006).

Successful adoption and implementation of such public-sector operating initiatives as knowledge management, enterprise architecture, e-government, and e-learning requires that public-sector organizations embrace even more complex changes—and address the need for transformative changes to their organizational cultures. That many public-sector organizations already have set goals to become learning organizations will provide rich opportunities for public administration research in the years to come.

Enterprise Architecture

The federal enterprise architecture framework (EA) is one of the chief forces helping to make the transformation of government possible. The EA concept involves a comprehensive overview of an agency's operations, the technology it uses and plans to add in order to conduct those activities, and the strategies it follows as it strives to achieve its mission. According to the National Association of State Chief Information Officers (NASCIO 2005, 3), EA involves following a "disciplined, or *management engineering,* approach" to the act of running a government agency. Management engineering refers to constructing the organization so that it has the tools, technology, and people to accomplish its mission despite potentially catastrophic changes in its environment.

The enterprise architecture concept is not a new one; it was introduced in 1987 by former IBM engineer John Zachman as a tool for managers to organize their organizations and integrate their IT systems (Ruby 2004). Zachman came up with what he termed an underlying "Enterprise Architecture Framework" to serve as a guide for managers in integrating IT into the business. However, Zachman soon concluded that the framework he had developed for designing IT systems could also be used to organize an entire enterprise, and was applicable for both public- and private-sector organizations. Thus, he saw that the architecture could be a framework for identifying and designing the "set of guidelines, policies, models, standards, and process that, aligned to business strategy and information requirements, guides the selection, creation and implementation of solutions that are aligned with future business direction" (Zachman 1987, 1).

Zachman's enterprise architecture framework consisted of 36 data points in a six-by-six matrix. The six areas of the business are (1) the objectives and/or scope of the enterprise; (2) a model of the enterprise—the *business architecture*; (3) the IT architecture; (4) a technology architecture; (5) detailed program design; and (6) facilities and personnel architecture. Architecture planners must come up with answers to these question areas for each of the enterprise areas: Data (what), function (how), network (where), people (who), time (when), and motivation (why). When completed by agency personnel, the EA can serve as "a blueprint for designing and implementing information technology solutions to serve current and future business functions. It can enhance coordination, reduce diversity, promote data sharing, and boost efficiency in the development of business [i.e., agency] solutions" (Leganza 2005).

Enterprise Architecture in Government

The Federal Enterprise Architecture (FEA) initiative includes a number of management policies and procedures that were not in Zachman's 1987 approach. The FEA requires agencies to identify architectures for at least these following management tasks and responsibilities (NASCIO 2005):

- Technology architecture
- Project management
- Architecture program management
- Security architecture
- Internal enterprise architecture consulting
- Data architecture
- Process architecture
- "Business" architecture, and
- Enterprise performance management

Initially, the goal for implementation of the federal enterprise architecture initiative focused on increasing efficiency, controlling IT costs, developing and implementing common solutions, and following up on the responsibilities of the E-Government Act of 2002. This also meant improving their electronic security and building an effective IT workforce. OMB evaluates performance on these program metrics: budget and performance, competitive sourcing, expanded electronic government, improved financial performance, and strategic management of human capital (U.S. OMB 2002).

The FEA has far reaching ramifications, touching on almost every federal government management activity, as the following statement by the association of state chief information officers attests (emphasis in the original):

> Enterprise architecture is not an end in itself. Rather, it is the path to *government transformation.* And, government will need to adopt an iterative change management process in order to identify, understand, and respond to current and future increasingly *complex* demands and needs. The requirements for improved government performance, reduced spending, and greater accountability to the citizens calls for smarter management—which includes the adoption of EA. (NASCIO 2005, 3)

The federal government has come a long way since 2002 in implementing the federal enterprise architecture, but there is still much work to be done—and even more work required at the state government level. As part of the PMA's objective to improve federal management, the Office of Management and Budget (OMB) measures the progress of each federal agency and department every quarter. Results are reported on OMB's "balanced score card." The measurements compare an agency's achievement against where approved goals indicate it should be. Results are reported on the scorecard as a "stop-light" with red, yellow, and green symbols making it easy to see which agencies are achieving the goals and which are not. A green score indicates the agency is achieving its goals; it is the highest rating possible. A yellow score indicates needs for greater efforts, while a red score signals that the agency is in real danger of not achieving the planned objectives (Weigelt 2006).

Enterprise architecture is obviously of great focus in the federal government and significant results have already been accomplished. But what about the individual states? Are they working just as hard on implementing enterprise architecture?

Enterprise Architecture at the State Level

While enterprise architecture requirements are close to being fully implemented at the federal level, many of the program's components are also being implemented at the state level. To determine the level of implementation by the states, in August 2005 NASCIO conducted a census to find out how far the individual states have come in adopting enterprise architecture. The results of that survey, published in October 2005, listed results from 37 states and the District of Columbia—a response that represented more than 80 percent of the U. S. population.

The survey found that the states have made significant progress toward adoption of enterprise architecture since 1999, when the last survey was done. Key results include that 95 percent of the states had adopted some level of enterprise architecture; 71 percent believed it necessary to have dedicated enterprise architecture staff; and 92 percent believed it necessary to have a defined process for enterprise architecture. However, most of the states' emphasis had only focused technology architecture, although a minority of states had broadened their architecture to include business architecture, performance management, and process architecture.

Approximately 85 percent of the states responding to the NASCIO survey had adopted technology architecture; nearly 70 percent had adopted program management architecture; and close to 65 percent had adopted architecture program management. A somewhat surprising find is that only about 60 percent of the states have implemented security architecture. NASCIO finds it noteworthy that cyber security is a top priority for state CIOs, while the implementation apparently has fallen behind.

The survey also revealed that 70 percent of the states either had or planned to have full-time staff dedicated to managing the enterprise architecture program; 30 percent of the states have no plans to employ full-time staff to their enterprise architecture.

Enterprise Architecture: A Case Example

Washington State is typical of the states now beginning to implement enterprise architecture throughout its operations. The implementation process is under the direction of the State Department of Information Services (DIS). A complete statement of the state's e-government program is spelled out in a planning document published in February of 2000 (DIS 2000). Follow-on plans for managing the state's e-government program was released as an initial draft on September 7, 2005, as version 1.0 on September 21, 2005, and as version 1.1 on November 2, 2005. The plan discussed procedures for managing the state's enterprise architecture program and includes items such as program management principles, an architecture lifecycle, and program iterations and architecture releases.

To provide overall guidance and oversight, the state's Information Services Board (ISB) has established an Enterprise Architecture Committee (EAC). The mission of the EAC is:

> [T]o build and maintain an enterprise architecture program that guides and optimizes state resources; enables agencies to meet their strategic goals;

facilitates the management of organizational and technological change and complexity; and helps agencies manage the state's IT resources as assets within its portfolio of investments." (ISB 2006)

As of 2006, Washington had standards for one initiative (networking architecture) established and three initiatives underway: Voice-over Internet Protocol (VoIP), integration architecture initiative, and a geographic information technology (GIT) initiative. A charter has been written for each initiative, but only the charter for the networking architecture networking standards initiative had been approved by the Enterprise Architecture Committee; charters for the other initiatives were still under development (DIS 2006). These initiatives were to be delivered by June 30, 2006, so that they could be used to make investment decisions for 2007 through 2009.

The purpose of the networking standards initiative is to develop policies, standards, and guidelines for network infrastructure solutions, assets, and services that are common statewide. The initiative seeks to evolve a set of early adoptions-components (Tier One) in the statewide Enterprise Architecture. The purpose of the Voice-over Internet Protocol (VoIP) initiative is to provide telephony tools that will assist agencies in making decisions about the deployment of Voice-over IP technologies. These tools focus on:

- Establishing a standard set of measures to assess agencies' technical readiness to implement Voice-over IP
- Establishing standard factors that agencies should consider in making a business case for implementation of Voice-over IP
- Defining standard features of Voice-over IP implementations and establishing potential standard techniques or protocols for implementing those features

The initial usage of these standards, guidelines, and solutions are to support the financial and administrative systems "roadmap" initiative. Information about the roadmap can be found at its website: www.ofm.wa.gov/roadmap.

The purpose of the state's integration architecture EA initiative is to simplify implementation of business capabilities and to allow state agencies to benefit from all agency IT capabilities. This initiative's intent is to support the integration of information systems between government agencies without compromise and wherever operationally and technically feasible. The infrastructure solutions established by this initiative will be documented within the statewide enterprise architecture's solution architecture. Standards and guidelines will be documented within the technology architecture. The integration architecture initiative also expects to establish information architecture components that are relevant to the integration of information systems. For example, this initiative expects to develop data modeling conventions and metadata, and standards for the representation of information as messages between systems.

Finally, a geographic information technology (GIT) initiative is planned to identify a standard approach for integrating all GIT systems in the state. This initiative is jointly sponsored by the ISB committees on enterprise architecture and geographic information technology (DIS 2006).

E-Learning

Closely related to the federal e-government mandate is the new *e-learning initiative*. Under its original title of "GoLearn.gov," this program was instituted under the Office of Personnel Management's *e-training imitative,* which was one of the first 24 e-government initiatives included in the PMA. The GoLearn.gov site was launched in July 2002 to make available a wide variety of free, high-interest, and agency-mandated courses. By the end of FY 2004, the site recorded 314,952 completed courses out of the 441,537 registrations since its beginning (U.S. OMB 2005d). The GoLearn.gov site was renamed the USALearning.gov to become "the official learning and development site for the U.S. federal government" (USALearning n.d., "Introduction"). USALearning has become the portal for access to all federal government e-training and e-learning products and services.

E-learning has roles to play in such PMA-directed elements as personnel management, knowledge management, information architecture, and e-government. Thus, it is also coming to be seen as an important tool for implementing and maintaining the momentum of government transformation.

According to Al Corbett, a U.S. Department of Energy spokesman, the original goals for the e-learning/e-learning initiative are:

- To support and move forward the PMA by unifying and simplify e-training programs across all government agencies.
- To improve the efficiency and effectiveness of government operations by providing training as and where it is needed.
- To support federal agency human capital initiatives by leveraging existing e-training resources.
- To serve as a focal point for e-training access across agencies.
- To aid in the transformation of government by providing learning opportunities to all employees.
- To push lifelong learning as a strategic goal, improving agency ability

to react to changes and challenges, and become more cost effective in the performance of their services. (Corbett 2002)

By 2006, these goals had been amended to go beyond just offering e-training courses as the following OPM statement attests:

> The goals of the e-Training initiative extend far beyond offering e-training courses. The Gov Online Learning Center is evolving into an online learning center of excellence focused on easily accessible, high quality learning and performance support. In addition to the myriad e-training course and e-mentoring offered through GoLearn [now USALearning], employees can obtain targeted learning objects on demand and make use of performance support tools for research and career management; supervisors and managers can use performance support tools to provide skill gap analysis and integrate into plans for the strategic development of human capital. (U.S. OPM 2006, n.d.)

Developments in the capacity, functionality, and declining cost of information and communications technology (ICT) have greatly increased access to and the availability of information for everyone (Dirr 1999). Moreover, ICT has shown itself to be an effective medium for delivering instructional content. ICT and the Internet have resulted in learning that is "constructivist, interactive, collaborative, learner centered, and just in time" (Wonacott 2002).

Both the rate and the extent of change occurring in the economic, social, and technological foundations of higher education delivery systems are increasing dramatically. In addition, the knowledge base in many disciplines is expanding so rapidly that it is almost impossible for most people to stay current in a field. At the same time, existing knowledge becomes obsolete often before it can be fully absorbed. Imparting information and sharing knowledge among government workers at all levels involves imparting practical experience with current e-government applications, including the ability to diagnose, prescribe, and monitor the design and application of solutions to management problems.

The E-Training Initiative was included in the 2002 President's Management Agenda to meet these challenges. The program is one of five e-government initiatives managed by the Office of Personnel Management.

E-learning is generally considered to be synonymous with distance learning (or distance education), with the terms often used interchangeably. However, this is not entirely correct. Distance education does not necessarily involve computers, the Internet, or any electronic media at all; e-learning does. For most of its history, distance education meant correspondence courses, with student-teacher interaction taking place via the mails. E-learning, on the other hand, has been defined as a "process of delivering instructional material to remote sites via the Internet, intranet/extranet, audio, video, satellite broadcast, interactive TV, and CR-ROM" (Holsapple and Lee-Post 2006, 67–68).

The Role of the Internet

The Internet has brought about significant changes in the way business, government, and education transfer knowledge. Today, organizations increasingly use such strategies as e-commerce, e-government, and e-learning to deliver content to their respective stakeholders. Personal computers, the Internet, and the World Wide Web have entirely reshaped the way that products and services are developed, produced, and delivered (Sternstein 2006).

The Internet is the chief component in many e-learning systems, resulting in what is often referred to as Internet-based, Internet-enhanced, or Internet-enabled learning. Internet-based instruction can take many forms. Figure 14.3 is an illustration of just a few of the many different approaches that are being used to deliver instructional content. In practice, however, distance learning programs appear to fall into two mutually exclusive camps, with a smaller number of schools providing more than one avenue for program completion (*Online University Directory*, www.online-university.us/mba-degrees-on-line.htm).

Instructional delivery systems range across this continuum, with traditional classroom-based systems at one pole and completely external delivery systems at the other. The exclusively distance-learning model is positioned at the opposite pole of the content-delivery continuum. This model may be defined from both an educational and a technological point of view. From the instruction view, e-learning is seen as the *use of print or electronic media to deliver instructional content when learners and teachers are separated in time and/or place.* From the point of view of technology, it has been defined as *the means of getting people together* (including through video conferencing) *in the same electronic space, thereby facilitating mutual learning* (Kerka 1996).

The combined models are sometimes collectively referred to simply as *e-learning*. They have been defined as "education created and delivered by using technologies related to (the) computer, the Internet and telephony, in combination or in isolation" (Chadha and Kumail 2002, 31). Clearly, if judiciously applied, distance or online learning is not a substitute for the classroom, but an extension of the classroom.

272

Figure 14.3 **A Continuum of Content Delivery Models with Illustrative Pedagogies**

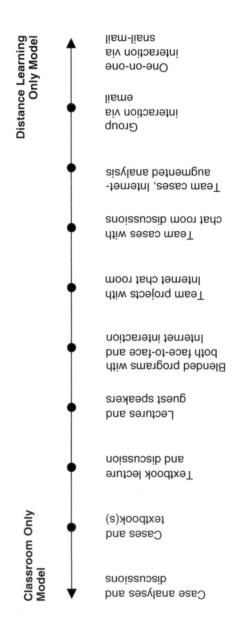

Classroom Only
Model

Case analyses and
discussions

Cases and
textbook(s)

Textbook lecture
and discussion

Lectures and
guest speakers

Blended programs with
both face-to-face and
Internet interaction

Team projects with
Internet chat room

Team cases with
chat room discussions

Team cases, Internet-
augmented analysis

Group
interaction via
email

One-on-one
interaction via
snail-mail

Distance Learning
Only Model

Source: MacDonald and McNabb (2006).

The central positions on the continuum employ many of the best components and pedagogies of both of the two opposite approaches. The use of the World Wide Web and the Internet are cornerstones in these combined approaches. These combinations benefit from the chief strength of the Internet by overcoming the barriers of time and space in teaching and learning. Moreover, they also maintain the important benefits that accrue from onsite learning by enabling face-to-face student/teacher interaction.

Whether it occurs in the classroom or at a distance, Internet-based instruction typically takes one or more of the following forms: (1) electronic mail, including delivery of course materials, assignments, giving and receiving feedback, participation in discussion groups, and other interactive activities; (2) electronic bulletin boards serving newsgroups and special-topic discussions; (3) student accessing and downloading of course materials, handouts, or tutorials; (4) interactive tutorials on the Web; (5) real-time, one-on-one or group interactive conferencing; (6) intranet websites with limited access; (7) sharing of online databases, catalogs, and other library information; and (8) sharing and/or contributing to research related to specific study issues or questions (Kerka, 1997).

Conclusion

This chapter examined four closely related transformational initiatives contained in the President's Management Agenda, comprehensive program designed to make the federal government more transparent, accessible, and better able to perform its many services. The four interrelated activities included in this drive for the transformation of government are knowledge management, enterprise architecture, e-learning, and e-government. This chapter has shown how closely each activity depends on what happens with the others, and how critical it is for all levels of government to coordinate their implementation.

The key integrating element in all of these initiatives is information and communications technology. Technology is one of the key pillars of knowledge management programs: enterprise architecture is all about how technology is planned and used in organizations, and without communications technology e-learning and e-government programs simply could not exist.

A key objective for the knowledge management initiative is to make sure that critical operational knowledge held by government workers is collected, shared, and retained. This often requires a major change in the culture of an organization. As large numbers of government worker retirements are expected from now through 2015, KM is becoming particularly important. As the baby boom generation workers retire, without KM much of what they know about their agencies' functions typically leaves with them.

The enterprise architecture initiative has three chief objectives: to make all government information and communication technology systems compatible, to avoid duplication and waste in technology purchases, and to ensure the development and acquisition of the latest advances in technology. The federal government's implementation of a combined e-training and e-learning initiative is designed to provide continuous training and education to all government workers. Again, the training of new workers needed to replace large numbers of retirees in the next few years makes e-learning and KM critical requirements for all government agencies. E-learning is also necessary to help prepare current administrators by providing them with the management and technological skills they need to transform government.

Perhaps the most important concept to take away from this chapter and the book as a whole is that all the government's management initiatives are closely interrelated. It is not possible to design and implement a program to collect, archive, and share knowledge, for example, without also coordinating the program with a detailed enterprise architecture analysis and design to accomplish the many knowledge tasks. Once such a coordinated program is in place, implementing the necessary culture change and program actions will require establishing and implementing e-learning and e-training policies, procedures, and programs.

Public sector managers and administrators seeking to raise their e-government accomplishments to acceptable levels in their annual performance assessments need to address these programs as an integrated whole—with full recognition of the synergistic contribution that they can make together—in the mandated drive to transform the way our governments function. The far-reaching goal of e-government—to make it possible for all citizens to access most if not all government information and programs electronically—cannot be achieved without also completing the complimentary tasks incorporated into knowledge management, enterprise architecture, and e-learning.

Glossary

This glossary was developed from a variety of public- and private-sector sources. Because most if not all public-sector knowledge management activities were first developed and tested in business and industry applications, until recently there has not been a need for a sector-specific glossary. In addition, knowledge management practitioners in both the private and the public sectors employ extensive use of jargon and acronyms—most but not all of which are found in both sectors. Ergo, this glossary focuses on the limited number of core terms commonly found in the international KM literature, regardless of sector. The glossary is arranged in alphabetical order. In those instances where more than one term is used for the same activity or thing, these are also included as often as possible. This is still a rapidly evolving discipline; the terms and definitions used today may not be the same tomorrow. Therefore, some mistakes may appear and some important terms may be omitted. These reflect the best information available at the time of the book's preparation.

Adaptive Learning. Also known as *single-loop learning,* adaptive learning is the use of knowledge to solve specific problems based on existing assumptions and on what has worked in the past. It is the first step in *double-loop learning.*

After-Action Review. A process developed by the U.S. Army to help teams learn quickly from their successes and failures by sharing their learning with other teams. The review is a structured discussion that takes place as soon as possible after a project has been completed. The purpose is to determine what should have happened, what actually happened, and why it happened. This allows team members to emphasize their strengths and improve on any weaknesses when engaging in subsequent tasks or projects.

Compiled from a variety of sources, including the UK National Electronic Library for Health (2004), Daniel Stuhlman of Stuhlman Management Consultants (http://home .earthlink.net/~ddstuhlman/defin1.htm), and others, and are used with permission.

Artificial Intelligence: A broad term that describes computer programs designed to simulate human thought processes and behaviors to solve human-like problems.

Balanced Scorecard: A performance evaluation model developed by Robert S. Kaplan and David P. Norton (1996) as a tool to measure organizational performance against both short- and long-term goals. The balanced scorecard encourages administrators to focus their attention on the factors that most help the organization with its strategy. It measures other factors alongside the traditional financial or budgetary measures, including customer or client satisfaction, internal processes, employee learning, and the like. It is sometimes used in setting and measuring performance with knowledge management initiatives.

Benchmarking: Benchmarking is the practice of comparing the performance of an agency, department, or other government entity against the performance of a "best" agency, department, or organization similar to yours. The purpose is to determine how well your agency is doing compared to others in the same field. It also allows agencies to learn from the identified best practices.

Best Practices: A "best practice" is the performance, a process, or a method that has been identified as working well; it is, therefore, an exemplar that can be recommended for emulation. The term "good practice" is sometimes substituted by people who feel that it is impossible to identify a single "best" practice. Best practices may be found in behaviors, routines, scripts, and other approaches that are related to certain situations, problems, an organization, or organizations.

Best Practices Index (BPI): A performance management tool. The BPI is the degree to which an organization, agency, or unit has implemented seven key management practices: strategic planning, long-term financial planning, risk management planning, optimized asset management, performance measurement, customer involvement, and continuous improvement.

Budget and Performance Integration (BPI): One of the five key initiatives in President G.W. Bush's management agenda, BPI consists of efforts to ensure that performance is routinely considered in funding and management decisions and that those programs achieve expected results and work toward continual improvement.

Business Process Reengineering (BPR): This organizational transformation tool focuses on detecting the core processes that together constitute the agency or business, and reconstituting them in a more efficient way, without functional barriers. BPR was designed to reduce complexity by reengineering operational and customer-directed activities into normal processes.

Capacity Building: A term in knowledge management that identifies a process of improving an organization's ability to implement a KM initiative, principle, or practice.

Champion: An important concept that refers to a high-level member of the organization who actively supports and promotes a management concept such as KM inside the organization, thereby persuading other managers, administrators, and staff of its benefits.

Chief Information Officer (CIO): A senior-level administrator or manager who typically manages the organization's entire IT or ICT program. The CIO has responsibility for information management and information technology; in some organizations, the chief knowledge officer reports to the CIO.

Chief Knowledge Officer (CKO): A senior-level administrator or an administrator who is responsible for ensuring effective knowledge collection and transfer of knowledge held by members of the organization, and manages information assets (technology) to achieve gains in performance and competitiveness.

Codification: The process of putting knowledge held in the organization into a form or forms that enable it to be communicated to others in the organization. A collection of "codes" is sometimes referred to as a "taxonomy" of knowledge. One way this is done is by writing things down, putting them into documents, and entering them into databases. Other methods include illustrations and sound and video recordings. *Knowledge harvesting* is a related term. A number of software programs, using keywords and/or descriptors, may be used as an aid in the codification process.

Collaboration: A process that leads to innovation of business processes, ultimately increasing organizational productivity and competitiveness through the sharing of information and knowledge among partners, clients, and suppliers.

Communication Processes: Information and communications technology with social processes that enable people to share information.

Community: The core group of members of an organization or group from which a community of practice or community of interest is formed. A community may include conveners, core members, and active, inactive, and peripheral members. Leadership in the community is exercised by a community coordinator.

Community of Interest (CoI): An informal network of people who share a common interest in a particular topic, either work related or peripheral to work, and who come together informally to share knowledge on that topic.

Community of Practice (CoP): A group of individuals that is informally bound to one another through a common class of practices and in pursuit of greater knowledge. Communities of practice make up the knowledge structures of an organization. In practice, CoPs are informal groups that complement formal structural groups such as departments and teams.

Community Workspace: A virtual team accomplishing a project goal through collaboration. The work of the group accelerates success, improves solutions, and captures work and knowledge for the organization.

Competitive Sourcing (CS): One of the five key initiatives in President G.W. Bush's management agenda, CS calls for regularly examining commercial activities performed by the government to determine whether it is more efficient to obtain such services from federal employees or from the private sector (often referred to as *outsourcing*).

Content Management: *Content* refers to computer-based information such as the content of a Web site or a database. Content management is about making sure that content is relevant, up-to-date, accurate, easily accessible, and well organized so that quality information is available to users when it is needed.

Core Competencies: Core competencies are what an agency does best. They are a combination of knowledge capabilities that represent the agency's key strength. Core competencies are considered to be sustainable over time.

Cultural Knowledge: The shared assumptions and beliefs that are used by people in organizations to (1) perceive and explain reality, and (2) assign value and significance to new information.

Customer Capital: The combined value of all the relationships an organization has with its customers or clients, past, present, and future. Customer capital includes tangible and intangible factors, including customer opinions, customer loyalty, and preferences. Customer capital is a component of a larger value concept, intellectual capital.

Customer Relationship Management (CRM): CRM is a business strategy based on selecting and proactively managing the most valuable customer relationships. It requires a customer-focused philosophy to support effective marketing, sales, and customer service processes. A number of commercially available software programs have been developed to enable organizations to do a better job of managing their customer relations programs.

Data: Data are facts, concepts, or statistics that can be collected, stored, or analyzed to produce information.

Data Mining: A technique for analyzing data in very large databases and making new connections between the data in order to reveal trends and patterns. Data mining is also known as knowledge discovery in databases (KDD); it is the extraction of implicit, previously unknown, and potentially useful information from databases. The process uses machine learning, statistical correlations and statistical analysis, and sophisticated search strategies to extract data in such a way that the information is easily comprehensible.

Document: A record of an event or recorded knowledge so that the information will not be lost. Documents are usually written, but may also be made up of images and/or sound. Documents can be put into electronic or digital form and stored in a computer.

Document Management: Systems and processes for managing documents, including the creation, editing, production, storage, indexing, and disposal of documents. This usually refers to electronic documents and uses specific document management software.

Domain: The domain of a community of practice includes the key issues or problems that members of the larger group seek to resolve, or that they consider essential to the group's primary mission. Members typically have a passion for the domain topic and understand how it contributes to a greater social good.

Double-Loop Learning. Different from single-loop learning, double-loop learning involves questioning existing assumptions in order to create new insights. Consider the problem, How can we prevent earthquakes from killing people? Single-loop learning would involve learning how earthquakes happen, then trying to predict them to be better prepared to survive them. The double-loop response would be to question the idea of "earthquake" and might conclude that earthquakes do not kill people; falling buildings do. Double-loop learning is also known as *generative learning*.

E-Business: The use of electronic information technologies (especially Internet technologies) in business practices. E-business may be business to customer (B2C) or business to business (B2B).

E-Commerce: The use of electronic information systems (especially Internet technologies) to perform business transactions (buy and sell).

E-Government: The delivery of governmental services using electronic information systems (especially Internet technologies).

E-Government Act of 2002: H.R. 2458/S. 803 was signed by President G.W. Bush on December 17, 2002, with an effective date of April 17, 2003. The act establishes an office of e-government within the OMB, and authorizes the naming of an e-administrator. It requires an annual report to Congress; calls for dialogue with state and local as well as tribal governments, the general public, and the private and nonprofit sectors to find innovative ways to improve the performance of governments in collaborating on the use of information technology to improve the delivery of government information and services; sets standards for federal agency Web sites; and creates a public directory of agency Web sites.

E-Learning: The use of electronic information systems to deliver learning and training.

E-Mail: Short for electronic mail. Uses Internet technologies to send messages and documents to and from computers around the world in a matter of seconds. Sending or receiving e-mail requires Internet access and an e-mail address.

Enterprise Architecture: A comprehensive model of all the key elements and relationships that make up an enterprise, agency, or organization. The federal enterprise architecture initiative forbids federal agencies to purchase technology without first completing an enterprise architecture study of their organization and its IT needs.

Expanded Electronic Government (EEG): One of the five key initiatives in President G.W. Bush's management agenda, EEG refers to programs to ensure that the federal government's $60-billion annual investment in information technology (IT) significantly improves the government's ability to serve citizens, and that IT systems are secure, delivered on time, and on budget.

Expertise: A tacit ability of individuals, ratified through a community of practice, to approach a problem with a large bag of tools, practices, and relationships that lead to new ways of doing things, which are then emulated in "best practices."

Expert System: A computer program developed to simulate human decisions in a specific field or fields; expert systems are considered to be a branch of artificial intelligence.

Expertise Directory (Experts Directory or Skills Directory): A staff directory in the form of a database that includes details of people's skills, knowledge, experience, and expertise. The directory allows users to search for people with specific know-how, using search engines and key words.

Explicit Knowledge: Knowledge that can be easily expressed in words or numbers, or both, and that can be shared through discussion or by writing it down and producing it as documents, manuals, or databases. Examples might include a telephone directory, an instruction manual, or a report of research findings.

Externalization: The process of making tacit (or implicit) knowledge explicit.

Extranet: A Web site that links an organization with other specific organizations or people. Extranets are accessible only to those specified organizations or people and are protected by passwords.

Federal Enterprise Architecture (FEA): A business reference model–based initiative designed to provide a common framework for improvement in such areas of federal government operations as budget allocations and budget and performance integration, horizontal and vertical information sharing, performance measurement, cross-agency collaboration, e-government, and component-based architectures, among others. Led by the Office of Management and Budget, FEA's fundamental purpose is to identify opportunities to simplify processes and unify work across agencies and within the lines of business of the federal government. A key goal of FEA is to help agencies become a more citizen-centered, customer-focused government that maximizes investments to better achieve mission outcomes.

Federal Enterprise Architecture Management System (FEAMS):
FEAMS is a Web-based management information repository and analysis system designed to provide agencies with access to initiatives aligned to the federal enterprise architecture (FEA) and associated references models. FEAMS was issued by the OMB in December of 2003 to provide users with an intuitive approach to discover and potentially leverage information technology components, business services, and capabilities across the federal government.

Firewall: Software that protects an organization's computer systems from such problems as viruses that can be carried by Internet technologies or hackers seeking to gain unauthorized access to a database or system.

Government Secure Intranet (GSI): A limited-access intranet that links government departments.

Groupware: Computer software applications that are linked together by networks, and so allow people to work together and share electronic communications and documents.

HTML: Abbreviation for *HyperText Markup Language.* The major language of the Internet's World Wide Web. Web sites and Web pages are written in HTML, which basically consists of a set of instructions for creating Web pages.

Human Capital: The knowledge, skills, and competencies of the people in an organization. Human capital is one component of intellectual capital.

ICT: Abbreviation for Information and Communication Technology (plural: ICTs)

Implicit Knowledge: *See* Tacit Knowledge.

Improved Financial Performance (IFP): One of the five key initiatives in President G.W. Bush's management agenda, IFP is concerned with accurately accounting for taxpayers' money and giving managers timely and accurate program cost information to improve management decisions and control costs.

Information: The organized data that has been arranged for better comprehension or understanding. What is one person's information can become another person's data.

Information and Communication Technology (ICT): Technology that combines computing with high-speed communications links carrying data, sound, and video.

Information Technology (IT): IT includes the physical components of computing, including servers, networks, and desktop computing, which enable digital information to be created, stored, used, and shared. IT is one of the chief components in a KM system.

Innovation: The creation of something new or different; the conversion of knowledge and ideas into a new benefit, such as new or improved processes or services. A related term is *invention,* which implies something entirely new, while innovation can also mean new uses for old or existing tools, materials, and/or processes.

Intellectual Assets: *See* Knowledge Assets.

Intellectual Assets Management (IAM): The management of an organization's intellectual assets in order to improve the performance of the organization. In theory, IAM is synonymous with knowledge management, but, in practice, intellectual assets management tends to focus more on issues relating to intellectual property such as exploiting patents, copyrights, trademarks, and other intellectual property rights.

Intellectual Capital: The same as the knowledge assets of an organization. This capital is the set of intangible assets that includes the internal knowledge employees have of information processes, external and internal experts, products, clients and customers, and competitors. Intellectual capital includes internal proprietary reports, libraries, patents, copyrights, and licenses that record the company history and help it plan for tomorrow.

Intellectual Property Rights: The legal rights associated with intellectual property. Intellectual property is often copyrighted or trademarked.

Internalization: The process by which explicit (easily communicated or shared) knowledge is absorbed and made tacit (internal or personal).

Internet: The Internet is the system of computers that are linked together (networked) in order to allow the exchange of information and resources. Using computers connected via communications media (such as telephones), the Internet makes it easy for people all over the world to communicate with one another. The Internet is a shared global resource that is not owned or regulated by anyone (although authoritarian governments control some content and/or access by their citizens).

Intranet: A computer network that functions like the Internet, but in which the information and Web pages are located on computers within an organization or a restricted group of organizations. Intranets are not accessible to the general public.

Knowledge: One definition of knowledge is the facts, feelings, or experiences known by a person or group of persons. Knowledge is derived from information. However, it is much richer and more meaningful than information. It includes familiarity, awareness, and understanding gained through study, results or comparisons and combinations, identifying and weighing consequences, and making connections. Wisdom and insight are also included in some definitions of knowledge. In organizations, some synonyms for knowledge include know-how, applied information, information with judgment, and other phrases.

Knowledge Assets: Also known as *intellectual assets,* these are the parts of an organization's assets that relate to knowledge, including know-how, best practices, intellectual property, and others. Knowledge assets are sometimes divided into three separate parts: human (people, teams, networks, and communities), structural (the codified knowledge found in processes and procedures), and technological (the technologies that support knowledge sharing, such as databases and intranets).

Knowledge Audit: A method for reviewing and mapping information and its transfer in an organization. An audit examines such things as what information is needed, what information is currently available, where the information is located, in what form(s), how it flows in the organization, the location of gaps in the network, and where duplication exists. It also establishes the value of the information. In first-generation knowledge management systems the knowledge audit may be referred to as an information audit.

Knowledge Base: The body of knowledge available to an organization. It includes the knowledge held by people, supported by collections of information and data, and can also include patents, trademarks, etc. In some organizations, subject-specific knowledge bases are developed to collate information on key topics or processes. *Knowledge base* is also the term used to describe a database of information.

Knowledge Broker: A knowledge broker is some person or group in an organization who facilitates the creation, sharing, and use of knowledge. The term is also sometimes used to refer to companies or individuals that operate commercially as knowledge traders, or to firms providing knowledge-related services.

Knowledge Flows: The paths that knowledge takes in moving around and in and out of an organization.

Knowledge Integration: Integrating the tacit knowledge of two or more individuals to create new agency-level knowledge.

Knowledge Management: One definition of knowledge management is the creation and subsequent management of an organizational culture that encourages knowledge to be created, shared, learned, enhanced, organized, and used for the benefit of the organization and its stakeholders.

Knowledge Management Strategic Plan: A detailed plan that outlines how an organization intends to implement knowledge management principles and practices in order to achieve organizational objectives.

Knowledge Manager: A member of an organization with the developmental and operational responsibility for promoting and implementing knowledge management principles and practices in an organization or one or more of its units.

Knowledge Mapping: A process for identifying and recording where knowledge assets are located in an organization. A knowledge map also indicates how knowledge flows between and among members of the organization. This makes it possible to evaluate relationships between knowledge holders, a process that results in identifying the sources, flows, limitations, barriers, and losses of knowledge in the organization.

Knowledge Repository: A place where explicit knowledge is collected and stored. The term is also used to refer to the collection of information and knowledge organized according to categories of interest to the agency. A low-tech repository might be simply a set of file folders; a high-tech repository might be retained on a database platform that is accessible through such technologies as intranets and browsers.

Knowledge Segment: Everything an agency's staff and electronic systems know about a specific domain. For example, the FBI's knowledge total of firearms constitutes one of that agency's knowledge segments.

Knowledge Worker: An employee of an organization whose performance relies on his or her ability to find, process, combine, and even reject knowledge from within and without the organization.

Learning Organization: A learning organization is one that considers its future success to be based on maintaining continuous learning and adaptive behavior. Through learning from and reacting to its environments, the organization is able to develop skills in creating, acquiring, interpreting, and retaining knowledge. The organization then makes future modifications to its behavior in ways that reflect its new knowledge and insights.

Leverage: A process by which managers gain benefits from the use of a physical or knowledge-based resource that exceed the inherent value of the resource.

Lessons Learned Database: A database in which examples of previous experiences are stored, along with the reasons why they succeeded or failed, and the lessons that staff members learned from them.

Mentoring: Mentoring is a one-to-one learning relationship in which a senior member of an organization supports the development of a newer or more junior member by sharing his or her knowledge, experience, and wisdom with the junior member. A related term is *coaching.* The strength of mentoring lies in transferring the mentor's specific knowledge, experiences, and wisdom. In coaching, the strength lies in the ability of the coach to help the student develop his or her own personal qualities and abilities.

New Technology: Technology that is new to the organization, but not necessarily newly created or installed.

Organizational Best Practices Index: *See* Best Practices Index.

Organizational Culture: Often paraphrases the feeling of an organization's members expressed in the phrase "the way we do things around here." More formally, an organization's culture is a mixture of its traditions, values, beliefs, attitudes, and behaviors. Different organizations performing similar tasks can have vastly different cultures. An organization's culture is important in knowledge management; it must value and promote such qualities as trust and openness. If it does not, then KM initiatives are not likely to succeed.

Organizational Learning: Popularized in Peter Senge's 1990 text *The Fifth Discipline, organizational learning* refers to the ability of an organization to gain knowledge from experience, through experimentation, observation, analysis, and a willingness to examine both successes and failures, and then to use that knowledge to do things differently. Organizational learning cannot occur without individual learning, although individual learning does not necessarily promote organizational learning. For organizational learning to take place, the organization as a body must become more knowledgeable and skillful in pursuing its goals and objectives.

Organizational Memory: This is the sum of the knowledge and understanding embedded in an organization's people, processes, services, or products, along with its traditions and values. Organizational memory can either promote or hinder the progress of the organization.

Peer Assist: A practice in which an individual or team calls a meeting or a workshop in order to tap the knowledge and experience of others before embarking on a project or activity.

Portal: A special Web page that organizes access to all of the online resources about a topic, an organization, an agency, or an individual, providing a one-stop shop of sorts. It is often referred to as a *Web portal.*

Practice: A core concept in communities of practice, practice denotes both methodologies and skills; it includes the job or task-related techniques, methods, stories, tools, and professional attitudes of the members of the community.

President's Management Agenda (PMA): The PMA was launched in 2002 as a strategy for improving the management and performance of the federal government. It focuses on the areas where deficiencies were most apparent and where the government could begin to deliver concrete, measurable results. PMA includes five federal government-wide initiatives and ten program-specific initiatives that apply to a subset of federal agencies. The five key government-wide areas are: strategic management of human capital, competitive sources, improved financial performance, expanded electronic government, and budget and performance integration (see individual entries for definitions of each area). For each initiative, PMA established clear, government-wide goals (termed *standards for success*), and developed aggressive action plans to achieve those goals. A government-wide scorecard reporting individual agency progress is published quarterly.

Process Team: A group of skilled workers responsible for an agency's operational and/or strategic processes.

Quick Win: An initiative or solution that yields rapid positive results. Building quick wins into a change initiative often promotes greater willingness to stay with the project.

RDI Methodology: Results-driven incremental methodology; a way of implementing a complex project or program such as a knowledge management system so that each phase builds on a learning experience gained from the preceding phases.

Records Management: Every organization creates records, whether they are on paper, on film, electronic records, or some other format. Records management helps an organization ensure that it is creating and maintaining an adequate documentary record of its functions, policies, decisions, procedures, and essential transactions. It then helps the organization to decide which records to keep and which to destroy, and how best to organize them all. Hence, it involves processes relating to the generation, receipt, processing, storage, retrieval, distribution, usage, and retirement of an organizations records.

Return on Investment (ROI): An estimate of the financial benefit (the return) on the money spent (the investment) of a particular program, system, or initiative. ROI is often used to aid in cost-benefit decision making.

Search Engine: A software program that carries out searches for information. Search engines are what facilitate literature searches on the Internet and in various informational databases.

Server: A computer that shares resources with other computers in a network.

Single-Loop Learning (*see* Adaptive Learning): Single-loop learning involves using knowledge to solve specific problems, using existing assumptions. It is often based on what has worked in the past. In contrast, double-loop learning goes a step farther and questions existing assumptions to create new insights and ideas.

Storytelling: The use of stories in organizations is a way of sharing knowledge and helping learning. Stories can be very powerful communication tools, and may be used to describe complicated issues, explain events and their antecedents, communicate lessons learned, and contribute to changes in organizational culture.

Strategic Knowledge Management: A way of focusing a KMS application that links the development of the agency's knowledge to a competency strategy.

Strategic Management of Human Capital (SMHC): One of five government-wide initiatives included in President G.W. Bush's management agenda, SMHC consists of processes to ensure the right person is in the right job, at the right time, and is not only performing, but performing well. It is closely associated with human resources planning (HRP).

Structural Capital: A term that refers to an organization's captured knowledge, such as best practices, processes, information systems, databases, etc. It is often used to describe the knowledge that remains in the organization after employees depart. Structural capital is one component of intellectual capital.

Tacit Knowledge: Knowledge that resides in the heads and hands of individuals. It is the implicit knowledge used by members of an organization to perform their work and to make sense of their worlds. It is very difficult to use documents or other media to transfer tacit knowledge to others without learning by doing. Tacit knowledge tends to be shared between workers through discussions, stories, and personal exchanges. It includes skills, experiences, insight, intuition, and judgment.

Taxonomy: A hierarchical organizing structure for categorizing a body of information or knowledge. A taxonomy facilitates an understanding of how that knowledge can be broken down into logical parts, and how these parts relate to each other. Taxonomies are used to organize information in systems.

Thesaurus: An organized language, used for inputting and searching information systems. It predefines the relationships between terms and concepts used in its vocabulary.

Virtual Team: *Virtual* is a term used to describe something that exists or is brought together via electronic networks, rather than existing in a single physical place. A virtual team is a group of individuals who are not located together, but who use electronic networks for communication, collaboration, or work processes.

Web Browser: A software program that resides on a computer and enables access to the Internet and viewing of World Wide Web pages and documents. Netscape and Internet Explorer are examples of Web browsers.

White Pages: In knowledge management, *white pages* refers to a structured directory of people within an organization. It is usually in electronic form, and is often the basis for an expertise directory.

World Wide Web: The terms *the Internet* and *the Web* are often used interchangeably. However, the World Wide Web is actually a collection of Web pages that can be accessed on the Internet. The Web has become the most popular area of the Internet because everyone can view the pages regardless of what kind of computer they are using.

XML: An abbreviation for *eXtensible Markup Language.* XML is a successor technology to the markup language HTML, which is used for creating Web pages and documents.

Bibliography

Acs, Zoltan J. 2002. *Innovation and the Growth of Cities.* Cheltenham, UK: Edward Elgar.

AGIMO. 2004. *Better Practice Checklist: 13. Knowledge Management.* Australian Government Information Management Office. www.agimop.gov.au/practice/delivery/checklists/knowledge. Accessed July 6, 2005.

Aichholzer, Georg. 2003. "Scenarios of E-Government in 2010 and Implications for Strategy Design." *Electronic Journal of E-Government* (www.ejeg.com) 2(1): 1–9.

Alavi, M., and D. Leidner. 2001. "Knowledge Management and Knowledge Management Systems: Conceptual Foundations and Research Issues." *MIS Quarterly* 25(1): 107–36.

Alberts, David S., and Richard E. Hayes. 2003. *Power to the Edge: Command and Control in the Information Age.* Washington, DC: U.S. Dept. of Defense, Center for Advanced Concepts and Technology.

Altshuler, Alan A., and Robert D. Behn. 1997. "The Dilemmas of Innovation in American Government." In *Innovation in the Public Sector,* ed. Alan A. Altshuler and Robert D. Behn, 3–37. Washington, DC: Brookings Institution.

Altshuler, Alan A., and Marc D. Zegans. 1997. "Innovation in Public Management: Notes from the State House and City Hall." In *Innovation in the Public Sector,* ed. Alan A. Altshuler and Robert D. Behn, 68–80. Washington, DC: Brookings Institution.

Anantatmula, Vittal. 2005. "Knowledge Management Criteria." In *Creating the Discipline of Knowledge Management,* ed. Michael Stankosky, 170–87. Burlington, MA: Elsevier Butterworth-Heinemann.

Andre, John. 2003. "Chief Knowledge Position Description." KM.gov (June 25). Available at http://ioa-qpnet-co.gsa.gov/QuickPlace/km/PageLibrary85256C6B005EDD06 .NSFH_7a67. Accessed May 20, 2005.

Apple, Diana Dravnieks. 2000. "Evolution of the Forest Service Toward a Learning Organization." Policy White Paper (May 15). Available at www.fa.fed.us/publications/policy-analysis/fs_learning.html. Accessed June 24, 2005.

APSC. 2002. *Australian Government Use of Information and Communication Technology.* Report of the Australian Public Service Commission (October 14). Available at www.apsc.gov.au/mac/technology.htm. Accessed June 26, 2005.

Argyris, Chris, and Donald Schön. 1996. *Organizational Learning II: Theory, Method, and Practice.* Reading, MA: Addison-Wesley.

Aristigueta, Maria P. 2002. "Reinventing State Government: Managing for Results." *Public Administration Quarterly* 26(2): 147–73.

Ash, Amin, and Patrick Cohendet. 2004. *Architecture of Knowledge: Firms, Capabilities, and Communities.* Oxford: Oxford University Press.

Auditore, Peter J. 2003. "Governments Worldwide Poised to Exploit Knowledge Management." *KMWorld* 13(9): 54–55.

Bahra, Nickolas. 2001. *Competitive Knowledge Management.* Houndmills, UK: Palgrave.

Baird, Zoë, and James Barksdale. 2004. "There Is Security in Sharing: Information Network Would Aid Terror Fight." San Jose, CA, *Mercury News* (August 16): Op-Ed page. Available at MercuryNews.com. Accessed June 16, 2005. .

Barzelay, Michael. 2001. *The New Public Management.* Berkeley: University of California Press.

Baxter, Helen. 2002. "A KM Initiative Is Unlikely to Succeed Without a Knowledge Audit." *KnowledgeBoard* editorial. Available at www.knowledgeboard.com/cgi-bin/item/cgi?id=78415. Accessed July 8, 2005.

Bennett, W.L. 1997. "Why Government Innovation Is Not News: The View from the Newsroom." In *Innovation in the Public Sector,* ed. Alan A. Altshuler and Robert D. Behn, 177–201. Washington, DC: Brookings Institution.

Bhatta, G. 2001. Enabling the Cream to Rise to the Top: A Cross-Jurisdictional Comparison of Competencies for Senior Managers in the Public Sector." *Public Performance and Management Review* 25(2): 194–209.

Blessing, Luciënne M., and Kenneth M. Wallace. 2000. "Supporting the Knowledge Life-Cycle. *Proceedings of the 3rd Workshop on Knowledge-Intensive CAD,* Tokyo. Exerpt (The Learning Cycle). Available at www.adbn.ac.uk/hr/esdu/docs/box1.doc. Accessed June 22, 2005.

Bock, Freiderich. 1999. "The Intelligent Approach to Knowledge Management: Viewing KM in Terms of Content, Culture, Process and Infrastructure." *Knowledge Management Review* 7 (April): 22–25.

Bontis, Nick. 2002. "The Rising Star of the Chief Knowledge Officer." *Ivey Business Journal* (online version) (March/April): 20–25. Accessed March 6, 2005. www.ivebusinessjournal.com/view_article.asp?inArticleID=370.

Borras, John. 2003. "International Technical Standards for E-Government." *Electronic Journal of E-Government* (www.ejeg.com) 2(1): 76–80.

Bresciani, Paolo, Paolo Donzelli, and Angela Forte. (2003). "Requirments Engineering for Knowledge Management in Government." In *Knowledge Management in Electronic Government,* ed. Maria A. Wimmer. Berlin: Springer-Verlag.

Breu, Karin, David Grimshaw, and Andrew Myers. 2000. *Releasing the Value of Knowledge: A Survey of UK Industry.* Cranfield, UK: Cranfield University.

Brown, Mary M. 2001. "The Benefits and Costs of Information Technology Innovations." *Public Performance and Management Review* 24(4): 351–66.

Burk, Mike. 1999. "Knowledge Management: Everyone Benefits by Sharing Information." U.S. Department of Transportation, Federal Highway Administration. *Public Roads* 63(3). Available at www.tfhrc.gov.pubrrds.novdec99/km.htm. Accessed June 14, 2005.

Butler, Tom, Joseph Feller, Andrew Pope, Paul Barry, and Ciaran Murphy. 2003. "Promoting Knowledge Sharing in Government and Non-Government Organizations Using Open Source Software: The pKADS Story." *Electronic Journal of Electronic Government* 2(1): 81–93.

Canadian Centre for Management Development. 1999. *A Primer on Knowledge Management in the Public Service.* Available at www.myschool_monecole.gc.ca/research/publications/pdf/LO-Primer-REV.PDF. Accessed July 18, 2005.

Chadha, Gaurav, and S. M. Nafay Kumail. 2002. *E-Learning: An Expression of the Knowledge Economy.* New Delhi: Tata McGraw-Hill.

Choi, Yang-sik. 2004. "Government Innovation in Korea." In *General Information on Innovation in Korea* (May 25). Seoul: Ministry of Government Administration and Home Affairs. Available at www.mogaha.go.kr/warp/wegapp/english/board/notice/view?id=428500. Accessed July 22, 2005.

Christensen, Tom, and Per Lægreid. 2002. *New Public Management: The Transformation of Ideas and Practice.* Aldershot, UK: Ashgate.

City of Fremont. 2002. "Learning Organization." Available at www.ci.fremont.ca.us/Employment/WorkingForTheCity/LearningOrganization.htm. Accessed July 21, 2005.

Conectándonos al Futuro de El Salvador. 1999. *Strategy for Building a Learning Society in El Salvador.* Available at www.conectando.org.sv. Accessed July 20, 2005.

Corbett, Al. 2002. *The President's Management Agenda: E-Learning Initiative.* "E-Training Initiative Goals." PowerPoint presentation, Department of Energy Office of Training and Human Resource Development. Accessed May 21, 2006 from www.doeal.gov/qtd/internet/trn-conf/tc-presentations/The%20Presidents%20Management%20Agendar.ppt.

Cummins, J.M., and E.C. Stonebraker. 1989. "Total Quality Management of Telecommunications." *Business Communications Review* 89(12): 36–41.

Curda, E.H.1993. "Reinventing Government: Moving Beyond the Buzzwords." *The Public Manager* 22: 33–36.

Daft, Richard L. 2004. *Organization Theory and Design,* 8th ed. Cincinnati, OH: Thomson South-Western.

Dastmalchian, A., P. Blyton, and R. Adamson. 1991. *The Climate of Workplace Relations.* London: Routledge.

Davenport, H. Thomas. 1997. *Information Ecology: Mastering Information and Knowledge Environment.* New York: Oxford University Press.

Davenport, H. Thomas, and Laurence Prusak. 1998. *Working Knowledge.* Cambridge: Harvard Business School Press.

Defense Contract Management Agency (DCMA). 2004. "Knowledge Management in Government." *DCMA Communicator.* Washington, DC: Defense Contract Management Agency. Available at www.dcma.mil/communicator/archives/spring%20summer%202004/km_govt.htm. Accessed April 7, 2006.

DeLong, David W. 2004. *Lost Knowledge: Confronting the Threat of an Aging Workforce.* New York: Oxford University Press.

Dempsey, James X. 2005. *Building a Trusted Information Sharing Environment.* Presentation at the 6th annual E-Government Institute Conference on Knowledge Management, Washington, DC, April 17–21.

Department of Information Services (DIS). 2000. *Washington State Digital Government Plan.* Olympia: Washington State Dept. of Information Services. Available at http://www.public.iastate.edu/~ycchen/eGovernment/IT_Plan/Washington_State_DGPlan_0200.pdf. Accessed May 20, 2006.

———. 2006. *Enterprise Architecture Update.* Olympia: Washington State Dept. of Information Services. Available at http://www.dis.wa.gov/technews/2006_01/20060111.aspx. Accessed May 20, 2006.

Dingwall, John. 1998. "Knowledge Management: Approach for the Public Sector." *Canadian Government Executive* 4(1): 2–10.

Drucker, Peter F. 1995. *The Post-Capitalist Society.* Oxford: Butterworth-Heinemann.

———. 2005. "Trading Places." *The National Interest* 79 (Spring): 101–7.

Duffy, D. 1998. "Knowledge Champions: What Does It Take to Be a Successful CKO?" *CIO* 12(4): 66–71.

Earl, Michael J., and Ian Scott. 1999. "What Is a Chief Knowledge Officer?" *Sloan Management Review* (December). Available at http://itmnet.cba.hawaii.edu:82/OldVersions/What?is?a?Chief?Knowledge?Officer. Accessed March 6, 2005.

Eddowes, Lee Anthony. 2003. "The Application of Methodologies in E-Government." *Electronic Journal of E-Government* (www.ejeg.com) 2(1): 114–25.

Edvinsson, Leif, Ron Dvir, Norman Roth, and Edna Pasher. 2004. "Innovations: The New Unit of Analysis in the Knowledge Era." *Journal of Intellectual Capital* 5(1): 40–58.

Edwards, J.S., and J.B. Kidd. 2003. "Knowledge Management *sans frontiers.*" *Journal of the Operational Research Society* 54: 130–39.

Entman, R.M. 1997. "Mass Media and Policy Innovation: Opportunities and Constraints for Public Management." In *Innovation in the Public Sector,* ed. Alan A. Altshuler and Robert D. Behn, 202–16. Washington, DC: Brookings Institution.

Environmental Protection Agency (EPA). 2005a. "Great Lakes: Regional Collaboration: Interagency Task Force." Washington, DC: Environmental Protection Agency. Available at www.epa.gov/glnpo/collaboration/taskforce/. Accessed July 12, 2004.

———. 2005b. "Regional Collaboration: Interagency Task Force Executive Order" (May 18). Washington, DC: Environmental Protection Agency. Available at http://epa.gov/glnpo/collaboration/taskforce/eo.html. Accessed July 12, 2005.

———. 2005c. "Remarks Announcing the Great Lakes Executive Order of 2004." Speech delivered in Chicago, IL, May 18. Washington, DC: Environmental Protection Agency. Available at http://yosemite.epa.gov/administrator/speeches.nsf/blab9f484b098972852562e7004dc686/. Accessed July 12, 2005.

——— 2005d. "A Strategy to Restore and Protect the Great Lakes—Draft Action Plan, July 2005." Washington, DC: Environmental Protection Agency. Available at www.epa.gov/greatlakes/collaboration/strategy.html. Accessed July 12, 2005.

Eskildson, L. 1994. "Improving the Odds of TQM's Success." *Quality Progress* 27: 61–63.

Evans, C. 2003. *Managing for Knowledge: HR's Strategic Role.* Boston: Butterworth-Heinemann.

Faget, Nancy. 2004. "KM Learning Objectives." KM.gov (January 14). Available at http//:km.gov/QuickPlace/km/PageLibrary/85256C79002EE74E.nsf. Accessed May 23, 2005.

Fast, William R. 2002. *Knowledge Strategies: Balancing Ends, Ways, and Means in the Information Age.* Available at www.ndu.edu/inss/siws/ch1.html. Accessed May 22, 2005.

Federal Aviation Administration (FAA). 2003. "Traffic Flow and Enterprise Management Collaborative Communications System." Washington, DC: Federal Aviation Administration. Available at www.fas.gov/aua/news/apr03/tfmmo.htm. Accessed June 18, 2005.

Federal Energy Regulatory Commission (FERC). 2005. "Chief Knowledge Manager Job Announcement." KM.gov.

Federal KM Working Group (FKMWG). 2000. "Chief Knowledge Officer." Available at www.ndu.edu/irmc/km-cio_role/km-cio_role.htm. Accessed March 6, 2005.

Fredericks, Col. Brian. 2002. "Information Warfare: The Organizational Dimension." In *Sun Tzu Art of War in Information Warfare,* ed. Robert E. Neilson. Washington, DC: National Defense University Institute for National Strategic Studies. Available at www.ndu.edu/inss/siws/ch4.html. Accessed May 22, 2005.

Fuller, Steve. 2002. *Knowledge Management Foundations.* Burlington, MA: Butterworth-Heinemann.

Gagnon, Yves C. 2001. "The Behavior of Public Managers in Adopting New Technology." *Public Performance and Management Review* 24(4): 337–50.

Gardner, Christopher. 2000. *The Valuation of Information Technology.* New York: John Wiley and Sons.

Gaston, Stephen J. 1997. *Mining Data for Knowledge.* Toronto: Canadian Institute of Chartered Accountants.

Girard, John P. 2005. "The Inukshuk: A Canadian Knowledge Management Model." *KMPro Journal* 2(1): 9–16.

Gladstone, Bryan. 2000. *From Know-How to Knowledge.* Dover, NH: The Industrial Society.

Griffiths, Peter. 2005. "Performing an Information Audit." Paper presented at the Knowledge & Content UK conference, London, July 4–6.

Guimaraes, T.A., G.P. Angelim, D.S. Spezia, G.A. Rocha, and R.G Magalhaes. 2001. "Organizational Learning in the Public Sector: Lessons from a Brazilian Government Organization." Available at www.delft2001.tudelft.nl/abstract%20files/abstract1173.doc. Accessed July 18, 2005.

Haque, Akhlaque. 2001. "GIS, Public Service and the Issue of Democratic Governance." *Public Administration Review* 61(3): 259–65.

Harney, John. 2005. "A Sampling of Hosted Collaboration Products." *KMWorld* 14(6): 14, 24.

Harris, Shane. 2001. "In the Know." GOVEXEC.com (July 1). Available at www.govexec.com/story_page.cfm?mode=report&articleid=20393. Accessed June 14, 2005.

Hassounah, Jamil. 2001. "Developing a Learning Organization in the Public Sector." *Quality Progress* 34(1): 106–9.

Ho, Alfred Tat-Kei. 2002. "Reinventing Local Government and the E-Government Initiative." *Public Administration Review* 62(4): 430–44.

————. 2003. "Perceptions of Performance Measurement and the Practice of Performance Reporting by Small Cities. *State and Local Government Review* 35(3): 161–73.

Holley, L.M., D. Dufner, and B.J. Reed. 2002. "Got SISP? Strategic Information Systems Planning in U.S. State Governments." *Public Performance and Management Review* 25(4): 398–412.

Holmes, James. 2003. "E-Diplomacy: Using Technology to Advance Foreign Relations." Speech given at a U.S. Department of State Open Forum (February 20). Washington, DC: U.S. Department of State.

Holowetzki, Antonina. 2002. *The Relationship Between Knowledge Management and Organizational Culture: An Examination of Cultural Factors that Support the Flow and Management of Knowledge Within an Organization.* Eugene, OR: Applied Information Management Program, University of Oregon.

Holsapple, Clyde W., and Anita Lee-Post. 2006. "Defining, Assessing, and Promoting e-Learning Success: An Information Systems Perspective." *Decision Science Journal of Innovative Education.* 4(1): 67–85.

Hsu, Francis. 2004. *Taxonomies and Semantics Mission Statement.* Available at http://km.gov/quickplace/km/PageLibrary85256D1F0058823B.nsf/. Accessed July 9, 2005.

Human Resources Director's Council (HRDC). 2003. *Alberta Government Guide to Knowledge Management.* Alberta, Canada: Human Resources Director's Council. Available at www.pao.gov.ag.ca/learning/knowledge/guide.pdf. Accessed July 16, 2005.

Hylton, Ann. 2002. *A KM Initiative Is Unlikely to Succeed Without a Knowledge Audit.* Industry White Paper. Available at http://knowledgeboard.com/library/the_need_for_knowledge_audits/pdf. Accessed July 8, 2005.

Information Services Board (ISB). 2006. "Enterprise Architecture Committee: Mission, Objectives, and Goals. Available at http://isb.wa.gov/committees/enterprise/mission.aspx. Accessed May 24, 2006.

International Center for Applied Studies in Information Technology (ICASIT). 2003. 16th Knowledge Management Roundtable. (September 10). Available at www.icasit.org/km/kmrt/sept03/index.htm. Accessed July 9, 2005.

Joch, Alan. 2004. "Knowledge vs. Content Management." FCW.com (April 12). Available at http://www.fcw.com/article82580-04-12-04-Print. Accessed October 17, 2004.

Kaplan, Robert S., and David P. Norton. 1996. *The Balanced Scorecard.* Boston: Harvard Business School Press.

Kerka, Sandra. 1997. "Distance Learning, the Internet, and the World Wide Web." ERIC

Digest No. 168. Available at www.ericdigests.org/1997-1/distance.html. Accessed January 28, 2006.

Kettl, Donald F. 2002.*The Transformation of Governance: Public Administration for Twenty-First Century America.* Baltimore: Johns Hopkins University Press.

Kiel, L.D. 1994. *Managing Chaos and Complexity in Government.* San Francisco: Jossey-Bass.

Kloman, Erasmus H. 1972. *Unmanned Space Project Management: Surveyor and Lunar Orbiter.* NASA SP-4901. Washington, DC: NASA. Available at www.hq.nasa.gov/office/pao/History/SP-4901/chp5.htm.

KM.gov. 2004. "KM.gov Communities." Available at http://km.gov/quickplace/km/PageLibrary85256C6B00608688.nsf/h_toc/. Accessed July 9, 2005.

Knapp, E., and D. Yu. 1999. "Understanding Organizational Culture: How Culture Helps or Hinders the Flow of Knowledge." *Knowledge Management Review* 7 (April): 16–22.

Knox, Jim. 2005. "Giving the U.S. Navy a Knowledge Advantage." Paper presented at the 6th Annual E-Government Institute's Knowledge Management Conference, Washington, DC, April 17–21.

Kolb, David. 1984. *Experiential Learning.* Englewood Cliffs, NJ: Prentice Hall.

Kopelman, R.E., A.P. Brief, and R.A. Guzzo.1990. "The Role of Climate and Culture in Productivity." In *Organizational Climate and Culture,* ed. B. Schneider, 282–318. San Francisco: Jossey-Bass.

Kusunoki, Ken. 2004. "Synthesizing Modular and Integral Knowledge: Business Architecture Innovation in the IT Era." In *Hitotsubashi on Knowledge Management,* ed. Hirotaka Takeuchi and Ikujiro Nonaka, 309–37. Singapore: John Wiley and Sons.

Lane, Jan-Erik. 2000. *New Public Management.* London: Routledge.

Lawrence, Eton. 1998. "Some Thoughts on Turning a Government Organization into a Learning Organization." Public Service Commission of Canada White Paper (June). Available at http://www.psc-cfp.gc.ca/research/knowledge/learning_org_e.htm. Accessed June 24, 2005.

Lee, Geunioo, and James L. Perry. 2002. "Are Computers Boosting Productivity? A Test of the Paradox in State Governments." *Journal of Publica Administratin Research and Theory* 12(1): 77–102.

Leganza, Gene. 2005. "Making the Case for Enterprise Architecture." *PublicCIO* (Online version). November 8. Available at www.public-cio.com/story.print.php?id=97210. Accessed May 20, 2006.

Leiken, Robert S. 2005. "Europe's Angry Muslims." *Foreign Affairs* 84(4): 120–35.

Lesser, Eric L., and John Storck. 2001. "Communities of Practice and Organizational Performance." *IBM Systems Journal* 40(4): 831–41.

Lewicki, Roy J., Donald D. Bowen, Douglas T. Hall, and Francine J. Hall. 1996. *Experiences in Management and Organizational Behavior,* 4th ed. New York: John Wiley and Sons.

Lewin, Arie Y. 1999. "Application of Complexity Theory to Organization Science." *Organization Science* 10(3): 215.

Lewin, Kurt. 1946. "Action Research and Minority Problems." *Journal of Social Issues,* 2(1): 34–46.

Lewis, Bob. 2005. "Emerging Technologies for Knowledge Sharing with Case Study." Paper presented at the 6th Annual E-Government Institute's Knowledge Management Conference, Washington, DC, April 20–22.

Lyotard, Jean-François. 1984. *The Postmodern Condition: A Report on Knowledge,* trans. Geoff Bennington and Brian Jameson. Minneapolis: University of Minnesota Press.

MacDonald, Diane B., and David E. McNabb. 2006. "Developing a Blended Model for

MBA Content Delivery: Using Internet Capabilities to Enhance Graduate Education." Paper presented at the 2006 Academic Business World Conference at Nashville, TN. May 29–June 1, 2006.

Malafsky, Geoffrey. 2005. "Fitting KM into Enterprise Architectures." Paper presented at the 6th Annual E-Government Institute's Knowledge Management Conference, Washington, DC, April 20–22.

Malhotra, Yogesh. 2000. "Knowledge Management & New Organization Forms: A Framework for Business Model Innovation." *Information Resources Management Journal* 13(1): 5–14.

Markle Foundation. 2003. *Creating a Trusted Information Network for Homeland Security.* Available at www.markle.org/downloadable_assets/ntstf_report2_part1_homepage.pdf. Accessed June 16, 2005.

May, Thornton. 2005. "*CIO Habitat:* Technology's Great Divide: Where Do You Stand?" *CIO Decisions* (online version, June). Available at http://ciodecisions.techtarget.com/magPrintFriendly/0,293813.sid86_gci1092075,00. Accessed June 26, 2005.

McElroy, Mark. 2003. *The New Knowledge Management.* Burlington, MA: Butterworth-Heinemann.

McElroy, Mark, and J. Firestone. 2003. *Key Issues in the New Knowledge Management.* Burlington, MA: Butterworth-Heinemann.

McElyea, Brian E. 2002. "Knowledge Management, Intellectual Capital, and Learning Organizations: A Triad of Future Management Integration." *Futurics* 26(1, 2): 59–65.

McGee, James V., and Laurence Prusak. 1993. *Managing Information Strategically.* New York: John Wiley and Sons.

McKeen, James D., and D. Sandy Staples. 2001. "Knowledge Managers: Who They Are and What They Do." In *Handbook on Knowledge Management,* ed. Clyde W. Holsapple, 21–41. Heidelberg, Germany: Springer-Verlag.

McKinnon, Cheryl. 2005. "Challenges Facing the Public Sector." *KMWorld—Best Practices in Government Supplement* 14(6): S3–S4.

McNabb, David E., and F. Thad Barnowe. 2006. "Integrating Knowledge Management into Public Administration: Public Sector Enterprise Architecture Initiatives." Paper presented at the 2006 Global Conference on Business and Economics (July 6–8), Cambridge, UK.

McNabb, David E., and F. Thomas Sepic. 1995. "Culture, Climate, and Total Quality Management: Measuring Readiness for Change." *Public Productivity and Management Review* 2 (June): 369–85.

Melkers, Julia, and Katherine Willoughby. 2004. *Staying the Course: The Use of Performance Measurement in State Governments.* Washington, DC: IBM Center for the Business of Government.

Moon, M. Jae. 2002. "The Evolution of E-government Among Municipalities: Rhetoric or Reality." *Public Administration Review* 62(4): 424–35.

———. 2004. *From E-Government to M-Government?* Washington, DC: IBM Center for the Business of Government.

Moore, Andy. 2005. "What Makes Government Different?" *KMWorld—Best Practices in Government Supplement* 14(6): S2.

———. 2002. *Strategic Plan for Knowledge Management* (April 2). Washington, DC: National Aeronautics and Space Administration Knowledge Management Team.

National Association of State Chief Information Officers (NASCIO). (2005). *Research Brief: Connecting the Silos: Using Governance Models to Achieve Data Integration.* Lexington, KY: NASCIO Interoperability and Integration Committee. Available at www.nascio.org/nascioCommittees/interoperability/connectingSilos.pdf. Accessed July 15, 2004.

National Association of State Chief Information Officers (NASICO). 2005. *The States and Enterprise Architecture: How Far Have We Come?* Washington, DC: NASCIO and Office of Justice Programs, U.S. Dept. of Justice. Accessed May 18, 2006 from https://www.nascio.org/ nascioCommittees/ea/eaAssessment.pdf.

National Defense University. 2005. *Sun Tzu Art of War in Information Warfare.* Washington, DC: Institute for National Strategic Studies. Retrieved May 22, 2005. www.ndu.edu/inss/siws/cont.html.

National Electronic Library for Health (NeLH). 2004. "Knowledge Management Glossary." UK National Health Service, National Electronic Library for Health. Available at www.library.nhs.uk/knowledgemanagement/Page.aspx?pagename=GLOSSARY. Accessed June 21, 2006.

Nicolay, John A. 2002. "The Wagging Tail of Technology. *Public Administration Quarterly* 26(1): 65–88.

Nonaka, Ikujiro. 1991. "The Knowledge Creating Company." *Harvard Business Review* 69(1): 96–104.

Nonaka, Ikujiro, and Hirotaka Takeuchi. 1995. *The Knowledge Creating Company: How Japanese Companies Create the Dynamics of Innovation.* Oxford: Oxford University Press.

O'Hara, Colleen. 2004. "Mr. Rogers' New Neighborhood." *Federal Computer Week* (April 9). Available at www.fcw.com/fcw/articles/2004/0809/mgt-commune-08-09-04. Accessed July 9, 2005.

Osborne, David, and Ted Gaebler. 1992. *Reinventing Government: How the Entrepreneurial Spirit Is Transforming the Public Sector.* Reading, MA: Addison-Wesley.

O'Toole, Laurence J. Jr. 1996. "Rational Choice and the Public Management of Interorganizational Networks." In *The State of Public Management,* ed. Donald F. Kettl and H. Brinton Milward, 242–63. Baltimore: Johns Hopkins University Press.

Papadakis, Vassilis, and Patrick Barwise. 1998. "What Can We Tell Managers About Making Strategic Decisions?" In *Strategic Decisions,* ed. Vassilis Papadakis and Patrick Barwise, 267–86. Boston: Kluwer Academic.

Parikh, Jagdish. 2005. "The Zen of Management Maintenance: Leadership Starts with Self-Discovery." *Working Knowledge* (May 9). Harvard Business School. Available at http://hbswk.hbs.edu/tools/print_item.jthml?id=4790&t=technology. Accessed July 13, 2005.

Payne, R.L. 1971. "Organizational Climate: The Concept and Some Research Findings." *Prakseologia.* NR 39/40/ROK.

Pedler, M., J. Burgoyne, and T. Boydel. 1991. *The Learning Company: A Strategy for Sustainable Development.* London: McGraw-Hill.

Perera, David. 2005. "UK Struggles with E-Gov Ignorance." *Federal Computer Week* (June 2). Available at www.fcw.com/print.asp. Accessed June 27, 2005.

Pettigrew, A.M. 1990. "Organizational Climate: Two Constructs in Search of a Role." In *Organizational Climate and Culture,* ed. B. Schneider, 413–23. San Francisco: Jossey-Bass.

Phillips, Bernard S. 1976. *Social Research: Strategy and Tactics.* 3rd ed. New York: Macmillan.

Polanyi, Michael. 1958. *Personal Knowledge.* Chicago: University of Chicago Press.

Probst, G., and S. Raisch. 2005. "Organizational Crisis: The Logic of Failure." *Academy of Management Executive* 19(1): 90–103.

Prusak, Laurence. 1997. *Knowledge in Organizations.* Burlington, MA: Butterworth-Heinemann.

PSC. 2005. *Leveraging Knowledge at the Public Service Commission of Canada.* Available at www.psc-cfp.gov.gc.ca/research/knowledge/km_psc_e.htm. Accessed July 18, 2005.

Qiao, Yuhua, and Khi V. Thai. 2002. "Reinventing Government at the Federal Level: The Implementations and the Prospects." *Public Administration Quarterly* 26(1): 89–116.

Quindi Corp. 2003. "New Techniques for Knowledge Capture." Paper presented at the TTI/Vanguard Conference, *Knowledge Management Comes of Age,* Washington, DC. September. Available at www.quindi.com/download/Quindi_knowledge_capture.pdf. Accessed March 5, 2005.

Rastrogi, P.N. 2000. "Knowledge Management and Intellectual Capital: The New Virtuous Reality of Competitiveness." *Human Systems Management* 19(1): 39–49.

Reichers, A.E., and B. Schneider. 1990. "Climate and Culture: An Evolution of Constructs." In *Organizational Climate and Culture,* ed. Benjamin Schneider, 5–39. San Francisco: Jossey-Bass.

Remez, Shereen, and Jon Desenberg. 2000. "Knowledge Management." General Services Administration (GSA) White Paper. Available at www.gsa.gov/gsa/cm_attachments/ GSA_DOCUMENT/8-SRemez_GSAR2GT56. Accessed May 20, 2005.

R/IS. 2003. "An Atlantic Case Study on Inter-Organizational Collaboration." Montreal, Canada: Regulatory/Inspection Secretariat. Available at http://ricommunity.gc.ca/documents/working_in_partnership_e.asp. Accessed July 9, 2005.

Robertson, James. 2004. "Developing a Knowledge Management Strategy." A *Step Two Designs* White Paper. Available at www.steptwo.com.au/papers. Accessed June 24, 2005.

Robson, I.A. 2003. "Creating the Future Using Intelligent Systems." *Public Performance and Management Review* 26(3): 291–301.

Ross, Mickey V., and William D. Schulte. 2005. "Knowledge Management in a Military Enterprise: A Pilot Case Study of the Space and Warfare Systems Command." In *Creating the Discipline of Knowledge Management,* ed. Michael Stankosky, 157–70. Burlington, MA: Elsevier Butterworth-Heinemann.

Ruby, Dan. 2004. "Erecting the Framework, Part I." *FTP Online* (February 19). Available at www.ftponline.com/ea/magazine/spring/online/druby/default_pf.aspx. Accessed May 21, 2006.

Ruggles, R. 1998. "The State of the Notion: Knowledge Management in Practice." *California Management Review* 40(3): 80–89.

Sakowicz, Marcin. 2002. "Knowledge Management in Polish Local Government." Warsaw School of Economics. Available at http://unpan1.un.org/intradoc/groups/public/ documents/NTSPAcee/UNPANO/8975.pdf. Accessed July 22, 2005.

SAP Public Services Inc. 2001. "Collaboration in Government." Report presented to the Congressional Internet Caucus Advisor Committee—E-Government Task Force (February 25). Washington, DC: SAP Public Services, Inc.

Saunders, Marcelline. 2005. "Emerging Technologies for Knowledge Sharing Environments." Paper presented at the 6th Annual E-Government Institute's Knowledge Management Conference, Washington, DC, April 20–22.

Schein, Edgar H. 1992. *Organizational Culture and Leadership.* 2d ed. San Francisco: Jossey-Bass.

Schwartz, Karen D. 2003. "Countering Terrorism with Technology." GOVEXEC.com (October 17). Available at www.govexec.com/story_page.cfm&articleid=26843. Accessed June 14, 2005.

Senge, Peter. 1990. *The Fifth Discipline: The Art and Practice of the Learning Organization.* New York: Doubleday.

Sepic, F. Thomas, and David E. McNabb. 1992. "Moderating Stress for Quality in the Workplace: Toward a Normative Model." *Proceedings of the 21st Annual Meeting of the Western Decision Sciences Institute,* Reno, NV, March 25–28.

Smith, Mark K. 2001. "The Learning Organization." *INFED: The Encyclopedia of Informal Education* (July): 1–14. Available at www.infed.org/biblio/learning-organization .htm. Accessed June 8, 2005.

Snyder, William M., and Xavier de Souza Briggs. 2004. "Communities of Practice: A New Tool for Government Managers." In *Collaboration: Using Networks and Partnerships,* ed. John M. Kamensky and Thomas J. Burlin, 171–272. The IBM Center for the Business of Government Series. Lanham, MD: Rowman and Littlefield.

Spira, Jonathan B. 2005. "Time to (Re)innovate the Office?" *KMWorld* 14(6): 1, 16.

Stankosky, Michael. 2005. "Advances in Knowledge Management: University Research Toward an Academic Discipline." In *Creating the Discipline of Knowledge Management,* ed. Michael Stankosky, 1–14. Burlington, MA: Elsevier Butterworth-Heinemann.

Sternstein, Heidi. 2006. *Designing and Teaching an Online Course.* Boston: Allyn and Bacon.

Sundbo, Jon. 2001. *The Strategic Management of Innovation.* Cheltenham, UK: Edward Elgar.

Sydänmaanlakka, Penti. 2002. *An Intelligent Organization.* Oxford, UK: Capstone.

Taylor, Robert S. 1986. *Value-Added Processes in Information Systems.* New York: Ablex.

Thompson, K.R., and F. Luthans. 1990. "Organizational Culture: A Behavioral Perspective." In *Organizational Climate and Culture,* ed. B. Schneider, 319–44. San Francisco: Jossey-Bass.

Tiboni, Frank. 2005. "Air Force Picks Hobbin for CIO." FCW.com. Accessed May 6, 2005. www.fcw.com/article88785-05-05-05-Web.

Tissen, Rene, Daniel Andriessen, and Frank L. Deorez. 1998. *Value-Based Knowledge Management.* Amsterdam: Addison-Wesley Pearson.

Tiwana, Amrit. 2001. *The Essential Guide to Knowledge Management: E-Business and CRM Applications.* Upper Saddle River, NJ: Prentice Hall.

———. 2002. *The Knowledge Management Toolkit.* Upper Saddle River, NJ: Prentice Hall.

Travis, Matthew. 2005. *Building a Successful KM Environment for the Homeland Security Community.* Presentation at the 6th Annual E-Government Institute's Conference on Knowledge Management, Washington, DC, April 20–22.

Turnipseed, David. L. 1988. "An Integrated, Interactive Model of Organizational Climate, Culture, and Effectiveness." *Leadership and Organizational Development Journal* 9(5): 17–21.

USALearning, n.d. "About USALearning," under "Introduction." Available at www.usalearning.gov/USALearning/index.cfm?room=about&roomaction=about. Accessed May 21, 2006.

U.S. Army Corps of Engineers (USACE). 2003. "Learning Organization Doctrine: Roadmap for Transformation" (November). Available at www.hq.usace.army.mil/cepa/learning.pdf. Accessed July 22, 2005.

U.S. Department of Agriculture (USDA). 2004. *Using Learning Contracts.* Washington, DC: USDA Animal and Plant Health Inspection Service. Available at www.aphis.usda.gov/mrpbs/training/learning_contracts.pdf. Accessed July 21, 2005.

U.S. Department of Defense (DOD). 2002. "Knowledge Management: Maximizing Human Potential." Washington, DC: OSD Comptroller iCenter. Available at http://www.dod.mil/comptroller/icenter/learn/knowledgemanconcept.htm. Accessed July 13, 2005.

U.S. Department of Defense (DOD). 2003. "Computer Specialist (Knowledge Management)." Washington DC: Department of Defense. Available at http://ioa-qpnet-co.gsa.gov/QuickPlace/km/PageLibrary85256C6B005EDD06.nsf. Accessed May 20, 2005.

U.S. Department of State (DOS). 2003. *Knowledge Management at the Department of State: Learning from Successful Principles and Practices.* Information Technology Audit, Report No. IT-A-03-08 (July). Washington, DC: Office of the Inspector General, U.S. Department of State. Available at http://oig.state.gov/documents/organization/23489.pdf. Accessed July 8, 2005.

———. 2004. "FY 2005 Performance Summary (The Plan)." Washington, DC: Bureau of Resource Management, U.S. Department of State (February). Available at www .state.gov/s/d/rm/rls/perfplan/2005/html/29306.htm. Accessed July 7, 2005.

U.S. Department of the Treasury (DOT). 2004. *Annual Report of the Results of the President's Management Agenda (PMA)*. Washington, DC: Department of the Treasury.

———. 2004. "PMA Results Document." Available at www.treas.gov/2004results. Accessed June 13, 2005.

U.S. General Accounting Office (GAO). 2003a. *Architect of the Capitol. Management and Accountability Framework Needed for Organizational Transformation*. Document Number FAO-03-231. Washington, DC: General Accounting Office.

———. 2003b. *Electronic Government: Potential Exists for Enhancing Collaboration on Four Initiatives*. Report GAO-04-6 (October). Washington, DC: General Accounting Office. Available at www.gao.gov/new.items/d046.pdf. Accessed July 5, 2005.

———.2004. *Performance Budgeting: OMB's Performance Rating tool Presents Opportunities and Challenges for Evaluating Program Performance*. GAO-04-550T. Washington, DC: General Accounting Office.

U.S. General Services Administration (GSA). 2006 *US General Services Administration: Knowledge Management Division*. Available at http://www.gsa.gov/Portal/gsa/ep/ contentView.do?contentType=GSA_OVERVIEW&contentId=17107&noc=T. Accessed April 15, 2006.

U.S. Office of Management and Budget (OMB). 2002. *The President's Agenda, FY2002*. Washington, DC: Office of Management and Budget.

———. 2005a. "About E-Gov: The E-Government Act of 2002." Available at www .whitehouse.gov/omb/egov/g-4-act.html. Accessed May 24, 2005.

———. 2005b. *Expanding E-Government: Improved Service Delivery for the American People Using Information Technology*. Washington, DC: Office of Management and Budget. Available at www.whitehouse.gov/omb/budintegration/expanding_egov_ 2005.pdf. Accessed May 18, 2005.

———. 2005c. *FY07 Budget Formulation FEA Consolidated Reference Model Document* (May). Washington, DC: Office of Management and Budget.

———. 2005d. *Presidential Initiatives: E-Training*. Washington, DC: Office of Management and Budget. Available at www.whitehouse.gov/omb/egov/c-4-1-eTraining.html. Accessed May 24, 2005.

U.S. Office of Personnel Management (OPM). n.d. "E-Gov: E-Learning," under "Overview." Office of Personnel Management, www.opm.gov/egov/training_overview.asp. Accessed May 24, 2006.

Voss, Angi, Stephanie Roeder, and Oliver Marker. 2003. "Optimizing Cooperation in Spatial Planning for E-Government." In *Knowledge Management in Electronic Government*, ed. Maria A. Wimmer, 239–49. Proceedings of the 4th IFIP International Working Conference, KM.gov (May), Rhodes, Greece.

Wang, Kesheng, Ove Rustung Hjelmervik, and Bernt Bremdal. 2001. *Introduction to Knowledge Management*. Trondheim, Norway: Tapir Academic Press.

Wasko, Molly M., and Samer Faraj. 2005. "Why Should I Share? Examining Social Capital and Knowledge Contribution in Electronic Networks of Practice." *MIS Quarterly* 29(2): 35–57.

Watkins, K., and V. Marsick. 1992. "Building the Learning Organization: A New Role for Human Resource Developers." *Studies in Continuing Education* 14(2): 115–29.

Watson, Hugh J., and Traci A. Carte. 2000. "Executive Information Systems in Government Organizations." *Public Productivity and Management Review* 23(3): 371–82.

Weigelt, Matthew. 2006. "Congress Blamed for Poor E-Government Performance." *Federal Computer Week* 20(15): 54–55.

Wenger, Etienne, Richard McDermott, and William M. Snyder. 2002. *Cultivating Communities of Practice: A Guide to Managing Knowledge.* Boston: Harvard Business School Press.

Wheeler, E.T. 1993. *Government that Works: Innovation in State and Local Government.* Jefferson, NC: McFarland.

Wiig, Karl M. 1994. *Knowledge Management.* Arlington, TX: Schema Press.

Wilson, J.Q. 1989. *Bureaucracy: What Government Agencies Do and How They Do It.* New York: Basic Books.

Wilson, T.D. 2002. "The Nonsense of 'Knowledge Management.'" *Information Research* 8(1). Paper no. 144. Available at http://InformationR.not/ir/8-1/paper144.html. Accessed May 18, 2005.

Wollner, G.E. 1992. "The Law of Producing Quality." *Quality Progress* 28: 35–40.

Wonacott, Michael E. 2002. "Implications of Distance Education for CTE." ERIC Digest No. 227. Available at www.ericdigest.org/2002-1/cte.html. Accessed January 28, 2006

Zachman, John. 1987. "Viewing and Communicating Information Infrastructure: Enterprise Architecture (EA)." Available at http://www.valuebasedmanagement.net/methods_zachman_enterprise_architecture.html. Accessed May 21, 2006.

About the Author

David E. McNabb is professor of business administration at Pacific Lutheran University. He has recently held academic posts of visiting professor at the Stockholm School of Economics at Riga, Latvia, and of visiting instructor in the Masters in Public Administration programs at the Evergreen State University and the University of Maryland–University College (Europe). He has also served as a visiting instructor in ethics and international courses at the University of Washington–Tacoma. He began his teaching career at Oregon State University, where he earned his PhD in 1980. Prior to beginning his academic career, he served as communications director for the Washington State Legislature's House of Representatives, majority caucus, and as a campaign manager for a variety of state office candidates. His municipal experience was gained as director of economic development for the city of Fullerton, California. He has served on citizen advisory boards for the cities of Seattle and Kirkland, Washington. He is the author of nearly fifty articles and conference papers. This is his third book published by M.E. Sharpe, Inc. The previous two books were *Research Methods for Public Administration and Nonprofit Organizations,* and *Research Methods in Political Science.* Professor McNabb is a member of the Academy of Political Science, the American Society for Public Administration, and the Academy of Management.

About the Invited Contributors

Dr. Jon Boyle is the program manager for the NASA Academy of Program and Project Leadership (APPL) at Arctic Slope Regional Corporation Management Services (ASRCMS), responsible for all products and services produced by the academy as well as strategic relationships for the program. Dr. Boyle teaches knowledge management at Virginia Tech, where he earned his doctorate. He also holds an MA from George Mason University and a MEd from Boston University. He has served as a U.S. Army officer and worked with many organizations during his career, including General Electric, Hewlett Packard, the National Aeronautics and Space Administration, the Department of Energy, and the Department of Education. Dr. Boyle resides in northern Virginia with his wife Allyson and sons Christopher and Zachary.

Dr. Maureen L. Hammer joined the Virginia Department of Transportation (VDOT) in November 2003 as knowledge management officer. The division includes the Knowledge Management Office, the Transportation Research Library, and the Technology Transfer program. Dr. Hammer has also served as the knowledge management administrator for the Virginia Retirement System and corporate librarian for the Montana Power Corporation, as well as holding several library and information technology positions in academic and health services organizations. She has a master's in library science from Emporia State University and a PhD in organization and management from Capella University. Her dissertation focused on the role of tacit knowledge networks in a state agency.

Dr. Edward J. Hoffman is the director of the NASA Academy of Program and Project Leadership (APPL). In this capacity, he is responsible for providing the leadership in supporting NASA's project people and teams in a variety of areas, including curriculum, consulting services for project teams, e-learning and automated project tools, knowledge sharing, and research in project management. Dr. Hoffman has published numerous articles on project management and leadership in modern organizations. Dr. Hoffman holds a doctorate, a master of arts, and a master of science degree from Columbia University in New York.

Mr. Anthony Maturo is the deputy director of the NASA Academy of Program and Project Leadership (APPL). As deputy director, Mr. Maturo is responsible for the procurement and financial position of the academy, as well as the career development of the NASA project practitioner community. He is also responsible for the management of contract arrangements and daily operations. Mr. Maturo holds two master of arts degrees in school administration and psychology from Southern Connecticut State University, a master of arts degree in guidance from the University of Bridgeport, and a bachelor of arts in education from Keene State College. He resides in Washington, D.C., with his wife Nancy.

Ms. Susan L. Nappi is responsible for the development, implementation, and oversight of knowledge capture activities for C-E LCMC's global workforce, over 8,000 civilians, military personnel, and contractors. A graduate of the College of New Jersey (magna cum laude) with a degree in business administration–marketing, she also holds a masters of science in management degree from Florida Institute of Technology (summa cum laude). Ms. Nappi's recognitions include the Department of the Army Superior Civilian Service Award, the Department of the Army Commander's Award for Civilian Service, four Department of the Army Achievement Medals for Civilian Service, and recognition in 2003 and in 1992 as one of C-E LCMC's Ten Outstanding Personnel. She is also the recipient of the U.S. Army 2002 Nick Hoge Award for her essay "Transforming Business Processes: The War the Civilian Workforce Wages and Why They Need Knowledge Management to Win It."

Index

C

California, 58–59, 130, *130*
Canada, 17, 40, *117, 119*, 125, 132, *133*, 264
Canadian Border Services Agency, *117*
Capacity building, **277**
Carroll, Tom, 235
Carte, Traci A., 4
C–E LCMC. *See* U.S. Army Communications–Electronics Life Cycle Management Command
Center for Program and Project Management Research (CPMR), 222
Center for Strategic and International Studies, 181–82
Central Intelligence Agency, 182, 186
Challenger tragedy, 211, 214
Champion, **277**
Change advocates, 110
Charlotte (North Carolina), 159–61
Charlotte–Mecklenburg Police Department (CMPD), 159–61
Chatzkel, J., 251
Chief information officer (CIO)
  challenges facing, 122–23
  chief knowledge officer and, 191, 197
  definition of, **277**
  emergence of, 170–71
  knowledge management trends and, 54
  leadership guidelines for, *123*
  in public sector, 170–71, 173
  at U.S. Department of Defense, 121–22
Chief Information Officers (CIO) Council, 100, 171
Chief knowledge officer (CKO)
  activities of, 173, 196–98, 200
  certification, government–approved, 201–03
  challenges facing, 122–23, 200–01
  characteristics of, 198–201
  chief information officer and, 191, 197
  definition of, **277**
  at Department of Defense, 203–04, *204*
  at Department of the Navy, 204–06
  emergence of, 190–91

Chief knowledge officer (CKO) *(continued)*
  at Federal Energy Regulatory Commission, 193, *193–94*
  at General Services Administration, 191, *192*
  information and communications technology and, 198–99
  innovation and, 156
  leadership guidelines for, *123*
  open enterprise and, 191–94
  overview, 188, 206
  practices shaping role of, 195–96
Chief transformation executive (CTE), 203
Chiem, P.X., 250
Clinger–Cohen Act (1996), 122
Clinton, Bill, 8, 11, 18, 73, 151, 159
Codification, **277**
Collaboration. *See also* Collaborative culture
  best practices, 70–72
  definition of, 68–69, **277**
  e–government and, 69, *70*
  examples of, 106, *117*
  in government, 69
  knowledge management and, 65
  monitoring agency progress with, 69–70
  President's Management Agenda and, 65
  requirements for, 116, 118–19
Collaborative business knowledge (CBK), 55–56
Collaborative culture
  barriers to organizational change and, 109–10
  in Canada, 116, *117, 119*
  change advocates and, 110
  definition and description of, *27*, 28, 41
  dimensions of, 113–14
  factors affecting, 111, *112*, 113
  Great Lakes Interagency Task Force and, 119, *120*, 121
  knowledge management and, 108
  knowledge sharing and, 36–38
  organizational climate and, 109–10, 114–15

Griffiths, Peter, 33
Grimshaw, David, 60
Groupware, **282**
Guzzo, R.A., 115

H

Halsey, Cyndia, 235
Harris, Shane, 188
Hjelmervik, Ove Rustung, 188
Ho, Alfred Tat–Kei, 3
Hobbins, William T., 197
Hoffman, Ed, 211–12, 215–17, 222,
    225
Holley, L.M., 151
Holm, Jeanne, 175
Holowetzki, Antonina, 114
Holtzman, J., 215
HTML, **282**
Human capital, 11, 196, 218–19, **282**
Human interactions
  challenge of, 86
  community of practice and, 30, 34–35,
      93, 95–103
  definition and description of, *27*, 28, 41
  importance of, 84–85
  knowledge audits and, 32–34
  knowledge registry and, 35–36
  knowledge repositories and, 85,
      103–04
  in local government, 98–99
  overview, 83–84, 104–05
  principles, successful, 89, *90*
  processes
    knowledge acquisition, 87–88, 104
    knowledge sharing, 87–88,
        104–05
    knowledge utilization, 87–88,
        104–05
    overview, 86–87
    at U.S. State Department, 88–93
  stakeholders and, 85–86
  in state government, 98–99
  value of, 85–86
Human Resources Planning (HRP), 15
Hylton, Ann, 83, 93

I

Illinois, 71–72
Implementation of knowledge
    management
  challenge of, 86
  community of practice and, 85, 93,
      95–103
  definition of implementation and, 83
  importance of, 84–85
  knowledge audits and, 85, 93–95, *94–95*
  knowledge base and, 85
  knowledge repositories and, 85, 103–04
  in local government, 98–99
  overview, 83–84, 104–05
  principles, successful, 89, *90*
  processes
    knowledge acquisition, 87–88, 104
    knowledge sharing, 87–88, 104–05
    knowledge utilization, 87–88,
        104–05
    overview, 86–87
    at U.S. State Department, 88–93
  in public versus private sector, 4–5
  stakeholders and, 85–86
  in state government, 98–99
  value of, 85–86
Implicit knowledge. *See* Tacit knowledge
Improved Financial Performance (IFP),
    14–15, **282**
Industry. *See* Private sector
Information. *See also* Information
    processes
  access to, 20, 172
  architecture, 48–49
  audits, 32–34, 85, 93–95, *94–95,* **284**
  converting, to knowledge, 30–31
  definition of, **283**
  highways, 8
  learning process and, 128–31
  management, 195
  sharing, in Europe, *185*
  technology in managing, 126
Information and communications
    technology (ICT)
  chief knowledge officers and, 198–99

Made in the USA
Monee, IL
25 August 2020